H.E. PRIME MINISTER
XANANA GUSMÃO

The Sky is Ours

Speeches on Unity, Prosperity, and
Development in a New Timor-Leste
2017-2024

I0082815

LONGUEVILLE
MEDIA

LONGUEVILLE
MEDIA

First published 2024 by
Longueville Media
PO Box 205
Haberfield NSW 2045 Australia
www.longmedia.com.au
info@longmedia.com.au

Cover design / Lisa Reidy

For the National Library of Australia Cataloguing-in-Publication
entry visit www.nla.gov.au

Print ISBN: 978-1-7635361-5-9
POD ISBN: 978-1-7635361-6-6
eBook ISBN: 978-1-7635361-7-3

Cover image: Prime Minister Gusmão delivers his Special
Remarks at the ASEAN Business Summit, Plenary Session,
September 2023.

Xanana Gusmão, the leader of Timor-Leste's transformation into an independent country, a democratic country, a country that respects human rights and a country that is asserting itself internationally with growing influence. Timor-Leste won the battle for independence, Timor-Leste won the battle for democracy … but now it needs to win the battle for development.

United Nations Secretary General António Guterres

Dili, 29th August 2024

The Speeches

The Photographs

Presentation of the 2023 Amending Budget Law Proposal, August 2023

On the Occasion of the Budgetary Days on the General State Budget for 2024, September 2023

Swearing-in of the New Governor of the Central Bank of Timor-Leste, September 2023

Presentation of the 2024 General State Budget Law Proposal, December 2023

National Seminar: *Rules and Procedures in the Development of Timor-Leste's Infrastructure*, February 2024

My Sea of Timor

If I could
capture between my fingers
the sighs of the sea
and share them with
children

If I could
caress with my fingers
the wave's gentle breeze
and feel the hair of
children

If I could
feel between my fingers
the kiss of the foam
And hear the laughter of
children

If I could touch
with my fingers
the sleep of the sea
and coax to slumber
the eyes of the
children

If I could
take between my fingers
pretty little shells
and make the necklaces for
children

Oh, sea of mine!
Why do you wait?
Why don't you give?
Why don't you feel?
Why don't you hear?
Immersed in my thoughts
I was suddenly shaken

From the sea, my sea,
out of the bellies of ships
tremors came

I looked at the erupting sky
the sights of the sea were
cries of agony
the gentle breeze
the smell of dust and blood
the kiss of foam
the death-rattle
the sea's slumber
the pebbles of the gravestone
and the pretty selves
traced
the destiny of the homeland!

Cipinang
8 October 1995

Foreword

I met Xanana Gusmão in September 1999, 25 years ago, on the day he was released from Cipinang prison in Jakarta. A small group of people were waiting in Darwin for him to arrive late at night, at a villa that was to be his headquarters in those leaden days that followed the referendum on August 30, when the Timorese people voted unequivocally in favour of independence from Indonesia.

Portugal was still the administering power of the non-self-governing territory of East Timor and the Portuguese government was anxiously following the bloody events in Dili after the result of the referendum was announced. The whole country was watching the terrorist actions of the pro-Indonesia militias with growing indignation and Antonio Guterres, then Prime Minister of Portugal, asked me as Secretary of State for Foreign Affairs and Cooperation to go to Darwin and, from there, follow the course of events in Timor. So, being there, I had the opportunity to welcome Xanana's arrival to freedom.

A few days after that meeting, I flew to Dili on an INTERFET flight. A quick tour of the rubble of a ghost town that had been practically destroyed, and then I accompanied Ross Mountain, who led the United Nations humanitarian mission, on a reconnaissance flight outside Dili. I was able to anticipate the difficulties of the process that would then begin until the formal Declaration of Independence and the effort that would have to be made by the international community and the Timorese to make East Timor rise from the ashes and be recognised as a state. That's why, having seen what I saw that day, I was never surprised by the incidents along the way or the vicissitudes of a necessarily complex process.

After that eventful trip to Dili, I visited East Timor countless times. I followed almost every difficult crisis the country went through, without surprise or disappointment. From the first day I flew over its literally devastated territory, I was always aware of the challenge it was - and still is - to build a nation and a state on those ruins, in that historical and cultural reality, in that geography, and on the memories of so much violence and suffering.

East Timor continues to be a country in the making, now without the tutelage of the United Nations. As Xanana so wanted, the Timorese are fully responsible for their destiny and contrary to what many feared, their democratic institutions have been consolidating and responding to the challenges. Today, Timor-Leste is an example of tolerance and peace, a safe and stable country, having managed to overcome the most serious situations it faced in the early years of independence and, on the other hand, has a well-defined and stabilised geopolitical insertion plan in the region and the international system. It cultivates relations with its neighbours and with regional powers on a bilateral level, develops its relations with countries from all continents and, on a multilateral level is an active member of the CPLP and aims for full economic integration into ASEAN.

Today, the decisive role of Xanana Gusmão's leadership throughout these 25 years of untiring dedication and work for the cause of independence, peace, democracy and development in Timor-Leste is recognised and can easily be deduced from the scripts of his most recent speeches, delivered in the different conditions and circumstances, brought together in this book.

The first country of the 21st century was born out of a difficult birth, assisted by the international community, under the firm leadership of Xanana. East Timor's independence had great repercussions around the world, and the most dramatic events that took place there were widely covered by the media, making Timor-Leste known to the world. The first merit of Xanana's leadership, a tribute to his prodigious political intuition, was that with the support and experience of Ramos Horta, he was able to transform a tragedy into a unique opportunity for Timor-Leste's international affirmation. Xanana's leadership also had the merit of being able to emphasise Timor-Leste's unique identity and differentiate it in the space in which it is inserted by intelligently managing a strategic and civil border line between southwest Asia and the Australian continent, which is extremely sensitive for the regional balance. This is even more important now, as the world is rapidly sliding towards a new 'cold war'.

In Cipinang, Xanana would have begun to understand that the identity of the Timorese nation would be based on the two close neighbours that geography imposes on it, Indonesia and Australia, and the 'distant neighbour' that history has destined for it, Portugal. It was these three countries that were directly involved in the independence process, and it is still on them that the country's geopolitical stability is based. It is, therefore, understandable that particular attention continues to be paid to their relations with Timor-Leste and the different borders that both separate and unite them. A genuine obsession with the delimitation of borders, which has so irritated its neighbour, Australia, is after all, the primary task of founding a state and the primary responsibility of the 'founder'.

But, after the conflict, the priority is development - Xanana's current obsession. Timor-Leste's economic and social development necessarily involves the full integration of its economy into ASEAN, which has been systematically postponed. As can be seen from his most recent speeches, Xanana is now placing particular focus on this process, which has been dragging on for more than a decade. This will be another legacy of his leadership.

Xanana is, everyone recognises, a natural leader, but he is no ordinary leader. He imposed himself on Timor-Leste as a democratic leader, based on a direct and intuitive relationship with his people. He led the resistance, was president, prime minister, head of the opposition and prime minister again. But in truth he was always a guerrilla fighter and a poet. An unusual leader.

Luís Amado
Former Minister of State and Foreign Affairs of Portugal

Introduction

After decades of suffering and heroic resistance, the people of East Timor unequivocally expressed their will to become a sovereign state with the People's Consultation of August 30, 1999. In this democratic vote, they affirmed with an overwhelming majority to exercise their right to self-determination and, ultimately, to the restoration of independence.

This year, we celebrate the 25th anniversary of that historic moment that marked the beginning of the transition process under the United Nations, which put an end to a final wave of brutal violence unleashed by the occupying forces and began preparations for the transfer of power to the Timorese and leaders freely chosen by them. The significance of the 1999 referendum lies in the courage, determination, and love of freedom that the Timorese People demonstrated against all threats and attempts at intimidation. For this reason, the liberation of East Timor was recognized globally as a triumph for humanity through peace, solidarity and international law.

Kay Rala Xanana Gusmão was the central protagonist of the epic resistance and liberation struggle in the mountains of Timor and later in Cipinang prison. For him, the hard-won victory was only the beginning of a new struggle to build a political community which, while respecting the memory of its heroes, dared to immediately strive for reconciliation among all Timorese and, overcoming old resentments, to promptly establish relations of cooperation and friendship with neighboring peoples. The complexity of the new challenges meant that no one was exempt from assuming responsibilities. For this reason, Xanana Gusmão – the *Maun Bo'ot*, as he is called in Timor-Leste – would be the first President of the young republic elected by his people, would always remain involved in the political running of the country, both as a government official and as a member of the opposition, and now as Prime Minister since July 2023.

While acknowledging how much remains to be done, it's remarkable how far we've come in the last 25 years. The first

Presidential Palace in Dili was called the "Palace of Ashes" by its first tenant in 2002 – a most eloquent metaphor to describe the ruins, the desolation, the methodical destruction that in September 1999 marked the entire territory of the eastern half of the island of Timor. This was the terrible starting point: no facilities or infrastructure, no public administration or qualified staff, no institutions, and no sign of democratic procedures. Even at the local level, UNTAET (the United Nations Transitional Administration), from 1999 to 2002, deployed international officials to administer each of the districts. This scenario confronted the first President, the first national parliament, the first government and the first courts that took on the sovereign mission of governing Timor-Leste by choice and on behalf of its own People.

Xanana Gusmão's speeches, which we have selected and offer to the public in the following pages, are a powerful illustration of the obstacles we have overcome and the successes we have achieved. We thank Dr. Luís Amado, former Minister of State and Foreign Affairs of Portugal, for his solidarity during the most difficult times and for the Foreword he kindly provided to this volume. The successes we have achieved are on four decisive fronts.

Firstly, the construction of the rule of law in accordance with the order defined by a consensual constitutional democracy approved by the freely elected representatives of the people.

Secondly, the international affirmation of an independent republic, capable of defending its own interests and the sovereign autonomy of its people in the face of powerful neighbors at the center of dangerous global tensions.

Thirdly, the flourishing of a coexistence that respects common values and rules, the practice of plural and tolerant citizenship, where democratic electoral results have never been contested.

Fourthly, the ecologically sustainable economic and social development conditions in created to satisfy the legitimate aspirations of our people and meet the increasingly demanding expectations of the new generations whose task it is to continue building our future. The goal of integration into the ASEAN regional cooperation area is of decisive strategic importance here.

This year, on the occasion of the Future Summit at the United Nations General Assembly in New York, the Prime Minister of Timor-Leste, Kay Rala Xanana Gusmão, reaffirmed his commitment to Peace and Development:

> "The Independence of Timor-Leste was an achievement of the Timorese people, but also a triumph of the international system … We know that without peace, there are no conditions for development. That is why investing in our young people – on educational, social and citizenship skills and behaviors – is an investment in sustainable development and lasting peace."

Agio Pereira
Minister of the Presidency of the Council of Ministers
Díli, October 2024

ASEAN

The ASEAN Regional Forum on Dispute Resolution and Law of the Sea. Welcome Keynote Address

Díli, Timor-Leste
27 February 2020

International Guests,
Members of the National Parliament,
Members of Government,
Heads of Our Sovereign Bodies,
Members of the Diplomatic Corp,
Co-chairs,
Distinguished Guests,
Ladies and Gentlemen,

It is a great pleasure to welcome you to Timor-Leste for this important ASEAN Regional Forum Workshop on dispute resolution and the law of the sea.

I would like to thank our international guests for joining us. I see many long-time friends of Timor-Leste here today, as well as those visiting for the first time. I trust that you will all enjoy this visit to our country. I would also like to thank the other co-chairs of this forum, Malaysia and Australia, for organising this event with Timor-Leste. The work of the co-chairs reflects their commitment to dispute resolution and international law.

It is excellent to see the many countries represented here today. This demonstrates the strength of ASEAN and its promotion of regional and global peace and cooperation.

We are also fortunate to welcome so many experts on dispute resolution and the law of the sea, including practitioners, legal and technical experts, diplomats, and academics. We look forward to hearing from you all and learning from your experiences.

I am pleased to welcome senior representatives from our two maritime neighbours, Indonesia and Australia. This includes Mr Damos Agusman, Director General for International Law and Treaties from Indonesia's Ministry of Foreign Affairs and my counterpart in our maritime boundary delimitation discussions. We are also fortunate that Ambassador Gary

Quinlan has joined us. As Australia's agent in our compulsory conciliation, he will be able to share his perspective on the process.

In the absence of H.E. Judge Koroma, who was scheduled to deliver the keynote address, please allow me to stand in his place. While I will not be able to speak with his legal knowledge and his legal experience, I can provide the humble point of view from the perspective of a lay person. Governance of the oceans presents some of the most pressing security, economic, and environmental issues of this century.

The ocean is critical to our survival. It is home to up to 80% of all life, is essential to combatting climate change, nurtures incredible biodiversity, and produces food, jobs, and energy resources that nations depend upon.

Effective ocean governance through the law of the sea is critical to protect our future and promote global peace and security. This includes the resolution of maritime disputes that can create geopolitical tensions dividing countries and people at a time when we should be coming together.

Globally there are around 400 unresolved maritime boundary disputes.

These disputes cause conflict and insecurity. We know this only too well in our own region, where maritime boundary disputes have caused unease and distrust.

We also know this from Timor-Leste's experience, where a long-running dispute with Australia prevented maritime cooperation and economic development. Over the two days of this forum, we will discuss this dispute in more detail, but please allow me to give some context to the Timorese situation.

While we are a small island nation, we have a big story to tell. Our people have emerged from conflict and fragility to build a strong foundation for national development, guided since 2011 by our 20-year Strategic Development Plan.

We have built a resilient country. We have built a safe, tolerant, and open society with a free media. Importantly, we have been working hard to consolidate our state and build effective institutions.

This has not been an easy or straightforward task for the Timorese people; it has not been without struggle and hardship. We are a fragile state, and we have stumbled along the way; but we have never lost sight of our dream: an independent, sovereign nation.

An important part of this dream is achieving sovereignty over our lands and our seas.

As a maritime nation, our waters are integral to our way of life. The seas have a spiritual significance to us.

By legend, the Timorese are the grandchildren of the crocodile – upon its death, its body became the land of Timor, the ridges on its back became the mountains and the valleys, and the oceans its final resting place.

Many Timorese depend on the oceans for their sustenance and livelihood. And the development of a blue economy and a petroleum industry based on the reserves of oil and gas under our seabed will underpin our economic future.

To achieve our dream of political and economic sovereignty, and realise our full national potential, we need sovereignty over our seas as well as our land.

That is why the permanent delimitation of our maritime boundaries is so important to us, and it is why our dispute with Australia was so significant. Since our independence in 2002, Australia had refused to agree to maritime boundaries that were in accordance with international law. This left us with no other option than to look to the constitution of the seas, the United Nations Convention on the Law of the Sea (UNCLOS), for a solution.

Timor-Leste had always been a strong supporter of the rule-based order and the international system established by the community of nations to uphold it.

During our struggle for independence, we called on international law to bring liberation to our people. In our struggle for our maritime sovereignty, we once again turned to international law to achieve a just outcome for our country.

Under the United Nations Convention of the Law of the Sea (UNCLOS), as well as customary international law, all countries have an obligation to negotiate permanent maritime boundaries with their neighbours.

As you know, UNCLOS also provides avenues for dispute resolution. If a negotiated agreement is not possible, disputes can be submitted to an international court, tribunal, or other body under UNCLOS.

The binding dispute resolution bodies under UNCLOS include the International Court of Justice, and the International Tribunal for the Law of the Sea, along with other arbitral tribunals.

However, we were in a predicament, because on the eve of our independence, Australia excluded maritime boundary disputes from the jurisdiction of binding dispute resolution bodies.

Fortunately, UNCLOS provided an alternative avenue that had never been used before: compulsory conciliation. Under this option, an independent panel of experts convenes to engage the parties in conciliation to try and achieve an agreement.

This mechanism was designed to ensure that no maritime boundary dispute is left unresolved, in the interests of maintaining international peace and security.

Compulsory conciliation is the option that Timor-Leste took to resolve our maritime boundaries with Australia — we became the first country to initiate a compulsory conciliation process.

On 13 April 2016, I personally delivered a copy of the notice initiating the compulsory conciliation process to the then Secretary-General, Ban Ki Moon, in New York.

The process involved an independent panel of conciliators, known as the conciliation commission, engaging with the parties in dialogue to reach an agreement.

At the end of the process, if no agreement is reached, the parties to the conciliation are required to negotiate in good faith on the basis of a report by the conciliation commission, which is presented to the Secretary-General of the United Nations.

The conciliation was difficult. It was intensive, and both Timor-Leste and Australia fought hard to defend their national interests.

After many rounds of negotiations, guided by the conciliation commission, a breakthrough was achieved on 30 August 2017, 18 years to the day since the people of Timor-Leste had voted for independence. An agreement was reached with Australia on a maritime boundary that was consistent with international law.

The story of the compulsory conciliation is set out in the book *New Frontiers: Timor-Leste's Historic Conciliation on Maritime Boundaries in the Timor Sea*. You have all been provided with a copy of this book in your delegate pack.

For Timor-Leste, the achievement of permanent maritime boundaries with Australia represents one of the last steps in our journey to full sovereignty. It is also a testament to the determination of our people who took a chance of testing a procedure that had never been used before.

The maritime boundary with Australia has brought pride to our young country and given us the opportunity to realise the potential of our seas. I also believe that the success of the compulsory conciliation can serve as an example for other countries in similar situations.

The UNCLOS conciliation shows the promise of the international system and the rule-based order at a time when it is under stress. In our increasingly disordered world, international law provides the foundation for peace and for development.

That is why this forum is so important – it brings together people who can defend the international system and who understand the importance of the law of the sea.

While Timor-Leste may be a small country, we want to do what we can to support the resolution of disputes, including maritime boundary disputes, that threaten global security and cooperation. We would be pleased to share our experiences, and what we have learnt, with other nations in a similar position to us. I see today's forum as part of that commitment and look forward to discussing our experiences with you all.

Ladies and Gentlemen,

I am pleased that this forum will also address the resolution of disputes in relation to fisheries and the environment. Over three billion people depend on marine and coastal biodiversity for their livelihoods, including the Timorese people.

However, our oceans are being over-exploited and are polluted, including by too much plastic. How we manage our oceans and its resources is critical to our future and to addressing the effects of climate change.

In 2012 I promised the then President of Kiribati, Anote Tong, that I would raise the matter of climate change in every global forum I attended. The very existence of his nation was, and remains, at risk.

As my dear friend UN Secretary General António Guterres said at the Global Economic Forum Meeting in Davos this year, '*We* will be destroyed by climate change, not the planet. This will be, for us, a clear indication that we absolutely need to change course.'

Sustainable Development Goal 14, to conserve and sustainably use the oceans and marine resources, is critical to humanity. It calls for the conservation and the sustainable use of ocean resources through international law. I hope that, at this forum, we have productive discussions about the importance of the law of the sea to resolve disputes about fisheries and the environment.

Like many countries, protection of the marine environment is critical to Timor-Leste's sustainable development.

Timor-Leste is a member of the Coral Triangle, working with our neighbours to protect this special ecosystem and the 3,000 species within it. In our northern seas, the Ombai and Wetar Straits are a major migratory route for many whale species – including the incredible blue whale – along with humpback and sperm whales. And a recent USAID study found that the coral reefs on Atauro Island are the most biodiverse in the world.

In June, I will be attending the 2020 UN Ocean Conference, in Lisbon. This will provide an opportunity to present Timor-Leste's vision for the blue economy and the steps we will take to meet Sustainable Development Goal 14.

This will include expanding our marine protected areas, conserving our coral reefs, protecting our mangrove forests, providing sustainable fisheries, and establishing a Marine Education Centre so that our youth become part of a Blue Generation. In implementing these initiatives, we will make sure we protect our traditional fishers who rely on the oceans to support their families and their communities.

Ladies and Gentlemen,

Before I finish, let me say some brief words about the importance of ASEAN.

Southeast Asia has a difficult history of colonialism and conflict; it has faced significant development challenges, and it is diverse in culture, religions, and languages.

Despite these challenges, it has successfully emerged as a vibrant and dynamic region and a global economic powerhouse. Importantly, Southeast Asia has come together in cooperation and solidarity, and with a sense of a shared identity and future. This has been the great success of ASEAN.

As the only nation in Southeast Asia not a member of ASEAN, Timor-Leste seeks ascension to this important body. ASEAN is part of the fabric of our region and the Timorese people look forward to becoming an active and positive member of this community.

I am very pleased that Timor-Leste could host this ASEAN Regional Forum Workshop. I trust you will find the workshop to be a valuable exercise in discussing the various avenues for dispute resolution under international law, in considering emerging issues in dispute resolution, and in supporting the rules-based global order.

I wish you all a productive and enjoyable visit to our country and I look forward to meeting with you during the workshop.

Thank you very much.

Special Remarks at the ASEAN Business Summit 2023 Plenary Session.
ASEAN Matters: Resilience and Stability in a Fractious Global Economy

The Sultan Hotel, Jakarta
4 September 2023

Excellencies
Ladies and Gentlemen

It is an honour to speak today at this important event, the ASEAN Business and Investment Summit 2023, and to speak on the topic of resilience and stability in a fractious global economy.

ASEAN has emerged as a critical driver of the global economy. With a market size of $2.3 trillion and 600 million people, ASEAN is an economic powerhouse that has transformed Southeast Asia.

A key reason Timor-Leste is seeking accession to ASEAN is to become part of this success story. Full membership of ASEAN will provide business and foreign direct investors the confidence and security to invest in Timor-Leste.

Attracting foreign direct investment is critical to grow Timor-Leste's economy, create jobs, and modernise and transform the economic structure of our nation.

We also want to be part of ASEAN's 'people-centred' approach to growth and development. This approach has allowed wide participation and ownership of ASEAN's affairs. It has helped increase per capita wealth, life expectancy, and health outcomes, lifting millions out of poverty.

This transformation has been achieved by building trust between ASEAN countries and by promoting stability, unity and peace in our region.

ASEAN has succeeded in bringing countries with diverse cultures and histories together to form a community bound by a shared commitment to tolerance, friendship, and cooperation.

Given the success of ASEAN, it is easy to forget that Southeast Asia was not always a region of such unity and cooperation. It was not that long ago that our region was a victim of colonisation and the Cold War; torn apart by other nations' greed, conflict, and war.

And the Timorese people were not immune. The dynamics of the Cold War, and the demands of Western powers, led to a period of occupation in our country and our difficult struggle for self-determination.

It is because we remember suffering the proxy wars of the Cold War that our region refuses to take sides in today's geo-strategic contest between the world's great powers.

It is with this understanding of how far our region has come that we can see how remarkable ASEAN's economic achievements are and can admire the rise of miracle economies within ASEAN, including in Vietnam, Malaysia, Thailand, Indonesia, and Singapore.

Friends, it is important that we recognise the international significance of ASEAN's success, and its ability to build strong and stable nations from fragility and conflict.

Sadly, however, the great successes of ASEAN, as well as those of East Asia, are not being replicated in other parts of the world.

Instead of the possibility of miracle economies, there is conflict and war. Instead of cooperation and harmony, there is the widespread loss of human dignity and hope.

Many countries in the world are unable to integrate, in any meaningful way, into the global economy. And this results in too many people without hope of meaningful employment, many living in slums, in societies that are in crisis.

We are also experiencing more extreme weather conditions - floods, droughts, cyclones, and rising sea levels - due to the failure of the global powers to respond to climate change.

And it is already fragile states that are experiencing the worst effects of climate change. Our neighbours in the Pacific Islands are proof of that, as they deal with the threat of being swamped by rising sea levels.

The failure of the global economic system to develop the poorest parts of the world is resulting in fragility and dangerous declines in state capacity.

It is fuelling mass migration and the tragedies we are seeing on the shores of Europe. It is feeding extremism, transnational crime, and the growth of militia groups.

It would, of course, be easy to blame these countries, or their people. But to do so would be to ignore the echoes of history.

It would be to ignore the impact of conflict, economic exclusion, and foreign intervention that keeps these countries trapped in a state of fragility.

And so, perhaps what we need to do now is to establish a better international order that is based on a vision of human solidarity and shared prosperity.

An international order that helps fragile states build resilience and stability.

It was with this realisation, and following a period of unrest in our own country, that Timor-Leste joined together with other least-developed countries who had also faced conflict and fragility.

We believed that it was important that our collective voice be heard – especially when decisions were being made about our countries without us.

We established the g7+ group of countries, which now has around 20 members from Africa, Asia, the Middle East, and the Pacific. [This group] works hard to support and represent our countries, and to make our voices heard on the international stage.

The g7+ now has observer status at the United Nations, which allows it to provide a collective perspective on the agenda and work of the United Nations.

The g7+ supports a more active role for the United Nations in promoting state resilience and stability.

We are fortunate that His Excellency António Guterres is Secretary-General of the United Nations. We believe that there is no better person to lead the United Nations and fight for a better international order that provides human dignity, justice, and equality for all.

Recognising ASEAN's extraordinary achievements, I believe ASEAN has a role helping build resilience and stability in fragile states.

ASEAN has built a region with high state capacity, effective governments, the rule of law and public order, and healthy and educated workforces. It has adopted a people-centred approach that emphasises tolerance and mutual respect.

While so many countries around the world struggle with fragility and unrest, ASEAN provides examples of strong emerging economies that are structured for the benefit of the people.

We must not only highlight ASEAN's stability, security, and contribution to global growth, we must ask how ASEAN can help support resilience and stability in fragile states.

ASEAN can provide models of sovereign development for building strong communities, social infrastructure, and economic resilience.

The West does not have the answers to global development. While we live in a world that is economically interconnected, too many fragile states face economic exclusion and poor development outcomes.

For over half a century, ASEAN has promoted stability, unity, and peace in our region. ASEAN has shown the world the power of dialogue and what can be achieved when nations come together with a common purpose.

And it has shown us the benefits of more inclusive economic growth, where prosperity is widely shared.

Ladies and Gentlemen,

I now urge ASEAN to do more. I ask it to look beyond our region and become part of a global network to support fragile states, where democracy and human rights should be the basis of building peaceful states.

In a volatile global economy, ASEAN can make an important contribution to building international resilience and stability, through tolerance and human dignity.

Working together, we can establish a better international order based on a vision of human solidarity and shared prosperity.

Thank you very much.

The 13th ASEAN–United Nations Summit

Jakarta, Indonesia
7 September 2023

Thank you, Co-chairs, Your Majesty,
Honourable Leaders of ASEAN,

Your Excellency Secretary-General of the United Nations António Guterres, Distinguished Ladies and Gentlemen,

It is a privilege to be here with ASEAN leaders, participating in this important summit of ASEAN and the United Nations.

As members of the United Nations, we share and observe the same values and principles as stipulated by the UN charter.

Timor-Leste became the 191st member state of the United Nations when our independence was restored in 2002.

We owe our existence as an independent state to the resilience and determination of our people and to the United Nations.

In the conduct of our international relations, Timor-Leste adheres to the core values of the United Nations – the right of all peoples to self-determination and independence, the permanent sovereignty of peoples over their natural wealth and resources, the protection of human rights, mutual respect for sovereignty, territorial integrity and equality between states and non-interference in the internal affairs of states.

We commend the leadership of His Excellency António Guterres as the Secretary-General of the United Nations.

We believe that there is no better person to lead the United Nations and strive for a better international order that delivers human dignity, justice, and equality for all in these current global dynamics.

The principles of the United Nations are, indeed, also enshrined in the Treaty of Amity and Cooperation of Southeast Asia as the code of conduct for cooperation with the ASEAN nations, a treaty that Timor-Leste signed in 2007, when we committed to adhere to ASEAN values.

Timor-Leste also supports the implementation of the ASEAN outlook on the Indo-Pacific, in which, among others, also puts forward the UN Sustainable Development Goals 2030 as one of its focus areas of cooperation.

We are eager to see more collaboration between ASEAN and the United

Nations in the implementation of this shared objective, which will be a major contribution to the region and the global community.

In today's fragmented world, with unprecedented challenges, Timor-Leste continues to believe that 'Right is might'.

Timor-Leste supports sovereign rights and international mechanisms such as United Nations conventions that build trust in the world system and help prevent tensions from escalating to violence.

I thank the ASEAN leaders and the Secretary General of the United Nations for this opportunity.

The 11th ASEAN–United States of America Summit

Jakarta, Indonesia
6 September 2023

Thank you, Chair.

Your Majesty, Honourable Leaders of ASEAN, Honourable Vice President of the United States of America, Distinguished Ladies and Gentlemen,

Firstly, allow me to express my sincere appreciation to the Chair of ASEAN for the invitation to observe the positive partnership between ASEAN and the United States of America, and to deliver these brief remarks.

I would also like to congratulate Indonesia for its excellent work as the country coordinator for ASEAN-United States of America dialogue relations.

Timor-Leste's participation at all of the ASEAN meetings as observer has significantly paved the way for our readiness to become a full member. Hence, I would like to express our sincere appreciation to the Republic of Indonesia, as the Chair of ASEAN, and all the ASEAN member states for their support of and strong commitments to our accession process.

The United States of America is an important development partner and a very good friend of Timor-Leste. The US and Timor-Leste enjoy excellent bilateral relations based on shared interests and values, and Timor-Leste is committed to strengthening and deepening our partnership.

Timor-Leste is also grateful for the United States' support for our ambition to join ASEAN, and we look forward to consolidating our collaboration in this regard for our eventual full membership in ASEAN.

Lastly, Timor-Leste appreciates the United States' recognition of ASEAN's centrality in the evolving regional architecture and commitment to implement the plan of action under the ASEAN-US dialogue partnership.

Thank you, co-Chairs.

The 24th ASEAN–The Republic of Korea Summit

Jakarta, Indonesia
6 September 2023

Your Majesty,
Honourable Leaders of ASEAN, Honourable President of the Republic of Korea,
Ladies and Gentlemen,

I wish to thank the co-Chairs for providing me the opportunity to deliver these brief remarks, and to have observed directly the positive dialogue between ASEAN leaders and the Republic of Korea.

I would also like to congratulate Vietnam for its excellent work as the country coordinator for ASEAN-Republic of Korea dialogue relations.

As the leader of the 9th Constitutional Government of Timor-Leste, I would like to take this opportunity to thank the Republic of Korea for its friendship and development support to Timor-Leste.

We admire and seek to learn from the Republic of Korea's development success. We are grateful for your support for our goal of food security.

We are also grateful for the opportunity the Republic of Korea has given thousands of our young people to access its Employment Permit System.

Our young people speak highly of their Korean employers and value the experience of living in your country.

The Republic of Korea and Timor-Leste have established a genuine development partnership since the restoration of our independence.

We highly appreciate the support for our accession to ASEAN and we are looking forward to strengthening our partnership in the future. Timor-Leste, as a prospective full member of ASEAN, continues to seek to understand the ways and relationship that ASEAN has with its partners, including with the Republic of Korea. We deeply appreciate the unwavering support from all the ASEAN member states throughout our accession process and are committed to continue to work with ASEAN and the Republic of Korea in this endeavour.

Thank you, co-Chairs.

The 26th ASEAN Plus Three Summit

Jakarta, Indonesia
6 September 2023

Your Majesty,
Honourable Leaders of ASEAN and the Plus Three Leaders,
Ladies and Gentlemen,

Firstly, I would like to express my sincere appreciation to the Chair of ASEAN for the invitation to observe the important dialogue at this 26th ASEAN Plus Three Summit Meeting, and to make these brief remarks. The meeting today has been one of the great opportunities for us to observe and follow the state of cooperation between ASEAN and the Plus Three countries as one of the most comprehensive cooperation frameworks in the region.

Timor-Leste commends the progress made since the establishment of ASEAN Plus Three mechanisms. This mechanism has strongly contributed to the ASEAN community-building initiatives.

ASEAN's partnership with China, Japan, and the Republic of Korea has evolved into a multi-billion-dollar trading partnership.

While the ASEAN Plus Three focuses in promoting practical cooperation in areas covering the three pillars of the ASEAN community, it has also worked to maintain and enhance peace, security, stability, and development in our region.

As a prospective full member of ASEAN, Timor-Leste values the commitments of the Plus Three nations in maintaining and concretely supporting ASEAN as the epicentrum of global growth.

We also deeply appreciate the unwavering support from all the ASEAN member states throughout our accession process and we look forward to continuing to strengthen this cooperation with ASEAN and partners for an eventual full membership in the future.

Thank you, co-Chairs, for this great opportunity, and congratulations to all.

The ASEAN–Canada Summit

Jakarta, Indonesia
6 September 2023

Your Majesty,
Honourable Leaders of ASEAN,
Honourable Prime Minister of Canada,
Distinguished Ladies and Gentlemen,

Let me start by expressing my sincere appreciation to the co-Chairs for providing the opportunity for Timor-Leste to observe directly how the partnership between ASEAN and Canada has progressed this year. I would like to express our sincere appreciation to the Republic of Indonesia, as the chair of ASEAN, and all ASEAN member states for their commitment to our ASEAN accession process.

I would also like to acknowledge the work of Malaysia, as the country coordinator for the ASEAN-Canada partnership which has further promoted a positive political engagement and solid relationship between ASEAN and Canada.

It is welcoming to recognise that Canada fully supports the ASEAN-led regional architecture and the ASEAN outlook on the Indo-Pacific, both of which have immensely contributed to peace, stability, and prosperity in the region.

Timor-Leste also acknowledges the important stepped-up efforts taken to enhance ASEAN-Canada trade and investment through the ASEAN-Canada Joint Declaration on Trade and Investment Work Plan of 2021-2025 and the activities of the Canada-ASEAN Business Council.

Timor-Leste enjoys a very good relationship, both bilaterally and in multilateral fora, with Canada. We look forward to strengthening this relationship in the future, especially in relation to our impending full membership in ASEAN.

We appreciate the continues support from all the ASEAN member states on the accession of Timor-Leste to ASEAN. As we are now focusing our attention on fulfilling all the future necessary requirements for our eventual full membership, we look forward to a stronger ASEAN-Canada relationship and to continue to work together with ASEAN and Canada throughout this process.

Thank you, co-Chairs.

The 26th ASEAN–Japan Summit

Jakarta, Indonesia
6 September 2023

Your Majesty,
Honourable Leaders of ASEAN
Honourable Prime Minister of Japan,
Distinguished Ladies and Gentlemen,

I wish to thank the Co-chairs for providing me the opportunity to deliver these brief remarks, and to observe the positive partnership between ASEAN and Japan.

I extend congratulations to the Head of Delegation of the Kingdom of Thailand for its excellent work as country coordinator for promoting ASEAN-Japan dialogue relations.

I would like to take this opportunity to acknowledge Japan's long-term assistance in support of Timor-Leste's goals to improve infrastructure and diversify our economy.

Japan has also consistently supported our efforts to join ASEAN and is providing assistance regarding human resource development.

Timor-Leste will be honoured to attend the commemorative summit for the 50th year of ASEAN-Japan friendship and cooperation in December this year.

ASEAN-Japan relations have made remarkable progress since 1973.

Japan has made every effort to build relations of mutual confidence and trust with ASEAN member states and is clearly as committed as ASEAN to peace and prosperity in the region.

Timor-Leste commends the steady progress in the implementation of the ASEAN-Japan plan of action.

We believe that, under the theme of 'ASEAN Matters: Epicentrum of Growth,' the ASEAN-Japan partnership will continue to thrive.

Thank you, co-Chairs.

The 43rd ASEAN–China Summit

Jakarta, Indonesia
6 September 2023

Your Majesty,
Honourable Leaders of ASEAN,
Honourable Premier of the People's Republic of China,
Distinguished Ladies and Gentlemen,

It has been an honour for me to observe the ASEAN/China partnership at this ASEAN-China Summit meeting.

As the Prime Minister of Timor-Leste, I would like to take this opportunity to thank the People's Republic of China for its friendship and development support.

The People's Republic of China has contributed to our country by supporting the building of essential power and transport infrastructure. We look to China as a model of sustainable and inclusive development.

We also appreciate China's support for our accession to ASEAN.

Timor-Leste will work bilaterally, and through ASEAN, to further strengthen our partnership with China.

Timor-Leste welcomes ASEAN and China's reaffirmation in this forum of your mutual commitments to strengthen the relationship in line with the ASEAN-China Comprehensive Strategic Partnership.

China's reaffirmation of its commitment to support ASEAN centrality will help ensure that the region remains the epicentrum of global growth.

Thank you, co-Chairs.

The 20th ASEAN–India Summit

Jakarta, Indonesia
7 September 2023

Your Majesty,
Honourable Leaders of ASEAN,
Honourable Prime Minister of India,
Distinguished Ladies and Gentlemen,

It is a great pleasure to have observed the positive dialogue in this ASEAN-India Summit, and to witness the progress of the partnership evolving under the theme of 'ASEAN Matters: Epicentrum of Growth'.

We acknowledge the excellent work by Singapore as the country coordinator for ASEAN-India dialogue relations. The partnership between ASEAN and India has continued to solidify over the years.

We commend the steady progress in the implementation of the ASEAN-India Plan of Action, and we are confident that the partnership will be even more mutually beneficial in the coming years. Timor-Leste welcomes ASEAN and India's renewed commitment in this meeting to intensify their longstanding relations.

We hope that under the theme of 'ASEAN Matters: Epicentrum of Growth', the partnership between ASEAN and India will continue to strengthen and progress. As a prospective member of ASEAN, Timor-Leste looks forward to intensifying our engagement with ASEAN and India for its eventual full membership in ASEAN.

As an advocate for democracy and human rights, Timor-Leste is also keen to build its strong relations with ASEAN and India to achieve a common goal of stability and prosperity in both the region and globally.

Thank you, co-Chairs.

The 18th East Asia Summit

Jakarta, Indonesia
7 September 2023

The East Asia Summit (EAS) is a forum that brings together leaders from ASEAN and its eight dialogue partners: Australia, China, India, Japan, New Zealand, South Korea, Russia, and the United States.

Your Majesty,
Distinguished Heads of Delegations of the East Asia Summit,
Ladies and Gentlemen,

First of all, I wish to thank the Chair of ASEAN for the invitation to participate as an observer at this 18th East Asia Summit Meeting.

I commend the leaders of the East Asia Summit's participating countries for the successful convening of this summit as an important leaders-led forum for dialogue on broad strategic, political, and economic issues of common interest and concern with the aim of promoting peace, stability, and economic prosperity in the region and beyond.

I congratulate ASEAN for initiating the East Asia Summit, a vitally important platform that brings all of the world's major powers together to focus on strategic issues affecting our region. This kind of dialogue is crucial to reducing the increasing geopolitical tensions and power rivalry.

Timor-Leste supports ASEAN in the evolving regional architecture, and at this critical juncture where current global security environment rests unpredictably, ASEAN and its ASEAN-led mechanisms, including the EAS, remain effective platforms for dialogue and cooperation.

Timor-Leste hopes this forum continues to provide an avenue for positive dialogue with world leaders focused on our region, particularly the devastating impact of climate change.

It was pleasing to see, from all of Your Excellencies' deliberations, a strong manifestation of on-going commitments to concretely support ASEAN centrality and ways to maintain the role of the region as the epicentrum of global growth.

As a prospective full ASEAN member, Timor-Leste's ongoing engagements with member states and partners will continue to strengthen our support for ASEAN's centrality and unity.

In this regard, Timor-Leste deeply appreciates the unwavering support from all the ASEAN member states and ASEAN partners on our accession to ASEAN. Timor-Leste looks forward to working with the East Asia Summit participating countries for our eventual full membership.

Finally, I want to reiterate that Timor-Leste shares the values of all nations that respect and uphold the principles of democracy and human rights, and which uphold international law in the conduct of international relations.

I thank you, Chair, for this great opportunity.

ASEAN

The 3rd ASEAN–Australia Summit

Jakarta, Indonesia
7 September 2023

Your Majesty,
Honourable Leaders of ASEAN,
Honourable Prime Minister of Australia Anthony Albanese,
Distinguished Delegates, Ladies and Gentlemen,

I appreciate the Chair of ASEAN for inviting Timor-Leste to attend this important meeting and for the opportunity to deliver my brief remarks.

As a close neighbour of both Australia and many ASEAN nations, Timor-Leste is delighted to see the positive partnership between ASEAN and Australia.

Australia is one of the major contributors to the development of Timor-Leste's nation building and state building.

We also appreciate Australia for providing the opportunity to thousands of Timorese to gain skills and work experience in Australia through its labour scheme program.

We thank Australia for the strong support for Timor-Leste's ASEAN accession and its commitment in assisting Timor-Leste to implement the roadmap for our accession to full ASEAN membership.

I would also like to thank ASEAN and Australia for the concrete and excellent collaborative effort done thorough the leadership of Lao PDR and Australia to support Timor-Leste's accession to ASEAN. With the support from Australia, many of our government officials have attended capacity-building programs for ASEAN in Vientiane, Lao PDR.

Finally, we appreciate the contribution of Australia to ASEAN community-building development cooperation efforts, and the priorities of ASEAN in 2023 under the theme of 'ASEAN Matters: Epicentrum of Growth'.

Thank you, co-Chairs.

The Launch of the Timor-Leste's Future Leaders for ASEAN (FLBA) Program

GMN Multi-Function Venue, Díli
3 April 2024

It gives me great pleasure to welcome you to the launch of Timor-Leste's Future Leaders for ASEAN Program.

We are honoured to have His Excellency ASEAN Secretary-General Dr Kao Kim Hourn with us this morning.

We are grateful for your visit as a demonstration of ASEAN's support for Timor-Leste's journey towards ASEAN membership.

Thank you very much for joining us, and for your guidance and advice.

May I also acknowledge members of Government, our friends in the Diplomatic Corps, and representatives from the private sector, international agencies, civil society, and academia.

I would also like to acknowledge and congratulate the first cohort of participants in the Timor-Leste Future Leaders for ASEAN program. Your selection for this program is both an investment in your future and in the future of our nation.

Developing the next generation of leaders is crucial for any country. It is particularly important for Timor-Leste now, as we embark on our final preparations to join ASEAN. This program is a sign of our commitment to regional integration and cooperation, and it marks a significant step in our journey towards national development.

Timor-Leste's development is dependent more than ever before on our human resources and the empowerment of our human potential, which is why we are investing in the next generation of leaders.

The 9th Constitutional Government has identified human development and social capital as priority areas for investment, along with economic diversification, infrastructure development, and good governance. We believe that our membership of ASEAN will augment these priorities.

Timor-Leste is a young nation with untapped potential. Our young people – including the future leaders here today – will play an essential role in accelerating our progress. We are committed to creating opportunities that enable young people to fulfil their potential and we are taking concrete action.

This year's annual budget increased funding in the education sector, so that we can improve the quality of education at all levels. The Human Capital Development Fund, established in 2011, continues to fund education and vocational training based on the greatest areas of need.

We believe that investing in future leaders will help our country better navigate global challenges, as well as foster innovation and contribute to a sustainable and prosperous future.

The Future Leaders for ASEAN Program is one way in which we are investing in our leadership, as we look to integrate further into our region.

Ladies and gentlemen,

To the 100 future leaders present here today, I wish you all a successful leadership program and a rewarding engagement with our ASEAN neighbours.

We look forward to you sharing the benefits of your experience on the program with your colleagues here in Timor-Leste and in your future leadership roles with our ASEAN partners.

Congratulations and good luck.

Plenary Session of the 44th and 45th ASEAN and ASEAN-Related Summits

Vientiane, Lao PDR
9 October 2024

His Excellency Sonexay Siphandone, ASEAN Chair and Prime Minister of the
Lao People's Democratic Republic,
Your Majesty,
Excellencies ASEAN Leaders,
Secretary-General,
Ladies and Gentlemen,

It is a privilege and honour to join you once again at this important ASEAN Summit.

I would like to begin by expressing my gratitude to the Government of the Lao PDR for its warm hospitality and for the progress it has achieved as the Chair of ASEAN this year.

It has been a difficult year in international affairs with rising tensions, hostilities, conflict and war.

We are witnessing a breakdown in the international system as powerful nations ignore international law at will.

We are experiencing the failure of developed countries to address the effects of climate change – a problem that they caused and which impacts Least Developed Countries and Small Island Developing Countries the most.

On behalf of the Government and the people of Timor-Leste, I would like to extend our heartfelt sympathies to the families and communities affected by the recent devastating typhoon Yagi in Thailand, the Philippines, Lao, Vietnam, and Myanmar. We stand in solidarity with the governments and people of the affected regions as they work to recover and rebuild.

We are seeing inequality rising to dangerous levels while the world struggles to achieve the Strategic Development Goals. In these difficult times, ASEAN holds more significance than ever as an international model for cooperation, unity, and trust.

As an observer country, I urge ASEAN to adopt a global vision and demonstrate to the world what can be achieved when we foster dialogue, when we work in solidarity, and when we strive for peace.

Excellencies,

For our country, we approach a significant chapter in our national journey. As we move closer to joining ASEAN, we understand both the responsibility of membership and the great potential of ASEAN.

We look forward to a future where Timor-Leste can grow together with the countries of Southeast Asia and where we can contribute meaningfully to peace and development.

It is with gratitude that we acknowledge the support of ASEAN member states and dialogue partners whose support has helped us on our path towards integration. And as we look ahead, I wish to offer my sincere best wishes to the Kingdom of Malaysia as it prepares to take on the ASEAN chairmanship next year.

I have no doubt that under Malaysia's leadership, ASEAN will continue to rise to the challenges of our time and to lead with vision, wisdom, and compassion.

Thank you very much

ASEAN Leaders' Interface with Representatives of the ASEAN Inter-Parliamentary Assembly

Vientiane, Lao PDR
9 October 2024

Esteemed ASEAN Leaders

Your Excellency, President of the ASEAN Inter-Parliamentary Assembly,

Members of Parliament and Secretary-General of the ASEAN Inter-Parliamentary Assembly,

Honourable Delegates,

Ladies and Gentlemen,

It is an honour to participate in this important interface with the ASEAN Inter-Parliamentary Assembly (AIPA).

Timor-Leste has been an observer at the ASEAN Inter-Parliamentary Assembly since 2018 in Singapore. Since then, we have witnessed the Assembly encourage dialogue, cooperation, and understanding among member parliaments.

We also commend the Assembly's work in helping to harmonise and strengthen legislative frameworks to align with ASEAN standards and practices.

We have seen how the Assembly's recommendations help national parliaments translate regional priorities into national laws and policies.

The National Parliament of Timor-Leste supports regional agreements. We have established an ad-hoc committee tasked with ratifying ASEAN agreements and protocols, enacting relevant legislation, monitoring the implementation of these agreements, and representing the interests of the Timorese people in regional forums.

By actively participating in AIPA activities, we have gained insights and learnt good practices that will further strengthen our legislative processes and governance structures.

In closing, I would like to reaffirm Timor-Leste's commitment to completing our internal processes for acceding to the priority agreements across the three ASEAN Community pillars by next year.

We look forward to continued collaboration with ASEAN Members of Parliament and development partners as we work towards our full membership of ASEAN.

Thank you, Chair

Culture

Opening of Timor-Leste's Inaugural Pavilion at La Biennale di Venezia

Timor-Leste Pavilion
Venice, Italy
19 April 2024

Ladies and Gentlemen,

It is a special privilege to be here to open Timor-Leste's first exhibition at la Biennale di Venezia.

Twenty-five years after the Timorese people voted in a United Nations' sponsored referendum to restore our independence, we are proud to participate for the first time in the world's premiere visual arts event.

Our path to independence was long and difficult. But we would not have been able to achieve our freedom without first having had a strong sense of national identity.

Over centuries we developed a unique culture, heritage, and spirit. The stories of our ancestors continue to echo throughout our ancient land. These stories guide us and bring us together as a people.

It was our distinct culture and heritage that unified the Timorese during our resistance struggle and fuelled our dreams of freedom.

Since independence, our culture and our storytelling have been an integral part of our peace- building and our state-building efforts.

And today, we are a free, open, and democratic nation.

Now, it is time to promote our culture to the world. Our painting, sculpture, weaving, craft, our theatre and film, and our dance and music. We want our rich cultural heritage to underpin the development of our tourism industry and create jobs for our people.

Just six months ago, last October, I appointed Jorge Soares Cristóvão to be Timor-Leste's inaugural Venice Biennale Commissioner. And here we are today! It is a remarkable achievement.

By opening this exhibition, Timor-Leste is making a statement that our art, culture, and heritage matter.

Our stories and our culture define who we are. But just as nations evolve, so does national culture. Art cannot just be about the past – it must also embrace the future and the potential of our country.

The art of Maria Madeira incorporates the timeless traditions of our people in contemporary works of truth-telling and beauty.

She uses materials that define our land and our heritage – red earth, betel nut, and tais – to tell a story of resistance, resilience, and renewal.

Maria speaks to the universal experience of women in war.

The stories of occupation can be difficult to tell. Maria is able to capture the darkness of war as well as the power of reconciliation and the possibilities of hope.

I would like to congratulate Timor-Leste's inaugural Venice Biennale Commissioner, the Secretary of State for Arts and Culture, Jorge Soares Cristóvão, and his team for making Timor-Leste's participation in la Biennale di Venezia such a beautiful reality.

I also congratulate the Minister of Youth, Sports, Art and Culture, Nélio Isaac Sarmento, for his steadfast support for Timor-Leste's exhibition. I would also like to thank the curator, Natalie King, for doing such a wonderful job, and all of the people who have worked so hard to support this exhibition.

I know that this exhibition will be an inspiration to Timorese artists and promote the development of contemporary art.

While this is the first time our country is participating in la Biennale di Venezia, we look forward to many more exhibitions in the future to celebrate our nation and share our stories with the world.

Thank you very much.

Economics & Growth

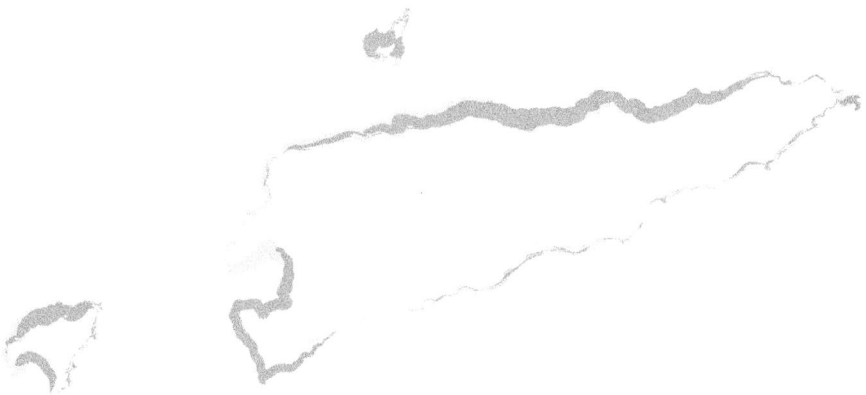

The Atlantic Council Global Energy Forum. Keynote Address

Abu Dhabi, United Arab Emirates
11 January 2019

Good afternoon.

It is a great pleasure to be back in Abu Dhabi for the Global Energy Forum. There is no better place than the United Arab Emirates to host this annual discussion about the energy challenges facing humanity.

Abu Dhabi itself is a dream in the desert, with a future founded on energy resources but built not by something you pump out of the ground but by a renewable resource: human imagination.

The UAE is committed to the future – in its thinking and in its economy. And it has responded successfully to many of the questions that we are discussing today, and which could not be more relevant to the people of my country, Timor-Leste.

How do we transition from a resource-dependent economy and avoid the resource curse?

What is the best way to marry successful resource development and economic diversification?

In addressing these challenges,

we must recognise that energy policy is economic policy, and that good economic policy must be sustainable. This is fundamental to good governance.

Today, there are many countries where the needs of the people are growing at a faster pace than ever before. We see growing populations of young people in places with limited access to education, jobs, and an opportunity for a better life.

Tomorrow, I will be speaking to college students at the UAE's diplomatic academy. The age of these students is a little more than the average age of half the population of Asia and Africa. Think about that for a moment.

In Timor-Leste about 60% of our population is under the age of 25.

From Africa to Latin America, to Asia, the challenge for many countries is how to meet the demands of a young and growing population.

This is an important question for all of us because failure will breed dissatisfaction, unrest, and conflict – it will result in both national and global fragility.

At last year's forum, I spoke about why this challenge is so fundamental to Timor-Leste, and it is why our maritime boundary agreement with Australia is so important.

In March 2018, Timor-Leste and Australia signed a Maritime Boundary Treaty, resolving jurisdictional issues over the resources in the Timor Sea.

Now that we have secured a majority of Greater Sunrise, one of the largest gas fields in Southeast Asia, with 70% of the revenue flowing to our country, the challenge is to develop it in a way that secures our economic future.

It is our aim to use our resources responsibly and to pass on a sustainable economy to the generations ahead.

With the ownership and jurisdiction of the resource resolved, we can move forward with the development plan for its exploitation.

We recently concluded an agreement with ConocoPhillips to sell us its shares in Greater Sunrise. We have also entered into a purchase and sale agreement with Shell to sell us its Greater Sunrise shares.

These investments represent an important step that will allow us to bring a gas pipeline to Timor-Leste – and build our own petroleum industry.

This is critical to ensure that the jobs and industries that come from Timor-Leste's resources stay in Timor-Leste – on our shores, and for our people.

But it is just the start. From the very beginning we have seen our natural resource wealth as the foundation of a diversified economy.

That demands long-term planning, and effective institutions that deliver for the people who need them.

Only a few years after the restoration of Timor-Leste's independence in 2002, we established a sovereign wealth fund to manage the revenue from our energy resources transparently and sustainably, for the benefit of all citizens and future generations.

Based on Norway's model, every dollar from our petroleum resources goes into the fund. From its opening balance of $205 million US dollars in 2005, I am pleased to say this has grown to $17.2 billion today.

We invest 60% in bonds and 40% in equities – and this has generated more than five billion dollars in returns.

We were also the third country in the world and the first across the whole of Asia to comply with the revenue transparency standards and requirements of the Extractive Industries Transparency Initiative – the EITI.

Timor-Leste recognises that diversifying a resource-based economy is the most sensible way to solve potential problems associated with resource dependence.

We also recognise that there is no magic formula for how to achieve diversification quickly – fostering diversification is a long-term process.

Eight years ago, we outlined a 20-year Strategic Development Plan that includes policies and programs to diversify our economy: social capital, and economic and infrastructure development, with a comprehensive infrastructure plan, headlined by the transformation of our south coast into a regional petroleum hub.

The Tasi Mane project, as we call it, will establish a 100-mile corridor along our southern coast that includes the construction and operation of a refinery, petrochemical plant, LNG plant, a linking highway, and seaports and airports.

This will open around 200,000 hectares of hinterland suitable for every industry from livestock to processing and packing exports.

When fully implemented, the Tasi Mane project will not only benefit the petroleum industries but help bring to a much bigger scale every other industry central to our future.

In other words: economic diversification. And this economic diversification guides us to develop and strengthen the agro-industry sector and tourism.

But our economic development will not be successful if we don't stay equally focused on another area critical to the development of our resources, and that is statebuilding.

If you look around the world, resource-based economies that succeed have strong institutions, good governance, political sustainability, effective and independent legal systems, and good leadership.

Those that fail too often tell the opposite story.

We are determined to succeed. We secured peace and we are consolidating our state. We have built a free and democratic country with an open economy and respect for the rule of law and the human dignity of our people.

The Economist *magazine deemed Timor-Leste to be the most democratic country in Southeast Asia*.

Revenue from our resource wealth has helped us with peacebuilding and statebuilding. Public spending has been directed to important areas that have had positive outcomes on health, education, social support, and infrastructure ever since our petroleum production began.

We are not alone in our challenge. Timor-Leste leads the g7+ body of fragile and conflict-affected states, many of which face the same challenge of how to harness resource wealth to give their people a sustainable future.

This inter-governmental organisation comprises 20 countries from across the world, from the Caribbean to Africa, and from the Pacific to the Middle East.

We all know too well that resource exploitation has not always been beneficial to small, developing countries – the so-called 'resource curse' can result in failed governments, economic stagnation, and corruption.

And so, our challenge is to make resource exploitation work to develop our countries and to build a future of opportunity for our people. We must learn from each other and our experiences, while recognising that the circumstances of all countries are different.

I have seen too much in my life to become a prisoner to the idea of a resource curse. There are no inevitable outcomes in life, or for nations.

And just as I have seen too many countries suffer from conflict and fragility, I have seen success stories of statebuilding supported by resource development. This includes not only the UAE but much closer to home, with Indonesia, and Malaysia and Brunei.

And so, rather than a resource curse, I believe in the curse of excuses. The curse that relies on resources as an excuse for unrest and underdevelopment or bad governance, when it is leadership that is the problem.

That is why countries need to plan for their future, to ensure that resource development benefits the people and not a few individuals or other interests.

None of our problems are without solutions. But neither will they solve themselves.

I am reminded of when Nelson Mandela travelled to Indonesia to visit me in prison. When he reflected on his country's long march to freedom he said, 'It always seems impossible, until it is done'.

It is leadership which decides whether resources will be a curse or a course towards a prosperous future.

Unfortunately, in under-developed or developing countries, there are still many political obstacles, especially the ego shown by political leaders, that prevent a smooth process towards democracy and consequently the development of the people and their nations.

And so, I look forward to our panel discussion and to learning more about resource management strategies in other countries from the distinguished experts here today.

Thank you.

The 'Specialisation Course in Economic and Financial Crime' Closing Ceremony

Hotel Timor, Díli
20 October 2023

Your Excellencies,
Madam Ambassador of Portugal,
Ambassador of the European Union Mr Marc Fiedrich,
Vice-Rector for External Relations of the University of Coimbra Mr João Nuno Calvão e Silva,
Judge Counsellor and President of the Court of Appeal Mr Deolindo dos Santos,
Professor Mrs Anabela Miranda Rodrigues,
Professor Mrs Maria João Antunes,
Appeal Court Judge Mr António Beça Pereira,
Public Prosecutor Mr Rui Cardoso,
Ladies and Gentlemen, Timorese Judges,
Distinguished Participants and Guests,

It's a great honour to come here and participate in the Closing Ceremony of the Specialisation Course in Economic and Financial Crime for Timorese Judges and the Round Table 'Criminal Justice and the Rule of Law'.

First, I would like to acknowledge the General Coordinator of this event, Dr Cristina Paula Baptista, for inviting me.

On behalf of the 9th Constitutional Government, I would also like to congratulate and thank the University of Coimbra, together with the European Union and the Camões Institute, for the partnership project to improve service delivery by strengthening the management and supervision of public finances in Timor-Leste – 'Osan Povu nian, Jere ho Di'ak' [Managing Public Money Wisely] – through the course, which ran from September 25th to October 19th, or more specifically, which ended yesterday.

The theme 'Osan Povu nian, Jere ho Di'ak' is a fundamental matter for the nation's life and transcends time boundaries.

Allow me, ladies and gentlemen, to address only this topic in its various guises, because it concerns the construction of the Democratic Rule of Law.

As a young state, Timor-Leste is not immune to the vicissitudes of the anomalies arising from the fragility of states in the making. When we identify ourselves as a fragile state, we only mean to recognise the crucial need to nourish the institutions of the state with the principles of seriousness and responsibility in our actions, from the functional to the merely administrative, from those of a decision-making nature to those of national scope, from those of a state nature to those that mainly involve political interests.

Having begun to rise in 2002 from the ashes of the 1999 destruction, the state of Timor-Leste carried a crushing weakness on its shoulders, not only because it lacked the capacity in technical and administrative resources but, above all, because it was penniless and thus totally submissive, and dependent on financial support from donors, and only a few years later did it begin to receive the first tens of millions from the Bayu Undang operation.

In 2005, the Petroleum Fund Law was created, and from then on, investment began in bonds – 90% of the fund's money, with an interest rate of 1.9%.

Back in the 4th Government, from 2007 to 2012, the Timorese State recognised the need to regulate the annual expenditure that would necessarily have to be borne by the Petroleum Fund, as well as the pressing need to give an accurate sense of responsibility to all those who would hold the reins of Government when the people so decided, in free and democratic elections.

Bearing in mind early discussion of the United Nations' Sustainable Development Goals which eventually came into force in 2015, we established the *Strategic Development Plan 2011-2030* (SDP). The primary objective of this SDP was to indicate the path and goals for the nation's development in all aspects, and this would allow the Government programmes to be formulated annually to initiate, continue, and consolidate the foundations of sustainable development for the period defined in the *Strategic Development Plan 2011-2030*.

This SDP would also allow the people to understand the various phases and stages of the development process, from social to infrastructural aspects, from the production of goods to the empowerment of the national private sector, in an integrated set of actions that would gradually and steadily advance the country's socio-economic development.

Furthermore, the SDP would serve as a point of reference requiring any political force that came to govern the country not to neglect participating in this process of national development, thus avoiding falling into the democratic vices of only seeing the interests of one's political organisation, rather than the interests of an entire people and an entire country, especially a country like Timor-Leste, which is underdeveloped and has no competitive strength in the economic field, having to import everything, even though it can produce for its consumption.

Thus, the 4th Government began with the electrification programme throughout the country, including the enclave of Oé-Cusse Ambeno. The Petroleum Fund Law required that, each year, the Government would only be allowed to withdraw 3% of the estimated sustainable income, and that, if necessary, it would have to prove its needs in Parliament in a coherently defined programme to be authorised to withdraw the proposed surplus. And so it went on, never exceeding 5% of the estimated sustainable income.

Given the amount of money spent on electrifying the country, the 4th Government considered alternatives for future basic infrastructure projects, such as roads and bridges and irrigation canals, schools, and hospitals, because all of this would require large outlays from the Petroleum Fund. The Government decided to take out loans, which would be paid back in stages, allowing less money to be taken out of the fund each year. This would give the fund increased capacity to be invested in shares and bonds moderately, thus being able to grow the fund's money.

In this vein, in 2011, the 4th Government also decided to amend the Petroleum Fund Law, thus allowing investment in equities, with the Government only having 35% of the Petroleum Fund and 61% in bonds. With the ups and downs inherent in the money market, there was a loss of 2 billion dollars last year, 2022. Still, during these years, we benefitted from a cumulative return of 8.3 billion dollars from the two investments mentioned. The Petroleum Fund currently has a reserve of 17.52 billion dollars.

Ladies and Gentlemen,

The whole scenario has been described with the sole intention to emphasise that the problem of corruption does not stem solely from the direct actions of the people involved in the decision-making process regarding expenditure. The judiciary must fulfil its part in this mechanism of prevention, and serious and responsible verification of expenditure.

In the 4th and 5th Governments, of which I was Prime Minister, we had the misfortune of seeing members of the Government accused and punished for corruption, which, honestly, did not constitute cases of 'stealing money' from the state. And the worst of all those cases is that of Emília Pires. I must state here that it was Emília Pires, Minister of Finance in the 4th and 5th Governments, who guided the Government to establish a very credible financial system. It was Emília Pires who showed admirable sagacity to suggest to the Government the successful option of loans and the unrivalled nationalistic sense of studying the international money market and proposing the investment of the Petroleum Fund in equities in a very moderate way to ensure the safe and sustainable vitality of the *Osan Povo nian*, to provide further confidence in the *Jere ho Di'ak*, bearing in mind that the country's development needed large amounts of money from the Petroleum Fund.

Today, Emília Pires is under tremendous psychological pressure, having been convicted by the Díli Court on a false accusation by the Public Prosecutor's Office, which only demonstrated a serious and biased manipulation of facts. She was falsely accused of single-handedly deciding to buy paediatric beds for the Guido Valadares National Hospital from Mac's Metalcraft Company. I must clarify this at this ceremony, because I didn't accept it from the start. I still don't accept the lack of analytical capacity of the judicial system and the routine simplicity of judicial actors in looking at cases, which has also been proven in various other matters in different areas, leading the justice system to define itself as incapable and unjust and, by society, seen as too vulnerable to pressure from third parties.

In 2011, the Ministry of Health bought 80 beds and other equipment from the Mac's Metalcraft Company, including mattresses, the cost of sea and land transport, installation, and user training, and this excellent quality material was distributed to hospitals. The purchase totalled US$366,168.

In 2012, there was an outbreak of dengue fever throughout the country, and the Ministry of Health saw the need to make more purchases, but it didn't have the money to do so. So, the Vice-Minister of Health requested to obtain the money from the Contingency Fund. I, as Prime Minister, authorised the transfer – because only the Prime Minister has this power – from the Contingency Fund to the Ministry of Health, for US$895,140, for the purchase of 180 beds, 100 bedside tables, four patient lifters, 180 hospital standard mattresses and pillows, and other equipment, including the cost of sea transport, from Australia to Timor-Leste, and land transport for distribution to hospitals in the national territory. As it fell within her remit, because the money was under one million dollars, the Vice-Minister awarded the contract to the same company.

Throughout the trial of Emília Pires, the courts, and the Public Prosecutor's Office in particular, were unable or unwilling to place the decisions in a proper chronology of the facts. The report on the dengue outbreak even disappeared from the Public Prosecutor's Office file, which abusively even denied that there had been a dengue outbreak, simply ignoring the statements of several witnesses, to falsely conclude that the entire decision on the purchase of the beds was solely and personally authorised by the Minister of Finance, Emília Pires.

I have never agreed, since the beginning of the process, and I still don't accept the Court's latest decision on the case of Emília Pires, who is totally innocent in this case - a woman who very decisively contributed to the Petroleum Fund now having a surplus of more than US$8 billion.

The training course provided to Timorese judges was on specialisation in economic and financial crime. Emília Pires was unusually professional in this area, and managed, under the rules she established in the financial system, to guide the Government not to sign contracts worth hundreds of millions of dollars with foreign companies that tried to deceive us with false identification.

Ladies and Gentlemen,

Today, we are faced with spending irregularities, over tens of millions of dollars, without Justice having shown the wisdom to demand responsibility for the loss of so much *Osan Povo nian*.

Jere ho Di'ak is not, and cannot, only be understood as a responsibility inherent to those who use the state's money for the common good. *Jere ho Di'ak* is also an act of responsibility consequent to the justice system itself, which, by law, must analyse the normative procedures that govern public spending. It must investigate the legality and transparency of acts carried out by public managers to be able to demand compliance with the duty of *Jere ho Di'ak*. The Attorney General of the Republic, who brought all that action against Emília Pires, bought earrings and chains for his wife in Brazil with the money of an advisor; in the annual Accountability Report, we only saw a piece of paper with a statement justifying that those thousands of dollars were spent to offer a dinner to colleagues from the CPLP, who had gathered there in Brazil for a meeting related to the Public Prosecutor's Office. In this case, the Court of Auditors didn't question the illegality of that paper, which was intended to justify the lack of a good few thousand dollars, because, as a rule, a receipt should be presented from the restaurant that provided the dinner.

In recent years, there has been a perception, manifestly resulting from the actions of the judicial system, that corruption only exists, or can only come, from acts carried out by a specific segment of society. This situation, we would say, has been politicised and 'legalised' by those in charge of the law, whereby, on one side of the scales of justice, there are those who are persecuted, and on the other, those who are immune from any blame.

Corruption doesn't just come from 'stealing' public money; corruption often manifests itself in the consent shown, consciously

or unconsciously, by judicial actors who create the impression in society that the 'law' ultimately protects individual interests, and puts the interests of friends and supporters above those of the state.

Jere ho Di'ak also means that it is unacceptable to encourage superfluous spending, and this should not only merit the attention of those involved in justice but also the heads of the institutions that have the role of monitoring, supervising, and drawing attention to violations of the *Jere ho Di'ak* rules.

Corruption is authorised by the handing over of public spending powers to directors who can now sign contracts worth more than one million dollars and the abusive use of public transfers to people's liking without properly proving what the activity is for, so it is impossible to know exactly what has or has not been done.

The changes to the financial system, which allowed total freedom of action and did not require the prior presentation of documents, is a fact that the 9th Government is discovering, with great regret. And to top it all off, in the financial system that Emília Pires helped set up, there was the fundamental and rigid rule of 'Budgeting by Programme', which was changed to an oasis, defined as 'Major Planning Options' (which didn't even exist, because it was unnecessary). This irregularity gave those responsible for managing public money total freedom of action to use Salaries and Wages money to buy items that would have been Goods and Services, and to use Minor Capital money to pay salaries. While, previously, the budget was valid annually, from January 1st to December 31st each year, each institution was recently allowed to deposit the money in commercial banks, and, in many cases, without spending it. In the 4th and 5th Governments, any money left over or unused by December 31st each year was returned to the state coffers. In recent times, this so-called 'management balance' has come to be regarded as 'revenue', and has not returned to the state coffers, and the institutions have held this revenue in banks to be used as they please.

'Osan Povu nian, Jere ho Di'ak' seems not to have been taken up by everyone yet. Institutions such as the Civil Service Commission, the General State Inspectorate, the Ombudsman for Human Rights and Justice, the Anti-Corruption Commission, and the Public Prosecutor's Office should act, in this monitoring and inspection plan, as the state's weapons in the fight against abusively illicit practices.

In this state-building process, from July until now, we have been identifying all the irregularities committed and will make the necessary corrections. I could define these months as the time spent completely cleaning house. Allow me to present here, for a better understanding, cases of so-called projects with the appropriate contracts signed – one relating to work on 800 metres of road at a cost of more than US$5 million, another of five kilometres at a cost of more than US$20 million, and another, in which a company is carrying out the work without a signed contract! These are just a few examples of what we have come across in these months.

As I have already stated, including in the National Parliament, our action has no retaliatory objective, and it is not our intention to bring these cases before the courts, not only because it would take years to decide, or not to decide, but also because the justice system no longer inspires confidence in society.

Therefore, we contacted these companies, and it was agreed that we would review the projects, and they agreed to continue carrying out the work, depending on the cost of each project. The idea is to educate these companies on how to participate, but with responsibility towards the people, because of *Osan Povu nian*. And that's what we did when we set up the National Development Agency, whose mission was to constantly monitor and supervise the work and tell the construction companies to correct the wrongs. This way of educating and mentalising the companies, national and international, about their duties in the execution of the works has helped enormously, so that many projects, when finished, have the appropriate level of execution and correspond to the value of the money spent by the state.

In 2015 and 2016, Timor-Leste was classified as the first country in Asia, and third in the world, to fulfil the requirements for transparency in money management, established by the Extractive Industry Transparency Initiative (EITI). It was a source of national pride for us, as *Osan Povu nian, Jere ho Di'ak* . Today, Timor-Leste continues to be the number one country in Asia for this, and regarding the world index, is in a more moderate position due to the change in the requirements of the EITI itself.

The 9th Government's programme for the next five years will focus on economic development, which will involve using public money to encourage and motivate entrepreneurship in the national private sector, productivity, and job creation.

To this end, in the plan for the successful execution of this programme, the Government has in mind the establishment of a Development Bank, whose mission is to provide credit support for continuing the activities that small- and medium-sized companies intend to carry out. This project will be regulated by the 'Grow-in Private Resource' system, and this bank, co-financed by the Government and the private sector, and will contribute to the economic return provided by the benefiting companies, as well as guarantee the financial recovery, so that the Development Bank can assume its sustainability in this process of active participation in the country's socio-economic development.

Ladies and Gentlemen,

I apologise for bringing up these subjects, but I ask for your understanding in that I was motivated to do so by the theme '*Osan Povu nian, Jere ho Di'ak*'.

This theme will have to guide all those involved in building and consolidating the state, starting from the realisation that the wages and working conditions each of us receives come from the *Osan Povu nian*, and if we don't respond with correctness and principled fairness to our duties, we are all contradicting the concept of *Jere ho Di'ak*. At the same time, the people continue to face the difficulties of daily life.

I hope that the initiative carried out by the University of Coimbra, co-sponsored by the European Union and the Camões Institute, will produce its practical effects, which we hope will finally be positive in the time to come, so that our people can genuinely have confidence in the fairness of the decisions that the country's justice system will have to prove with facts, as a result of the lessons learnt during the course and the possible recommendations that the Round Table may produce for a better synergy of thought and action in the institutions whose primary duty is to ensure that the *Osan Povu nian, tenke Jere ho Di'ak*.

Thank you all for your attention.

The Official Opening of the Timor-Leste International Business Forum 2023

GMN Multi-Function Venue, Díli
23 November 2023

Your Excellencies,
Ladies and Gentlemen,

It is an honour to be here at this Timor-Leste International Business Forum 2023.

Firstly, allow me to extend a warm welcome to those who have travelled from afar to take part in this event and honour us with their contributions.

I would also like to greet all the attendees who dignify this event, promoted by the Vice Prime Minister Coordinator for Economic Affairs and Minister of Tourism and Environment, in cooperation with the Timor-Leste Chamber of Commerce and Industry.

This Business Forum fosters the debate of ideas and solutions which, as you know, is the first step towards creating any business and entrepreneurship opportunity.

We are speaking of business opportunities not just for Timor-Leste but for our entire region, considering that Timor-Leste is creating conditions to become a more active and dynamic economic partner, particularly in the context of joining ASEAN and the World Trade Organization (WTO).

I think the challenges Timor-Leste faces as a young country are already well known to all. We have numerous weaknesses in terms of institutions, infrastructures, and human resources, as well as access to knowledge and technology.

But, today, I am not here to talk about weaknesses but, rather, about opportunities.

As such, I would like to address a crucial aspect for both businesses and the Timorese society, in general: our ability to adapt.

It is a fact that we live in a changing world where adaptability, innovation, and a youthful workforce are key factors.

In my time, it was said that 'You can't teach an old dog new tricks'. But in Timor-Leste, one of our main riches is the strength and youthfulness of our nation and, inherently, our adaptability. We have young people capable of 'learning new tricks', which include languages, skills, and technologies – youth who are eager to embrace development opportunities to transform themselves and the country.

We are witness to an impressive speed of social and technological changes that occur in months, or even weeks. Businesses must adapt to these changes, and they have to create modern and innovative business models, with the young being the most capable of driving this change.

Therefore, we must have more faith in the power of our youth! We need to create opportunities for young people, especially in the national productive sectors.

The time has come to launch start-ups in Timor-Leste, a strategy so popular around the world, for young people looking for challenges and opportunities.

The youth must take the initiative, and the Government will support local businesses to start and grow, as is foreseen in the National Industry Policy currently being prepared by the Government.

In addition to the youthfulness of our nation, another strong point that sets us apart is our geographical location. Situated in Southeast Asia, but very close to Australia and the Pacific, Timor-Leste is positioned to enjoy the vibrant economic dynamics of our region. ASEAN has recently emerged as a decisive engine of the global economy. With a market of $2.3 trillion and 600 million people, ASEAN is an economic powerhouse that has transformed Southeast Asia.

One of the reasons why Timor-Leste is working towards joining ASEAN is precisely to become part of this success story. Full membership in ASEAN will provide foreign businesses and investors with the confidence and security to invest in our country.

On the other hand, we also have deep ties that unite us with countries from various points of the globe, with Timorese youth adapting culturally, and even linguistically, to various worlds. This represents not only an advantage but also an opportunity to embrace all the innovative potential of developed or emerging economies scattered around the world. We may not dominate innovation, but we can easily reach it if we are predisposed to do so.

Therefore, I believe that Timorese businesses must make use of these opportunities. They should seek these differentiating innovation models, which can lead them to various sectors and markets.

Your Excellencies,
Ladies and Gentlemen,

We have another very important opportunity to explore: cooperation.

We are a country that resisted and became sovereign in the most unlikely of contexts, because we survived, despite the sacrifices and difficulties, the Cold War era. We survived, thanks not only to the Timorese Resistance but also to the invaluable foundations of cooperation and solidarity. Not just cooperation and solidarity with other countries but also cooperation and solidarity among the Timorese.

As such, the value of cooperation should not be underestimated. Cooperation should be encouraged for all Timorese entrepreneurs, to be able to capitalise on internal cooperation and strategic partnerships with international businesspeople, transferring knowledge, technology, and foreign capital to the country.

Timorese businesspeople should seek to step out of their comfort zone and build themselves up, as if it were a matter of survival.

They should not look exclusively to the Government to provide them with the support they need, to finance their ambitions, or extricate them from their difficulties.

On their own means, they must seek solutions favourable to their business area and move forward, looking themselves for the cooperation they need. These cooperative partnerships will certainly provide the sharing of resources and experiences that will enable their projects and investments to evolve.

And yet, Timorese businesspeople know they can continue to count on the cooperation of the Government. The Government is a strategic partner of national and international companies.

The Government is working to ensure that Timorese have access to education, professional training, and internships in friendly countries for the development of their skills.

The Government is working to develop basic infrastructures and access to markets. The Government is working to reform public administration systems and the management of finances and financing to the private sector. And, diplomatically, it is making every effort to establish cooperation frameworks that also contribute to the sharing of experiences, best practices, and expertise in all development sectors.

The *Strategic Development Plan 2011-2030*, which aims to develop social capital and the economic, infrastructure, and governance sectors, was reinforced through the 9th Constitutional Government Programme.

Diversifying the economy is one of the main goals of this Government, with the need to create the fiscal and bureaucratic conditions that allow greater predisposition to national and international investors to take a chance on Timor-Leste.

On the other hand, all cross-cutting policies that include the development of social and economic capital, infrastructure, and the governance sector are inseparable to boost economic development and create conditions for entrepreneurship.

The Government's priorities are clear. We want to diversify the economy through the development of productive sectors (agriculture, forestry, livestock, fishing, tourism, oil and minerals, and manufacturing industry), and we want to promote private sector investment, which also leads to the substitution of products that can be produced locally.

We believe that a comprehensive and transparent financial market facilitates investment in strategic sectors and drives economic growth within a sustainable and diversified non-oil economy.

We are working with the Central Bank of Timor-Leste to promote the development of the financial sector, by creating a favourable environment, facilitating the commercial activities of the banking sector, insurance institutions, microcredit institutions, and the financial market in Timor-Leste.

And we are working so that the private sector develops beyond the limits of state projects, having lacked access to long-term credit and financing, with the inherent accessible interest rates.

For this reason, we will create the Timor-Leste Development Bank, one of this Government's crown jewels, with the objective to facilitate access to long-term financing at affordable interest rates.

Your Excellencies,
Ladies and Gentlemen,

There are several necessary conditions to develop the national private sector, and the Government is acting on each of these conditions, namely:
- Political and economic stability
- Reform of the legal framework that offers security to investors, in terms of guaranteeing property rights, contract enforcement, and

resolution of commercial disputes, as well as in building a regulatory framework that favours commercial activity
- Improved basic infrastructures: including also the transport, energy, and communications sectors
- Education and training of national human resources, and
- Access to financing: with bank loans and investment capital for the private sector to grow

Ladies and Gentlemen,

I cannot conclude without coming back to something I highlighted earlier: the world is changing, unfortunately with increasingly tough challenges, which put our very survival at risk.

But for every disaster, there is an opportunity and an incentive to change. In this case, I refer to the transition to sustainable investment in green and blue opportunities.

Timor-Leste prioritises investing in areas that preserve and promote the country's natural environment. In this context, numerous opportunities arise to encourage the private sector to contribute to this goal.

From renewable energies, energy efficiency, waste management, and a more sustainable agricultural, fishery, and livestock sector, there are many opportunities to invest intelligently in the country and the planet. Timor-Leste, through its blue economy programme, whose action plan is under development, wants to focus on the protection and conservation of ecosystems, protecting its biodiversity and habitats, especially maritime biodiversity and habitats.

The truth is that environmental awareness for the protection of the marine environment also creates financial return opportunities for investors, including in the tourism area as a distinct brand in the region. And this is undoubtedly an area to develop:

We want to build a sustainable future for the Timorese, but also contribute to the sustainable future of the planet.

And if we all do our part: Government, businesses, and civil society, uniting our potential and our courage, we can create a competitive and innovative environment for the country, which creates income and employment and respects nature.

Please keep this in mind during the discussions that will take place today and tomorrow, which will focus more on the national priority development sectors.

Think of the power of adaptation, innovation, and cooperation to invest in businesses that bring income and pride to the nation.

Having a bold purpose, proper planning, clarity, and ambition, is the very nature of an entrepreneur.

A Timorese entrepreneur, who knows he or she can count on the Government and international strategic partnerships, is undoubtedly a promising and transformative agent of the national economic landscape.

I conclude by wishing success to the presentations and debates that follow.

Remember, the future is in our hands! Let us transform this future with energy, innovation, and cooperation.

Thank you very much.

Official Start of the Telkomcel Summit:
Driving Economic Growth Through Developing People's Digital Capability

GMN Multi-Function Venue, Díli
30 November 2023

Your Excellencies
Ladies and Gentlemen,

I wish to start by expressing my great pleasure to participate in this event, to discuss issues that are so important in today's modern and technology-driven world.

It is no secret that the 9th Constitutional Government is committed to creating development opportunities for the Timorese people. To do this, we must invest in a diversified economy with productive sectors driving economic growth.

This means there must be a focus on the development of the private sector, which includes removing obstacles to investment, ensuring a positive business environment, and providing concrete measures of support. This will allow the private sector to become true partners of the Government in the economic growth of our nation.

In the 21st century, the achievement of economic growth is closely linked to access to technology and telecommunications: to internet access and the ability to enjoy and exploit the opportunities it provides.

As such, I thank Telkomcel for hosting this important summit. It will foster debate on national digital empowerment and help drive our economic development and create jobs for our people.

In a world undergoing technological transformation, Timor-Leste cannot and will not remain indifferent to the opportunities the digital world provides in all areas of our life. This includes our social life, education, arts and culture, and, of course, in business and entrepreneurship.

Just last week, I had the privilege of participating in the Timor-Leste

International Business Forum. At this forum, I spoke about the importance of adaptability in a changing world, the importance of innovation and cooperation in creating entrepreneurship and business opportunities that bring revenue to Timor-Leste.

I also spoke about our country's greatest wealth, which is our young and ambitious workforce, who, like all youth today, are either adept at or attracted to all things digital.

The internet and social media have become ingrained in the lives of our youth, but there's still a long way to go to transform these tools into opportunities for development and economic growth.

We need to convert the ease and enjoyment of using the internet and social media into genuine skills and digital qualifications that link to the job market.

We must also leverage digital opportunities to create businesses that generate employment and income.

Using technology and creativity, it is possible to create business models with access to new markets, participating in the global digital economy with just a click.

Meanwhile, even traditional companies can use digital tools to increase their productivity and efficiency, generating more wealth for the country.

Improving digital skills of our people will contribute not only to more active participation in the country's economy, but also to caring for the democratic health of the country.

Ladies and Gentlemen,

We are aware that before investing more seriously in developing the digital skills of our people we must address the unequal access to technology in Timor-Leste.

In the information age, where access to technology is so critical to a person's social and economic opportunities, we must make sure we do not create a digital divide. And we must make sure that our people know how to make use of the information and communication tools that technology provides to us.

We cannot be left behind.

That is why the 9th Constitutional Government has been working on building and installing submarine fibre optic cable, which we have made a priority in the 2024 state budget.

A seabed study has been conducted and, currently, the submarine cable, branching unit, ROADM (reconfigurable optical add/drop multiplexer), and eight repeaters are being produced. Under the mandate of the 9th

Constitutional Government, the National Procurement Commission has also completed the procurement process and signed the contract for constructing the beach manholes related to the establishment of the terrestrial station in Bebonuk, Díli.

We also have the National Connectivity Project underway, to expand the connections of government agencies, state institutions, and public buildings, both in Díli and across the municipalities, including in hospitals and some health centres. We are also implementing the Electronic Governance Project to bring citizens closer to services provided by the Government.

Nevertheless, I admit there is much work to be done both to ensure that access is provided to all Timorese, including people who live in the remote areas of the country, and guarantee the quality and transparency of internet access services provided, particularly by telecommunications companies.

This includes setting policies and a regulatory framework that encourages competition and digital inclusion, as well as the much-needed protection of privacy.

Internet and digital media access must be fair and balanced, to avoid fostering inequalities and social exclusion.

In conclusion, investing in our people's digital skills means investing in qualifications to combat unemployment and in creating businesses and a private sector that can access the global economy.

It also means improving the connection between citizens and government services, which are undergoing technological modernisation for more efficient, rapid, and citizen-centric governance.

Cooperation is key to this sector. The Government has a duty to lead this transformation, to create the necessary infrastructure, to provide education, training, and digital capacity building; however, without the commitment of the private sector, and without civil society, success will not be possible.

The telecommunications operators in the country have a key role in fostering economic growth, and deserve the respect and support of the Government.

Their commitment and investment, coupled with greater digital capacity on the part of citizens, will provide us with opportunities for growth, improved social well-being and inclusion, and the economic development of our nation.

Thank you very much.

Environment

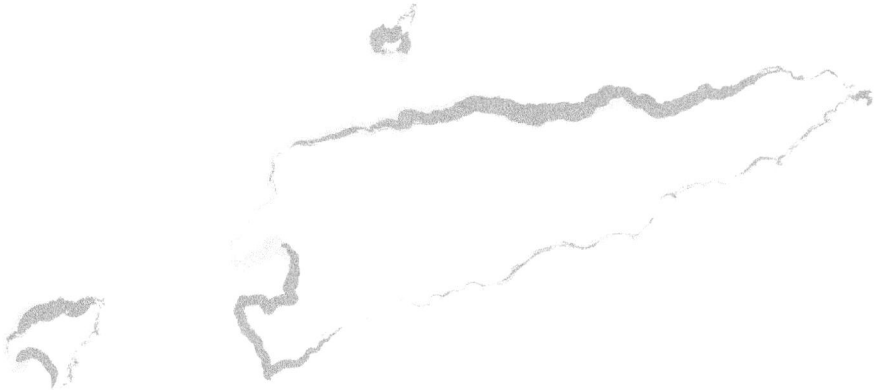

Blue Talks, Bridges to Lisbon: The 2022 United Nations Ocean Conference: Promotion and Strengthening of Sustainable Ocean-Based Economies.
Potential of the Sea of Timor-Leste: Perspectives on the Biodiversity of the Sea of Timor-Leste

Portuguese Cultural Centre, Dīli
8 June 2022

[Presentation of the videos 'Dircia', 'Adara', 'Tutuala', and 'Sal']

'Hau Nia Tasi, Hau Nia Timor', 'My Sea, My Timor'

These are the voices of our people. What you have just seen speaks for itself. It demonstates the relationship between the sea and our people. The sea nourishes us; we nourish the sea!

Your Excellency Ms Manuela Bairos, Portuguese Ambassador to Timor-Leste,
Your Excellency Mr Roy Trivedy, UN Resident Coordinator,
Your Excellency Ms Tuya Altangerel, UNDP Representative to Timor-Leste,
Your Excellencies,
Ladies and Gentlemen,
Dear friends,

Good afternoon!
    I would like to start by thanking the Portuguese Ambassador to Timor-Leste, my dear friend Manuela Bairos, and the UNDP, represented here by Ms Tuya Altangerel, for jointly hosting this important seminar on the potential of the sea in Timor-Leste.
    The sea is a core element in constructing the Timorese identity.
    Legend has it that the Island of Timor was born out of friendship and a

love of the sea. 'The legend says, and so I believe (...) From the bottom of the sea a crocodile sought to chase its destiny through that sliver of light' until it became the country that is Timor... 'Grandfather Crocodile – says the legend, and I believe it! It is Timor!'

The sea is part of the history and culture of our nation and the perception that the Timorese have of the world.

Thousands of years ago, different ethnic groups from the most diverse places in Asia and the South Pacific settled on our shores, and as others arrived, started to move deeper inland, onto the back of our grandfather crocodile.

As time went by, they moved from the coast into the interior. From fisherpeople, we became farmers. Still, the connection between nature and the people living in our island was never lost. We are deeply connected to that which houses, creates, and nourishes us, and even after we pass on, we still remain present in the lives of the living.

Centuries ago, the sea also brought European navigators from distant Portugal. Upon entering through the calm waves of the Lifau beaches, they were awestruck by our native resources and beauty.

And while the sea set the bounds of our country's territory, it was also the sea that provided easy access for a brutal invasion and an occupation that lasted a quarter century. The tears of agony cried by our people made the sea saltier than ever.

And yet, the Timorese never lost faith, or hope. The process that built our identity, resulting from a meeting of civilisations and cultures, also instilled in us an ideal of freedom that was to be the destiny of our people and our homeland.

Thanks to many friends all over the world who advocated for the restoration of our independence, the Maubere miracle did ultimately come to pass.

As such, in these crossroads between Asia and the Pacific, there exists today a small but proud sovereign country, located among more than 17,000 islands in the neighbouring archipelago of Indonesia and the vast continent of Australia to the south.

Because our country is Portuguese-speaking, we share our cultural identity and language with eight other maritime nations.

Your Excellencies,
Ladies and Gentlemen,

As we have seen, the sea is in the DNA of the Timorese. Perhaps that is why during the first years of our independence we felt incomplete. It was unacceptable to look at the sea that shaped the destiny of our nation, to feel the promise in its waves, when the international community would not acknowledge our maritime jurisdiction over that very sea.

For a long time we sailed over murky waters with our neighbour Australia, trying to achieve a negotiated compromise on maritime boundaries.

Recently, making use of international law, we finally succeeded in establishing permanent maritime boundaries with Australia. We are presently holding talks with Indonesia, seeking to achieve the same goal.

This is no more than guaranteeing our full sovereignty, both political and economic, so as to honour the sacrifices made for our people, many of whom died in the hope of a better future for their children.

Once our sea was very salty. Once it was murky. But now it is blue!

> *[T]he time has come to look at our sea with a strategic vision, so that we may start thinking about the future.*

The history of Timor-Leste is one of hope. In addition to petroleum resources, the sea of Timor also houses areas with the greatest concentration of biodiversity in the world, such as the waters around Ataúro Island.

Therefore, if 'Portugal is Sea'[1], then we can say that Timor is TASI. This is an acronym in Portuguese for a Timor that is blue, sustainable, and innovative.

Our proximity to the ocean gives us access to broad and rich biological, geological, mineral, and geostrategic resources. This means that our economy and the sea are inseparable. Still, this interdependency must be managed in a manner that is balanced and, most importantly, sustainable.

This is the difference in all that entails the blue economy. The blue economy seeks to utilise the ocean, as well as to protect it. We are all aware that we are using resources at a much faster rate than nature can replenish.

This means that biodiversity faces very serious threats.

> *The loss of biodiversity is a ticking time bomb: it is detrimental to the health of living beings, it hurts sustainable development, and it worsens climate change.*

And so, it is urgent to balance economic activity and the long-term ability of ocean ecosystems to support that activity.

---

1. Portugal is Sea, the new chart drafted by the Portuguese Task Group for the Extension of the Continental Shelf (EMEPC). Portugal's land area covers around 92,000 square kilometres. However, if we consider Portugal's maritime dimension under the Law of the Sea, we have a country with around four million square kilometres, 40 times more than Portugal's land area. EMEPC is still waiting for a response to its request to extend Portugal's continental shelf, which it submitted to the United Nations in 2009.

Ladies and Gentlemen,

Like I said, in Timor-Leste we have coral reefs containing the greatest biodiversity in the world. We have warm waters and beautiful tropical beaches. We also have an annual migration of blue whales and dolphins around the coast that, in my opinion, is worthy of establishing an International Centre of Cetacean Research and Control, in partnership with international academic institutions.

Fishing is a vital activity for our subsistence economy. Some experts claim that the best tuna in the world spawns in our waters. However, the vastness of the seas makes it easy for foreign commercial fleets to carry out illegal fishing, which causes us severe economic and environmental damage. We must put an end to this, and we must ensure the sustainability of the species of fish being exploited in an out-of-control and illegal manner.

Tourism is another key industry for our economy. We must ensure that it is done in such a way as to attract tourists without sacrificing our biodiversity. We want to develop tourism sustainably, contributing to poverty reduction without lowering the quantity and diversity of our precious maritime resources.

This is why our communities follow Tara Bandu, an ancestral practice that respects and protects our nature, as it is sacred to us. This traditional custom seeks both to manage our natural resources sustainably as well as to contribute to the development of our communities.

Together with five other states, Timor-Leste is part of the Coral Triangle Initiative. We are working with our neighbours to protect maritime life and diversity. The Coral Triangle is an epicentre of diversity in terms of coral, fish, and other marine organisms, representing around 3,000 species of fish and 76% of the types of coral in the world.

And yet, like many other areas throughout the world, so too is the Coral Triangle under threat. The ocean is becoming more acidic and warmer, with less oxygen. Populations, economies, and international trade are growing fast, which in turn leads to an increase in marine plastic and marine debris.

As in the case of climate change, it is urgent to make changes in order to mitigate the current trend of biodiversity loss and the terrible impacts it will have on humankind.

Responding to Madam Ambassador, who raised four very timely questions, I must state that we can no longer delay debate on how to improve the ability of island states to develope their blue economy.

This requires investments that are both intelligent and adapted to local realities. It entails serious commitment, particularly by those wealthier nations that, in addition to having greater financial resources and stronger technologic and scientific abilities, are the very ones that have been punishing our ocean the most, so that they adhere to a rule-based international order for the ocean.

The United Nations Secretary-General, António Guterres, told countries to 'bring plans, not just speeches'. I would like to add: bring concrete and feasible programmes, not merely pieces from international legislation.

Timor-Leste is one of 38 small island developing states – or, like we prefer to say, one of the small states of the vast ocean. Although we are resilient, we live in a time where climate change is a serious threat to our very survival. As such, we must waste no time in finding strategies to protect the ocean and its biodiversity, by focusing on genuine alliances.

We are linked to each other by the ocean and by common challenges. This bond must be heard by the international community.

It is incomprehensible that there is not a stronger and unanimous international response to mitigate climate change, which compromises both the global development agenda and the safety of millions of people.

Ladies and Gentlemen,

We Timorese must improve the way in which we understand and use our sea. This requires wisdom and a great deal of respect. There are many opportunities for a blue development that safeguards and uses the sea responsibly.

And here we have good news and bad news.

The good news is that we are a blank slate, or, better yet, a *blue* slate. We have the opportunity to implement from scratch a blue economy that contributes to the development of current and future communities.

We can boost economic growth, job creation, and food security through balanced economic activity that enables ocean ecosystems to replenish, thus protecting and preserving the seas and the ocean.

The bad news is that, despite all our efforts to establish maritime boundaries, the issues leading to loss of biodiversity are global. They are not stopped by national boundaries, much less maritime boundaries.

Ladies and Gentlemen,

As the Government's Special Representative for the Blue Economy, I can say that Timor-Leste wants to play an active role in the international arena, particularly within the UN, so as to promote and protect the ocean, as well as to ensure that maritime resources are managed responsibly. Timor-Leste advocates strengthening global governance towards this purpose.

Although we are aware of the challenges we face in protecting our biodiversity, we have concrete plans to do so, starting with greater awareness by our society. This entails greater civic education on ocean issues.

We want to start precisely with our children and young people, 'distributing breaths from the sea'... This is a project that we will announce very soon, acknowledging that education is an important starting point for promoting the long-term construction of the blue economy.

Still, awareness, by itself, is not enough. We require a combined political, economic, social, and cultural approach – a changing of mindsets – that once and for all changes the relationship between humans and nature.

Until then, we are all responsible to be a part of this change.

Thank you very much.

UN Ocean Conference, Plenary Session.
Scaling up Ocean Action Based on Science and Innovation for the Implementation of Goal 14: Stocktaking, Partnerships, and Solutions

Altice Arena
Lisbon, Portugal
28 June 2022

Distinguished Presidents and Vice-Presidents of the Conference,

Your Excellencies,

Ladies and Gentlemen,

On behalf of the Democratic Republic of Timor-Leste, I want to start by thanking the United Nations and the Governments of Portugal and Kenya for hosting this timely second UN Ocean Conference.

It is both a privilege and a joy to be here today to state once more our commitment to Sustainable Development Goal 14, the ocean, and our collective future.

I have the honour of representing His Excellency the President of the Republic of Timor-Leste, Dr José Ramos-Horta, who passes on his best wishes for a successful conference.

Timor-Leste is a small island developing state – our identity is anchored in the sea. The ocean has traced our past and is a cornerstone of our vision for the future.

As such, we want to add our voices and, most importantly, our actions to those committed to defending the ocean on which we all depend.

The ocean is a vital organ that is sick, putting our planet and all of humanity in peril. Throughout human history, power, selfishness, and ambition have caused great suffering. War, hunger, poverty, and inequality are tragedies that we could prevent and solve. Instead, we are treating nature with the same hubris.

And even though we are not all equally responsible for the pressure put on nature, we will all suffer from it.

The first victims are always those most fragile and most vulnerable. It is a cruel fact that these are often the very people who live in greatest harmony with nature.

Scientific reports provide data on the degradation of the seas and the oceans. Our largest carbon filter, which is essential to tackle climate change, is becoming clogged.

In some countries in the Pacific, Asia, Africa, and Latin America, we do not need to look at reports. We are already suffering with these effects.

Global threats demand global responses. I hope the COVID-19 pandemic has at least taught everyone this important lesson.

Your Excellencies,
Ladies and Gentlemen,

Supported by international law, particularly UNCLOS, we recently succeeded in delimiting permanent maritime boundaries with Australia. We are currently working with Indonesia to achieve the same.

UNCLOS is essential for the good governance of the ocean and for achieving Sustainable Development Goal 14. Areas 'without governance' are areas where uncertainty breeds.

Timor-Leste is located at the heart of the Coral Triangle. In fact, our seas have areas with the greatest biodiversity in the entire world. We also have one of the largest concentrations of cetaceans on the planet, as well as whale migration corridors, including for the incredible blue whale, humpback whales, sperm whales, and dolphins.

We want to establish a Marine Education Centre, with the support of international institutions, including global academics. We are committed to a Blue Economy, which protects the ocean in a balanced way.

Cooperation with neighbouring countries is fundamental, as well as partnerships with other states. We want to bring know-how, technology, and investment that could be a turning point for the sustainable development of Timor-Leste.

In my country we have young people who, recognising the importance of preserving the ocean and biodiversity, wish to study marine science. I want to believe that it is possible to make these young people's dreams come true and ensure that Timor-Leste will, with knowledge and conviction, implement a Blue Economy from scratch.

We reiterate our commitment to the Paris Agreement and are pleased with the COP 26 initiatives, even though greater effort is required to help developing countries address climate change.

We also support the United Nations Decade of Ocean Science for Sustainable Development to come up with transformative solutions linking people and oceans.

We encourage young people to develop science-based solutions. I am certain that the Youth and Innovation Forum has already contributed a great deal towards this goal.

A blue future requires a blue generation.

We renew the commitment we made at the 2017 Ocean Conference and our voluntary commitments.

And later today, the Pacific Small Island Developing States and Timor-Leste will adopt a Joint Declaration on Climate Change Adaption Alliance.

Timor-Leste is very much hoping to be a part of the global commitments, solutions, and partnerships that will derive from this Ocean Conference.

Thank you very much.

First High-Level Meeting of the Archipelagic and Island States Forum: *Fostering Collaboration, Enabling Innovation for Our Ocean and Our Future.*

Bali, Indonesia
11 October 2023

Your Excellency the President of the Republic, Joko Widodo.
Your Excellencies Heads of State and Government,
Your Excellencies, Ladies and Gentlemen,

It is a privilege to take part in this First High-Level Meeting of Archipelagic and Island States.

I would like to thank His Excellency President Joko Widodo for inviting me, and the Government of Indonesia for its warm hospitality.

All countries represented here are united by the ocean.

The ocean gives us life. It connects humanity. It gives us common identities and shared challenges and ambitions.

This forum promotes cooperation and solidarity, so that together we can achieve sustainable development and marine conservation.

Like most small island states, Timor-Leste is vulnerable to climate change and the destruction of our greatest asset – our marine environment, in all its diversity and wonder.

That is why, last month, Timor-Leste appeared before the International Tribunal on the Law of the Sea in Hamburg at the historic Advisory Opinion case on States' obligations concerning climate change and the marine environment.

While we are not all equally responsible for climate change, we will all suffer. And many small island states are already suffering more than the nations that caused the problem.

Recognising this, UNCLOS established the principle of common, but differentiated, responsibilities concerning the obligations of states.

Developing states cannot simply be left behind. We have a sovereign right to develop, and an obligation to protect our environment.

Like Indonesia, finalising our maritime boundaries is important to Timor-Leste. We have already settled with Australia, through the first-ever compulsory conciliation process under UNCLOS.

Now we are looking to finalise our maritime boundaries with Indonesia in a spirit of friendship and cooperation. Once we have concluded these negotiations with Indonesia, we will then be able to look at sustainable fishery projects in our seas and help put an end to the illegal fishing that is destroying our marine biodiversity.

We are also cooperating with Indonesia to establish a marine park for the sustainable management of our seas.

I would like this to be known as a Peace Park, not only for its symbolic value but to reflect its importance in conserving our biodiversity and our common development.

Timor-Leste and Indonesia are located in the Coral Triangle, an area with the highest marine biological diversity in the world.

Indonesia has established many wonderful national parks, including Komodo National Park, which is so close to our country. In Timor-Leste, we are developing a blue economy as another pathway for development.

Initiatives like the AIS Blue Hub, the Research and Development Centre, and the Blue Economy Development Index will support our endeavours.

Ataúro Island, which lies just 30 kilometres offshore from our capital, Díli, hosts some of the most biodiverse waters in the world. We are establishing a Marine Research and Education Centre on Ataúro Island and are preparing to declare the waters around the island a marine national park.

Friends, this forum is a welcome opportunity to embrace our shared connection to the ocean, and to work together to achieve sustainable development and marine conservation.

I conclude by conveying once more my appreciation to the leaders of Indonesia for facilitating collaboration among archipelagic and island states around the theme 'For Our Ocean and Our Future'.

Thank you very much.

Ninth Our Ocean Conference:
Intervention at the High-Level Panel.
An Ocean of Potential

Athens, Greece
16 April 2024

Excellencies,
Distinguished Guests,
Ladies and Gentlemen,

I am honoured to speak at the 9th Our Ocean Conference, and I would like to thank His Excellency Kyriakos Mitsotakis, Prime Minister of Greece, for his invitation, and for hosting this event.

When I was a secondary school student, I had learned of Greece as the cradle of philosophy, art, and democracy. It is therefore a great honour to be here in Athens at this important international conference – and as a small island developing state, I was also compelled to attend this conference to discuss ocean-related issues.

I can say that even though this is my first visit to Greece, when I first glimpsed the country – while still in the air – I was amazed by the beauty of its sea, and of its lakes, all one colour, the same blue as the sky!

The perfect union between sea and land, so clear and sacred. This perfect union dazzled me, of an ocean so serene and without ripples, in contrast to my Timor Sea. That is why, when I landed in Athens and saw the coastline outlined in blue, I reflected on the purpose of this conference and how it is being held in a perfect and inspiring location for us Timorese who are taking the first steps towards developing our Blue Economy.

As such it is a privilege to be here with the ocean's most passionate advocates to discuss our common interest – the health of our ocean and the potential it holds.

Timor-Leste was fortunate to be able to participate in the Our Ocean Conference in Bali, Indonesia, in 2018.

In 2022, Timor-Leste also attended the UN Ocean Conference in Lisbon. Timor- Leste is fully behind the international efforts to protect our ocean.

The ocean serves as a unifying force, connecting nations and communities across the globe. Our lives, identities, and cultures are all linked to the vastness of the sea.

And this panel – from Seychelles to São Tomé e Príncipe, ending with Timor-Leste – is the real evidence of this reality!

For Timor-Leste, our relationship with the ocean runs deep. Timor-Leste enjoys unparalleled marine biodiversity, with over 75% of the world's coral reef species calling our waters home.

Timor's seas are a sanctuary for marine life. Every year we welcome the migration of majestic creatures, like pygmy blue whales, along our north coast.

As a small island developing state, we are looking to build a Blue Economy so that we can conserve our environment and provide opportunities for our people.

Timor-Leste's commitment

To achieve this, my government is making every effort to develop a Blue Economy Policy and Action Plan, an initiative I personally oversee. This plan will set out concrete actions to protect our ocean, including efforts to:

- expand our marine protected areas to conserve our biodiversity and tropical reefs
- establish Ataúro Island as a national marine park to sustainably manage and protect its marine life
- develop a Marine Education Centre to improve marine literacy for our people, including our young people
- take action to combat illegal fishing
- stop plastic pollution of our seas

However, none of this will be possible without global cooperation and meaningful partnerships driven by concrete actions and urgent actions, as previous panellists, throughout the day, have called for.

In 2014, Timor-Leste took part in the Small Island Developing States Conference (SIDS) in Samoa. In October last year, Timor-Leste went to Bali to participate in the Archipelagic and Island States Forum. Next month, Timor-Leste will participate in the 4th International Conference on SIDS in Antigua and Barbuda.

We now have a better understanding of the need for these small pieces of land, anchored in the sea – our island-states united in our shared connection to the ocean – to work together to achieve sustainable development and marine conservation.

That is why we say: We depend on the ocean, and the ocean depends on us!

As a small island developing state, Timor-Leste is also here to learn from the experiences of other countries, and to forge partnerships to protect and sustain our ocean. We look forward to working together to protect our ocean.

Thank you.

Government

Inauguration of the 9th Constitutional Government

Presidential Palace, Díli
1 July 2023

Your Excellency the President of the Republic, Dr José Ramos Horta,
Your Excellency the President of the National Parliament, Mrs Maria Fernanda Lay,
Excellency the President of the Court of Appeal, Dr Deolindo dos Santos,
Your Excellencies, Distinguished Dignitaries of Neighbouring Countries and
Distinguished Representatives of International Organisations,
Your Excellencies, Ambassadors,
Honourable Members of the National Parliament,
Your Excellencies,
Distinguished Guests,
Ladies and Gentlemen,
People of Timor-Leste, to whom I bow with all respect,

First of all, I would like to extend a sincere welcome to all the dignitaries from neighbouring countries present at this ceremony.

I want to thank you for your kindness in coming to Díli. Your distinguished presence only dignifies the commitment of the Timorese, revealed in the recent Parliamentary Elections, to consolidate the Democratic Rule of Law in Timor-Leste and to continue on the path of progress and development, which will guarantee a better life for its citizens.

Excellencies, Honourable Guests,

In 2012, eleven years ago, I was sworn in in the Great Hall of Lahane Palace as Prime Minister of the 5th Constitutional Government. Today, I come before the People of Timor-Leste to again assume this heavy responsibility to continue the processes of statebuilding and nationbuilding.

It is now 21 years since we restored national independence in a solemn ceremony in Tasi Tolu on May 20th, 2002, witnessed by the highest international dignitaries, and thus Timor-Leste became the youngest country in the world.

Having emerged from a long struggle, the then new state was trying to rise from the ashes of violence perpetrated before, during, and after the historic Referendum of 1999, where the heroic and brave people of Timor-Leste did not hesitate to use their fundamental right to decide their fate.

We fully realised that we were a fragile state in all aspects, from management and operational capacity, to legal aspects. So, we introduced systems that would regulate all the actions of the state.

With the mission-driven vision of building and consolidating state institutions, the 4th Government laid the foundations to create a system of complete transparency and accountability, providing responsibility and transparency in administrative acts of governance and recruitment of civil servants on merit, regardless of political factors.

From this emerged a political conjuncture, in this process of statebuilding, with the motto 'From fragility to resilience', counting on the political and technical support of international institutions, such as the World Bank (WB), the International Monetary Fund (IMF), the Asian Development Bank (ADB), and several friendly countries, which recognised the safe steps taken by the state of Timor-Leste and called for a better strengthening of the state system and institutions.

As you have all noticed, I stand here today with a new alliance of two parties – the CNRT and the Democratic Party – in a shared commitment to restore the Democratic Rule of Law.

I realise that there is a bitter feeling that I have ultimately prioritised the former members of the Executive of the 4th and 5th Governments, of which I was Prime Minister. I can understand the disappointment of Timorese society at the need for more new political and technical staff. Therefore, to respond to the concern of Timorese society, it was essential to bring in people who were already familiar with the system so that the efforts to restore legality could bring concrete and immediate results.

I also understand some societal discomfort at the excessive number of government members. I could not help but bring all these Timorese together, as the 9th Government is committed to making a difference – planning, action, and managing responsibilities.

This is why the organisational structure of the 9th Government is enshrined in the philosophy of resuming the continuity of the progress achieved until 2017 and of leading the public administration once again towards the objectives of efficiency and effectiveness in the provision of services to the people and in the fulfilment of responsibilities towards the state.

Making the necessary corrections, doing more, and improving is the common platform of understanding for forming this new Government. Our governing practice will be guided by the principles of good governance, inclusiveness, and the principle that everyone must obey the law.

Our vision is of a nation where society is prosperous and healthy, educated and skilled, innovative and dynamic, with widespread access to essential goods and services, and where production and employment in all productive sectors match those of an emerging economy.

For this to happen, the structure of the 9th Government aims to give each member of the Government a mission to fulfil in the different areas and sectors, so that we can take decisive action in this crucial period of change, also bearing in mind the preparation, in each municipality, of the technical staff that will be needed for the process of decentralisation of powers.

Using their legitimate rights, the people have clearly given this message: Let us save the Democratic Rule of Law, so we can walk optimistically along the path of progress!

Today, we have sworn to everyone that we are fully aware of our responsibilities. Whenever any of us feels unable to fulfil his or her mission, he or she will not hesitate to resign from the office in which he or she has been invested.

This political message will decisively mark the history of the nation, because it also serves as a political lesson for the future leadership of the country, in order not to fall into the same mistakes that, if continued, would lead our state to a situation of a failed state!

Your Excellency, Mr President of the Republic,
Distinguished Guests,

To meet the expectations of the Timorese people and society, the 9th Government commits itself, within the first 120 days of governance, to:

1. Restore democratic normality through the legitimate Parliament, which has already started its 6th Legislature, and through a legal Government, to approve the Government Programme for five years, approve the Amending Budget for 2023 and the 2024 General State Budget. Every effort will also be made to repeal all legislation and regulations necessary for the state consolidation;

2. Repeal Law No. 3/2014, which established the RAEOA and ZEEMS, to subordinate the RAEOA Authority to better control the central Government, since the objective described in the law for the creation of ZEEMS was not outlined, even after nine long years, and proceed

to the immediate audit of all activities, including the process of the expensive acquisition of 'Ro Haksolok';

3. Repeal the law that established the municipality of Ataúro, due to the total lack of infrastructural and logistical conditions on the islet of Ataúro, such as roads, electricity, water, harbour, and airport;

4. Audit the Court of Auditors, the Anti-Corruption Commission and the Public Prosecutor's Office on the implementation of programmes and the lack of procurement processes for many projects;

5. Audit the Civil Service Commission and the State Inspectorate-General on illegal recruitments and termination of contracts without justification;

6. Audit the electoral fraud committed by the Electoral Administration in the recent parliamentary elections to put an end to the interests at stake and prevent it from recurring in the future to safeguard the Democratic Rule of Law;

7. Immediately restructure the management of TIMOR GAP and ANPM to ensure greater efficiency in the oil sector, which is crucial for the country's development;

8. Restructure the Criminal Investigation Scientific Police (PCIC) due to its total lack of integrity and professionalism;

9. Consolidate the peace and security necessary for national development, guaranteeing the fundamental rights, freedoms, and guarantees of all citizens;

10. Immediately review the illegal process of forced retirement of dozens of PNTL members;

11. Immediately reform and restructure the National Intelligence Service to ensure integrity and professionalism in this institution;

12. Alert all PNTL officers who have been sworn in to serve a particular party to renounce their oath bonds or else leave the PNTL;

13. Immediately abolish the brutal tax increase approved in January 2023;

14. Audit and review, where necessary, the major 'deals' made at the end of the previous government's term;

15. Ensure the immediate availability of all necessary medicines to hospitals and health centres;

16. Turn school meals into a real hot and nutritious meal for children;

17. Improve the conditions of assistance and treatment for the people with disabilities in the National Rehabilitation Centre and, in the future, create similar centres in all municipalities;

18. Conduct a nationwide survey of the main road maintenance and river standardisation needs to start urgent rehabilitation works next year.

Your Excellency, Mr President of the Republic,
Distinguished Guests,

In fulfilment of the mandate granted by the people, the 9th Constitutional Government will have the following commitments for the first 12 months of governance:

1. Implement the justice reform (through the establishment of the Supreme Court of Justice and the quality training of judges and prosecutors);
2. Revise the Strategic Development Plan 2011–2030, adapting it to the current circumstances of the country;
3. Start the process of developing the South Coast;
4. Secure the Greater Sunrise gas pipeline to Timor-Leste;
5. Finalise the land and sea border with Indonesia as a national priority;
6. Initiate the process of local government through the phased decentralisation of government and municipal assemblies, once the respective infrastructural and technical conditions have been created;
7. Create a coordinating committee of universities and higher education institutes to study a collective strategy to define better assistance from the state and to implement the objective of raising the quality of education;
8. Review the law on assistance to the elderly and handicapped so that the state recognises that the current so-called elderly were, and should continue to be, considered the true national heroes, since it was this layer of the Timorese population who suffered all the hardships of war, all kinds of threats, and much pain for the loss of their relatives, but did not step back, and faced everything to decide to vote for independence in August 1999.
9. Establish and support an Association of Timorese Art and Culture to encourage talented young people in various fields of art and culture to affirm Timorese identity and bring it to international forums;
10. Double the number of scholarships to be awarded, on merit and based on national needs;
11. Complete the construction and installation of the optical fibre cable and ensure a quality internet connection for all citizens across the country;
12. Significantly increase the number of people in employment;
13. Implement the registration of both movable property and real estate (houses and land);
14. Start the implementation of a CAFE school in all administrative posts;

15. Complete the country's electrification programme to reach the remaining 20% of the population that has not yet had access to electricity;
16. Create new seasonal work programmes with friendly countries;
17. Implement the one-stop shop in all municipalities' head offices to allow access to central administration services throughout the country.

Your Excellency, Mr President of the Republic,
Distinguished Guests,

The 9th Constitutional Government is committed to fulfilling its vision and mission for the development of the country.

In its programme, which will be presented in the National Parliament, this Government will focus on the themes of basic infrastructure, both in health and education. It will seek to emphasise the Economy as the crucial and vital factor for the development of the nation, starting from agriculture, fishing, livestock, tourism, and the beginning of small and medium industries, to gradually reduce the import of goods and products which can be produced in the country.

If statebuilding concerns state institutions and the entire public administration, nationbuilding encompasses civil society, in its technical and intellectual capacity, and necessarily the national private sector, which should encourage entrepreneurship, especially among women.

Therefore, the next five years deserve a tremendous collective effort, requiring from everyone a great spirit of responsibility, dedication, honesty, persistence, and courage.

We will start the long-awaited and necessary process of decentralisation. To this end, the Government counts on the participation and cooperation of all citizens in this process. This decentralisation process will require all intellectuals and technicians from each municipality to actively and constructively participate in the frank and genuine dialogue that will be implemented so that the multiple benefits that will contribute to the well-being of local populations will be achieved and strengthened from the potential of each municipality.

That is why I appeal to young people to get involved. Each generation has a role to play in the constant challenges emerging in our reality. Young people must embrace this new struggle for the country's development, thus strengthening the democratic values by which we live.

Young people will be the future leaders of this nation, because they will be the ones who, by practice and example, can transform our society and economy.

This Government is committed to creating opportunities for young people to develop their skills, experiences, and values to actively and fully participate in the nation's future.

Therefore, the economy, or the diversification of the economy, will be an essential pillar in this five-year term of the 9th Constitutional Government.

The Government is committed to bringing the Greater Sunrise pipeline to the South Coast of Timor-Leste. We will prove to the world that the pipeline to Timor-Leste is a viable, economically secure solution, and that our horizon lies in developing an oil industry capable of creating direct economic dividends for our people.

The development of the South Coast in the oil and gas sector will continue to be a priority. Establishing a supply base, a refinery, and a gas pipeline in this part of the country are necessary investments to create our oil industry and generate employment for the Timorese.

To this end, it will also be a national priority to finalise the land and sea borders with Indonesia, the solution of which must only comply with international law.

I take this opportunity to declare that the 9th Government will pay special attention to investment, and in this regard, foreign companies will be very welcome to help develop the country and create employment for Timorese.

Your Excellency, Mr President of the Republic,
Excellencies,
Ladies and Gentlemen,

The 9th Government will seriously focus on improving service delivery in the two critical areas of health and education.

In health, everything possible will be done to increase the technical capacity of medical staff to start treating the various diseases that usually require care abroad.

In education, we are committed to looking deeply at the problem of access to education, which has caused difficult situations in vulnerable families. Thus, the Government also intends to ensure quality at all levels of education by training teachers.

We propose to continue developing infrastructure that allows better and easier access to services for all citizens, especially those living in rural areas.

When we talk about a fairer society, we are talking about the fairness of our actions. In this challenging context of restoring the Democratic Rule of Law, the 9th Government will provide the necessary care to improve the justice sector. We will continue to give greater impetus to the capacity building of the existing Timorese human resources, both in courts and in the public prosecutor's office and the public defender's office, so that justice is served with seriousness and transparency, respecting the rule of law.

The Government will conduct a proper audit of several cases which revealed either the law officers' incapacity or dependence on third-party interests.

We will continue to raise the capacity of the Timorese legal profession, so that it can fully exercise its functions, through the formal constitution of a Bar Association, with management and training capacity in this critical sector of justice. We will continue to invest in the training of criminal investigators in all the necessary specialities to ensure greater credibility to the cases brought before the courts.

Mr President,
Excellencies,
Distinguished Guests,

We have already been admitted as Observers to ASEAN. Still, I must honestly state that we have not prepared ourselves sufficiently to be, in a constructive way for the country, a full member of this regional organisation. In this sense, the 9th Government is committed to initiatives with the ASEAN Member Countries for a more in-depth study regarding our capacity to participate, especially in areas that most affect this inclusion of Timor-Leste in ASEAN. Only in this way will we be able to proceed with the selection of the technical staff capable, in each area, of representing the country in this regional organisation.

As for the CPLP, our permanent problem is the mastery of the Portuguese language, so the 9th Government is committed, with a view to the future, to implement more CAFE schools in all administrative posts gradually and to train Timorese teachers in this area.

In terms of international relations, as neighbours, apart from Indonesia, we have Australia. I hope that with the current Australian Government, we will end all the differences of the past so that both Australian and Timorese people can see the future of the relationship in light of greater trust and mutual respect.

To conclude, I usually define our foreign policy as having this principle, which enshrines the sense of independence and sovereignty: 'For Timor-Leste, there are no allies or enemies; everyone will be FRIENDS!'. And this will be our motto, which will guide us in foreign relations in this currently very difficult international context.

We salute all the countries in the region which have given us unconditional support in various spheres, emphasising the good relations with Australia, New Zealand, China, Japan, South Korea, Indonesia, and other ASEAN countries.

We would also like to welcome the friendly relations and solidarity with countries such as Portugal, Brazil and the PALOP, Cuba, the United Kingdom, Ireland, and the USA, as well as with international organisations, namely the UN and its agencies, the World Bank, the International Monetary Fund, and the Asian Development Bank, with which we intend to strengthen the ties of technical and professional assistance, which we need to fulfil our mission to the people of Timor-Leste.

I commit myself, here and now, and on behalf of the 9th Constitutional Government, to govern responsibly, instilling in all the other members of the Government more enthusiasm in fulfilling their duties, always keeping in sight the future.

To the Timorese people, old and young, women and men, I address a special message: Today, we face the great challenge of developing the nation we fought so hard to obtain. With the same principles, values, and commitments that we all carried in body and soul during the long struggle for independence, we must continue working together to realise our dreams under the motto 'Mehi Povo nia mehi!'.

I know it won't be easy, but the Living Heroes, our elders, have already taught us that, united, they faced much more significant difficulties!

The time has come to put Timor-Leste and the Timorese back on the development path.

Thank you all for your attention.

Presentation of the Programme of the 9th Constitutional Government to the National Parliament

National Parliament, Díli
18 July 2023

Your Excellency Madam President of the National Parliament,
Your Excellencies, Vice-Presidents of the National Parliament
Your Excellencies Honourable Members of the National Parliament,
Members of the Government, Ladies and Gentlemen,

First, I would like to express my gratitude to the Timorese for the privilege of once again having the opportunity to stand in this great House and, together with the Honourable Members of Parliament, discuss the country's future for the next five years.

When, on September 12th, 2012, I presented here the 5th Constitutional Government Programme, I stated, 'We are aware of the pressing needs of the nation and the difficulties that the Timorese face, daily. (...) it has never been the lack of quality of our people that has limited our development, but rather the lack of opportunities.'

Unfortunately, 11 years later, these opportunities have not been created for our people, who continue to live in hardship.

Worse, in the last six years, we have witnessed a setback from the Democratic Rule of Law and the stagnation of development and economic growth directly impacting the population.

Therefore, the debate and appreciation of this programme, presented by the 9th Constitutional Government, is more than a constitutional formality. It is a vote of confidence that we ask for this qualified and experienced executive who wants to restore the rules of good governance, transparency, efficiency, and effectiveness, so that we can *all* aspire to the Timor-Leste we dreamed of during the struggle's difficult years.

I cannot promise miracles; nor can I promise immediate progress in national development. I can, however, promise that the inertia, inefficiency, and irregularities we have witnessed in recent administrations are not part of the structure of this governmental team.

Honourable Members of Parliament,

Grandmothers and grandfathers, mothers and fathers, young people of our nation, 'Freedom' is not living in misery and without hope!

The freedom we dreamed of included living in peace and security, and access to health, education, justice, and employment — in short: well-being.

Freedom, however, is earned! No strategic plan or government programme can be implemented with the sole effort of an individual or institution. The executive, of course, has the great responsibility of outlining and executing it, but this is an endeavour that requires the involvement of all citizens of the country.

I can understand that there is general weariness among our people, and even difficulty trusting the political promises and commitments made over these 21 years of independence. I understand a particular disappointment, but I want to remind you that we are still a young and, therefore, fragile state.

Therefore, once again, I am asking for your trust. Trust that we can preserve social peace, improve justice, and consolidate state institutions, which are fundamental pillars for attracting investment, and thus developing the economic and social sector sustainably.

My first request is, therefore, not only to my Government but to all the sovereignty bodies, civil society, and all of Timorese:

Let's embrace a new national cause.

Let's fight for our Democratic Rule of Law, armed with the will to work, with active and constructive participation, and encouraged by a vision of freedom and development!

This vision does not belong to the 9th Constitutional Government; it belongs to the Timorese, the same way that the Constitution of the Democratic Republic of Timor-Leste, which governs our Democratic Rule of Law, does not belong to a President of the Republic, to a Government or the members of the National Parliament - it belongs to the Timorese!

And the Timorese, using their legitimate right in the recent elections, were able to send that message clearly. They have, once again, given us a lesson in democratic culture. Let us now, as rulers, learn that lesson and act responsibly in carrying out our mission.

I will now present the set of commitments of this Government for your appreciation and debate, confident that the future begins today, and, as such, we want the agenda to be implemented in the country to be the result of a participatory and constructive dialogue from the outset.

Madam President of the National Parliament,
Vice-Presidents of the National Parliament,
Honourable Members of the National Parliament,

The Programme of the IX Constitutional Government, for the period 2023-2028, encompasses six main commitments:

First – Reaffirming the Democratic Rule of Law

We will correct the irregularities committed by the previous governance that broke the implemented system of good governance, transparency, and financial and administrative accountability.

This includes undertaking structural reforms to accelerate the necessary transformation of sectors that are not providing a valuable and timely response to Timorese society, and investing in improving state institutions – their systems, processes, and methodologies – to drive sustainable and inclusive development.

We will review all legislation and regulations necessary for state consolidation, including:

- The law that created the RAEOA and the ZEESM, ensuring the separation of powers between the two, and the establishment of a new authority in the Oe-cússe Ambeno region, with a total staff restructuring
  - The law that created the municipality of Ataúro, given that the concept of 'RAEOA' should continue to include Ataúro until the infrastructural and technical conditions are developed, for Ataúro to be then autonomously separated from the RAEOA
- The judicial organisation law
- The chamber of accounts law
- The recently approved Statute of Judicial Magistrates, Statute of the Public Prosecutor's Office, and Statute of the Public Defender's Office
- The legal framework of institutions in the internal security and civil protection sectors, including road legislation and the martial arts law
- The legal regime of the financial sector, by revoking outdated legislation that is still in force
- The budget and financial management law and the procurement and public contracts regime, by gradually transforming the state's

accounting system from the cash basis system to an accrual basis system
- The tax law that will introduce the value-added tax
- All existing anti-corruption legislation
- The lifetime pension law, so that this scheme is integrated into the contributory social security scheme regarding the pensions of the new members of the sovereign bodies
- The legislation regulating the framework law and the recently approved National Spatial Planning Plan
- The legal framework for the organisation and functioning of municipal authorities and municipal administrations, continuing the strategy of administrative decentralisation, and taking the opportunity to approve the regulations on the law on local government and administrative decentralisation, the municipal electoral law, and the municipal finance law

In the next 120 days, we will also carry out an immediate Audit of RAEOA and ZEESM, as well as other state institutions such as the Court of Auditors, the Anti-Corruption Commission, the Public Prosecutor's Office, the Civil Service Commission, the State General Inspectorate, and the Electoral Administration bodies, also including audits of 'deals' made by the previous Government, already at the end of his term of office.

We must speak of justice to speak of the Rule of Law. And the Rule of Law can only exist when justice wields the sword with the same skill with which it manipulates the scales. The 9th Government considers it a priority to pay greater attention to the justice sector, so that it is practised with more professionalism, seriousness, and transparency.

Also, to reaffirm the Democratic Rule of Law, we will thoroughly review the Strategic Development Plan in permanent consultation with civil society to update it to reflect the current state of the nation.

This plan will continue to focus on developing social capital, infrastructure, and the economy, to accelerate economic diversification and job creation in the country.

One of our most significant challenges, but also one of our most excellent opportunities, is the massive growth in the youth population. We need to find intelligent strategies to capitalise on this critical resource. In exploiting the country's energy resources, we want to escape the 'resource curse' by relying on the 'gift of youth'. In this combination of natural resources and young human resources lies the progress of the nation.

Thus, in addition to the investment in traditional diversification sectors, the investment in the transformation of the south coast into a regional oil centre – the Tasi Mane project – is the commitment of this Government with multiplier effects in all municipalities.

Implementing the Maritime Boundary Treaty between Timor-Leste and Australia in the Timor Sea is a priority for this executive, as is bringing the Greater Sunrise gas exploration pipeline to the south coast of Timor-Leste. And to ensure greater efficiency in this sector, we will immediately restructure the TIMOR GAP and ANPM Directorates.

Lastly, as an integral part of state- and nation-building, and because we want to be a *full* Rule of Law state, we will prioritise finalising the delimitation of the land and sea borders with Indonesia.

Second – Developing Social Capital

A just and developed nation guarantees access to quality health and education, fights inequalities, and promotes inclusion, creating opportunities for all, regardless of gender, age, place of residence, religion, social or economic status, or sexual orientation.

From 2007 to 2017, governments have given high priority to promoting social justice. In the long term, providing quality education and training and creating job opportunities will be essential tools for lifting people out of poverty.

Until this happens, the state must ensure that National Liberation Fighters (who have sacrificed for the homeland), women and children (where the success formula for sustainable development lies), as well as poor and deprived families, the elderly, and other vulnerable citizens (such as persons with disabilities), have access to fulfilment of their essential needs and well-being.

Therefore, we will continue to support this population while developing policies and creating strategies that reduce dependency on state support. In particular, we will:

- Consolidate the implementation of the national social protection strategy and the law on the general social security regime, ensuring the protection of citizens in precarious or vulnerable situations
- Consolidate the National Social Security Institute and the Social Security Reserve Fund to manage the social security system, including contributory and non-contributory schemes, with independence, transparency, effectiveness, and efficiency
- Approve the framework law on social protection

- Review and assess the legislative and operational documents of the social pension and the Mother's Grant New Generation (Jerasaun Foun) Programme
- Extend the construction of social solidarity centres, already existing in the municipalities, to all administrative posts, improve social care services through the social solidarity centres, and improve the support programme for social solidarity institutions
- Improve the National Rehabilitation Centre to provide better care and treatment for people with disabilities and extend the centre to all municipalities
- Create business opportunities for women in vulnerable situations, to ensure their economic independence
- Ensure equal opportunities for women and continue to implement gender-sensitive issues in all areas of governance
- Ensure that girls of school age complete basic education, and prevent women from dropping out of education when they reach their majority (18 years)
- Continue to implement the national action plan against gender-based violence and promote campaigns against domestic violence
- Support the elderly, particularly and urgently for those aged over 70
- Create centres for elderly care in all municipalities, as well as leisure and occupational therapy programmes for older people
- Stimulate the creation of self-sustainable businesses for citizens with disabilities; also investing in equipment and accessibility to equipment of public institutions
- Develop programmes to support not only people with disabilities but also families and communities who are responsible for people with disabilities
- Improve relief and assistance mechanisms for victims of natural disasters, including food assistance, infrastructure construction, and distribution of building materials and storage materials
- Continue to promote official recognition and support for national liberation veterans and combatants and their families
- Study the feasibility of creating a veterans' fund and support the creation of a commercial bank with funds from the veterans' investment fund

I have already mentioned that our young people are one of our nation's riches. Not only do they have the power to transform the country, but they will be our future leaders.

We will invest in a national youth policy that ensures coordinated action for the development and autonomy of these young people. This will be developed in conjunction with more responsible investment in sport and culture, essential instruments for developing civic, social, and leadership skills, while also promoting that young people have an occupation, contributing to social stability.

For these young people to know their past, honour the present, and cherish the future, we will complete rigorous research on the history of the national liberation struggle and promote the dissemination of the contemporary history of Timor-Leste.

Also in the area of culture, we want to create and support an association of Timorese art and culture to encourage talented young people in the arts and culture to reaffirm the national identity and expand it internationally.

We will also resume the old projects of building a museum and cultural centre in Díli, improve the legal framework associated with culture, and invest in cultural facilities and initiatives.

Honourable Members of Parliament,
Ladies and Gentlemen,

We must prioritise the health and education sectors to discuss social capital. And in these areas we will focus on things other than the policies already in place but also on improving the public provision of these essential services. We will work hard to improve planning, financing, management, and quality service delivery, as this is the main problem in these two crucial sectors for development.

In the health sector, the Government will continue to implement the national health policy and the National Health Sector Strategic Plan 2011–2030, maximising efforts to ensure better service delivery, as well as generalising access to quality health care, constantly assessing efficiency, transparency, and professionalism in the management of financial, human, material, and logistical resources, infrastructure, and equipment.

In particular, we will:

- Ensure the immediate availability of all necessary medicines to hospitals and health centres, guaranteeing a reform in the management and administration of the health sector so that, in the future, this fundamental right to the protection of citizens' health is never jeopardised

- Improve child nutrition, including through nutritious school meals for all children
- Ensure that all villages (*sucos*), especially in remote areas, have access to a health post with a comprehensive package of services
- Ensure that community health centres in administrative posts guarantee that more people are served
- Continue to improve maternal and child health through comprehensive policies that include preventive and integrated care, such as immunisation
- Improve and expand the provision of medical care at the Guido Valadares National Hospital, in various specialities, with more doctors and specialised technicians so that it is possible to treat various diseases which usually require care abroad
- Reform the National Health Laboratory and Blood Bank to improve the management of laboratory services and blood supply systems
- Regarding infrastructure, we will continue to build and rehabilitate Health Posts and improve Community Health Centres and Referral Hospitals, including the necessary supporting infrastructure
- We will also establish a psychiatric health hospital

Regarding the education sector, we want Timor-Leste to achieve a better-quality education by 2028, with a broader access opportunity for all. This education must be able to respond to the needs of the labour market, contribute to reducing unemployment through lifelong learning, and thus break the vicious circle of intergenerational poverty.

In particular, we will:

- Reform the management and administration of the education system, at the level of the Ministry of Education and the municipal and school levels, including the establishment of appropriate procedures and systems for monitoring and evaluation
- Improve the quality of teaching at all levels of education through more excellent teacher training
- Review school curricula, especially in general and vocational secondary education (high school), to ensure the acquisition of skills appropriate to the labour market and national development needs
- Continue to build, rehabilitate, and equip schools from pre-primary to secondary (high school) education
- Evaluate CAFE schools in terms of teaching development and financial aspects to consider expanding them to all administrative posts

- Double the number of scholarships to be awarded on merit and in line with national needs
- Improve higher education by ensuring adequate academic assessment and accreditation and continuous teacher training
- Expand higher technical education in areas strategic to the national economy by creating the Polytechnic Institute of Tourism, Hospitality, and Tourist Agencies and Guides in Lospalos, the Polytechnic Institute of Engineering in Suai, and the Academy of Fisheries and Marine Studies in Manatuto; we will also improve infrastructure, management, and teaching at the Polytechnic Institute of Betano
- Set up a coordinating committee of universities and colleges to study a collective strategy to define better assistance from the state and implement the objective of raising the quality of education

On the other hand, we will continue to focus on vocational training and employment, investing in the qualification of young people in strategic areas of development. We will also continue to work with friendly countries to create opportunities for vocational training and employment abroad through professional internships and seasonal work programmes, hoping that these Timorese will return to the country to apply the skills they have acquired.

Third - Developing Infrastructure

Between 2007 and 2017, the infrastructure sector was considered the engine of national development, capable of leveraging social capital, economic growth, job creation, and the consolidation of institutions.

The 9th Constitutional Government wants to recover this momentum and resume the integrated infrastructure plan with quality building works and proportionality of the investment.

In this regard, in the next 120 days, we want to survey the primary needs for road maintenance and river standardisation throughout the country to start urgent rehabilitation in 2024.

The Government has prioritised road sections in two phases. The most pressing phase refers to those roads linking administrative posts and rural roads, then moving on to urban roads in Ainaro, Baucau, Bobonaro, Ermera, Lautém, and Viqueque.

On the other hand, we must reinforce investment in access to drinking water and basic sanitation, essential conditions for public health and the quality of life of populations. To this end, we will approve and implement the Investment, Policy and Institutional Reform Plan 2023-2030 to fulfil the targets set in the Strategic Development Plan and the 6th Sustainable Development Goal. This plan will identify the investments needed for water supply and sanitation nationwide.

We will also continue to ensure that the entire population has access to electricity by expanding the national electrification programme. Regarding Ataúro, we will conduct a feasibility study to materialise a sustainable electrification plan for the island.

> *This Government will also establish a Renewable Natural Resources Office, which will coordinate actions at the cross-sectoral level, carry out analyses and feasibility studies relevant to this sector, and be responsible for implementing renewable energy projects, including management, monitoring, and evaluation.*

In this regard, we want to implement pilot renewable-energy projects, such as the construction of the Lariguto and Bobonaro plants for wind energy development, invest in solar energy systems, and develop a feasibility study for the construction of a thermoelectric plant to generate energy from household and industrial waste in Díli.

The 9th Government is also committed to completing the installation of the fibre optic cCable and ensuring a quality internet connection for all citizens throughout the country.

We also commit to resume investment plans in land, sea, and air transport, with emphasis on the following initiatives:

- Carry out a thorough review of the highway code, with a particular focus on improving safety, including the establishment of compulsory pre-test driving lessons
- Improve the harbour facilities at Com and Ataúro
- Build a harbour facility at Kairabela, in Vemasse, to facilitate access to the sea and support the tourism sector
- Carry out feasibility studies for the construction of the Manatuto harbour and the creation of a national shipping line
- Restructure and modernise the port of Díli to convert it into a city marina and cruise port
- Develop the international airport master plan and finalise its expansion
- Develop feasibility studies for municipal airports and operationalise Suai Airport

Fourth – Developing the Economy

Ladies and Gentlemen,

If we want to create opportunities for the people, we must develop a diversified economy based on agriculture, fisheries, livestock, and tourism, and invest in creating small- and medium-sized industries and businesses to reduce the import of goods and products gradually.

We can only talk about full sovereignty if we are self-sufficient in food.

The 9th Government will expand the agricultural sector, improve cultivation practices and agricultural productivity, and develop actions to improve the production of specific and systematic crops according to the potential of each region of the country.

We want to increase livestock production by 20% by 2028 to reduce imports of livestock products from abroad. We will also invest in incentivising fishermen and fishing efforts sustainably.

I would therefore like to highlight the following policies:

- Establish a public agricultural research laboratory to develop research programmes for all major agricultural products in Timor-Leste
- Establish an agricultural research and development institute dedicated to farmer-led production systems
- Continue to improve agricultural practices to increase and improve production and support farmers, including through training, equipment, and irrigation systems
- Continue to support the production of organic and high-quality coffee, including the promotion of Timor coffee at national and international levels
- Establish an animal production research centre to assess which species are best adapted to Timor-Leste conditions and improve genetic quality and selective breeding techniques
- Support the establishment of a cattle breeders association by facilitating its establishment and related policies and initiatives
- Promote the creation of small livestock support enterprises, including meat chilling, sorting, processing, and packaging infrastructure, to develop a safe and quality livestock industry
- Review the studies prepared on the fisheries sector to identify priority actions and strategies for the growth of the sector

- Regulate and control fisheries, and campaign with fishermen and their communities on fishing techniques that present less risk of depleting fish production capacity and the surrounding environment
- Invest in the training of human resources in the area of fisheries and aquaculture to support technical services at sea and in aquaculture and deep-sea fisheries with a future export orientation
- Prepare studies to establish a state indirect administration entity for fisheries and aquaculture, such as the National Institute for Fisheries and Aquaculture, which could promote and motivate private investment

As I have already mentioned, the 9th Government is genuinely committed to bringing the pipeline to Timor-Leste, proving to the world that this is an economically viable and safe solution.

Thus, the South Coast development will be a centre of oil and gas activity, with the establishment of a logistics base in Suai, an oil refinery and petrochemical complex on the south coast, and the installation of a liquefied natural gas plant from Greater Sunrise through the construction of a submerged pipeline to that region.

The Tasi Mane project will develop the entire southern coastal area by constructing new towns and supporting infrastructure. Not only the exploration but also the construction phase, as well as the operation of related infrastructure and services, will create more than 50,000 direct and indirect jobs.

The whole country will benefit from this project, not only by the increase in gross domestic product but by the economic dynamics provided by the productivity of economic factors that also include the subcontracting of services such as catering, engineering, security, fuel supply, management services, professionals and technicians, and agricultural product needs, to name but a few.

On the other hand, this Government is determined to look at the sea from a different perspective, since the sea is crucial for human life. It gives us almost everything we need: food, health, connectivity, entertainment, inspiration, and prosperity.

From the sea, a whole range of sectors presents itself as a potential driver for sustainable development, from traditional sectors, such as fisheries, ports, shipbuilding and shipping, port activities, tourism, and oil and natural gas, to strategic sectors, such as defence and security, to more recent sectors, such as biotechnology, marine renewable energy, and even the sea as a carbon sequester.

Building a sustainable sea economy is an opportunity for our country. I would even say a hope!

The Government will continue implementing the *Ha'u nia Tasi, Ha'u nia Timor* campaign to raise awareness of Timor-Leste's maritime areas. The Government will also prioritise the development of a Timor-Leste blue economy policy for the sustainable growth of the nation, including the preservation, conservation and sustainable use of our ocean resources and the promotion of initiatives and programmes aimed at environmental, economic and social sustainability.

This policy will require the joint and dynamic effort of several ministries and public entities, especially those with responsibilities in agriculture and fisheries, environment, foreign affairs, petroleum, state administration, defence, and security, for the successful and sustainable development of the blue economy.

This programme will also boost the tourism sector, combining its strategy of attracting tourists and improving and promoting tourism products and offers, sustainable maritime tourism, and ecotourism in Timor-Leste.

This strategy will also reinforce our strategy of preserving and valorising natural resources, our biodiversity, and safeguarding, in general, the environment, land and sea for the sustainable development of the economy.

Lastly, and before ending this commitment to the economy, I cannot fail to mention that we will focus on boosting foreign investment and developing the national private sector through attractive and safe conditions, removing obstacles and fostering entrepreneurship so that the private sector, national and international, is a true partner of the Government in economic growth.

Excellencies,
Ladies and Gentlemen,

I now want to talk to you about the fifth compromise.

Fifth – Consolidating Governance

In addition to the legislative reforms I have already mentioned, we will focus on an economic policy that contributes to the development of private investment, and a fiscal policy that contributes to a more significant fiscal balance through a tax system that collects more domestic revenue while maintaining a competitive tax regime, capable of attracting investment.

In the next five years, we want to create jobs for all and reduce the minimum poverty rate to 10% by developing infrastructure and the economic fabric, as I have already mentioned. A better financial sector policy will contribute to the shift in the structure of the economy, which is mainly dependent on public spending, towards a sustainable economy with increased private sector activities.

The private sector mainly fails to progress because it is limited to state projects and needs access to long-term, affordable credit and finance. Existing commercial banks only lend to international organisations and companies from their home country, and sectors that rely heavily on government contracts and public investment.

The Government will establish a Development Bank of Timor-Leste to facilitate access to long-term finance at affordable interest rates so that entrepreneurs can participate in the development of the nation.

On the other hand, we will support and expand the Banco Nacional de Comércio de Timor-Leste to municipalities and administrative posts, so that micro, small, and medium enterprises, both urban and rural, can also be an active part of this growth.

The Government also intends that, in its investment policy, the Petroleum Fund can consider the investments made by the companies in shares that it holds. To this end, the Government will strengthen the capacities of existing state-owned enterprises to orientate their activity to promote investments in Timor-Leste and assess the financial and economic effects for the state, promoting the activities of state-owned enterprises towards productive sectors.

It will also establish the Timor-Leste Investment Corporation (TLIC) as a state investment company, and capitalise on state-owned companies through business plans.

The Government will approve the state enterprise sector regime to improve the monitoring of state-owned enterprises, promote state participation in private investments, and contribute to their financial and economic return.

The Government also intends to implement the financial diversification mechanism of equity participation, as it will stimulate private sector investments, promote infrastructure development, and contribute to the diversification of the economy and job creation, to raise revenue for the state.

These commitments only make sense if the Government continues to strengthen fiscal policy and public finance management with transparency, accountability, efficiency, and sustainability. As one of the priorities during its mandate, the Government will reform public finance management.

We will also ensure a return to rigour in the execution of public expenditure by investing in financial decentralisation to public institutions and regional and municipal authorities, strengthening public institutions' capacities by interconnecting the public sector's IT system with the financial IT system. Linked to this, we will resume programme-based budgeting to avoid irrelevant expenditures that could be indicative of corruption.

Sixth – Promoting Good Governance and Fighting Corruption

We will work to ensure a robust, honest and efficient public sector, coupled with justice and internal security mechanisms that contribute to the country's security and prosperity.

We will act resolutely:
- On performance appraisals and merit-based promotion
- In the fight against corruption, also preventively. Members of the Government will be no exception, with the approval of a code of conduct
- In the association of information technologies, including eGovernment, and good cooperation with the country's media to promote good governance
- In public administration reform and modernisation
- On institutional strengthening, including the review of institutions' organisational matrix
- On training and capacity building of the state's local Government human resources to improve the delivery of local public goods and services

The Government will also, as I stated at the beginning of this speech, carry out the decentralisation process, focusing on the potential of each municipality, considering that this can be a second independence for the country, where everyone can contribute to their own development.

Therefore, in the next five years, we will start the process of local government through a phased decentralisation of the Government and municipal assemblies after the respective infrastructural and technical conditions are created. This objective will only be fulfilled with the active and responsible involvement and participation of all Timorese, from the East to the West.

In the context of good governance and the fight against corruption, we cannot fail to mention, once again, justice and defence and security. In this regard, the 9th Constitutional Government will prioritise the following actions:

- Implementation of the national defence and security strategic concept, including the review and approval of the respective legal framework
- Immediate reform and restructuring of the national intelligence system to ensure the integrity and professionalism of this institution
- Restructuring of the Criminal Investigation Scientific Police, also due to the absolute need for greater integrity and professionalism
- Review of the 2030 Internal Security Strategic Plan to adapt it to the current challenges of the internal security and civil protection sectors
- Elimination of the partisanship of the country's security and defence forces
- Implementation of a thorough reform in the justice sector, with the creation of the Supreme Court of Justice and impeccable training of judges and prosecutors

Madam President of the National Parliament,
Vice-Presidents of the National Parliament,
Honourable Members of the National Parliament,

The road ahead is full of challenges, challenges that we must face responsibly.

This programme requires a lot of determination, perseverance, and honesty, because sometimes it is easier to start again than to correct processes and systems, addictions, and established habits. Only then can we get back on the right track of progress.

And we have to be prepared for unpredictable conjunctures. It is not only the internal crisis of democratic irregularity that we have recently experienced in the country that has caused social and economic stagnation. The lack of capacity to analyse and overcome other crises, also on the international scene, has put us in the nation's current state.

We faced a global pandemic that had a tremendous impact on the whole world, which claimed millions of lives, forced the closure of borders, weakened global democracy, and led to a global economic and social crisis that further exacerbated poverty and inequalities.

Timor-Leste was no exception.

The 2021 floods, in addition to several fatalities, left severe damage in the country. More than two years later, we can still witness the signs of these floods all over the country, with roads and houses that have never been repaired, and many of those which have been, reminding us of the importance of spatial planning, especially in the capital of the country, Díli.

Less than a year after the floods, war breaks out in Ukraine. And not even our half-island, on the other side of the world, can remain indifferent to war in Europe. This war has caused even more uncertainty for our young state needing development.

War is not only the most abject action of human beings. This war is not only causing the greatest humanitarian crisis since World War II; it is causing democratic and economic disruption in many countries. And Timor-Leste, once again, is no exception, with disruptions in the supply chain, international inflationary pressure, and rising energy and raw material costs.

The international community, always swift and present in its support for Timor-Leste, has continued to show solidarity with our people during these recent crises. But donor countries and international agencies have many suffering peoples to look after.

Timor-Leste must be prepared to deal with national and international crises. In the face of the complexities and challenges that the world presents us with, from conflict to war, from the refugee crisis to fanaticism and terrorism, from maritime insecurity to climate change, it cannot simply shelter from the storms and forget that there is an ever-changing world out there.

We must face the world proactively, because no country can overcome global challenges alone.

We can have a more active voice on the international stage and have valid experiences to share within the g7+ countries and with all countries worldwide. Our success in resolving disputes peacefully in the case of maritime boundary delimitation, using UNCLOS and international law, has earned us global respect.

We want to continue to reciprocate the solidarity shown during the years of struggle and restoration of our independence by joining our voices to the international movement to promote reconciliation, peace, and stability.

Given the complexity of the international environment, we will promote multilateralism as a priority foreign policy objective. We will strengthen our engagement with the UN and other international agencies, participating in critical issues such as climate change, maritime affairs, and ocean sustainability, the blue economy, migration and refugees, and humanitarian initiatives.

And, of course, to strengthen relations of friendship, cooperation, and solidarity with all states, particularly with friendly countries and development partners, and in particular with the closest, whether they are our neighbours, the countries of the region, or the countries of the CPLP, but also with all those who have supported us unconditionally during the various phases of peace and nation building.

I cannot fail to mention with gratitude that in the same month that we took office, we were honoured with the visit of the Foreign Minister of Japan, the Foreign Minister of Australia, and the Prime Minister of Portugal. This friendship and bilateral cooperation reinforces our conviction that we are equal in fulfilling our mission to the Timorese.

And this commitment also includes being fully prepared to join ASEAN and the World Trade Organization.

And this is where my second request lies:

Let's all be diplomats for our country.

Let's build a credible image of an independent, responsible, and developing country which stands for tolerance, human rights, the Democratic Rule of Law, and a global system governed by internationally accepted rules.

And we will, regardless of our professional, social, or economic status, dignify our presence abroad while caring for our country to attract investment, trade, and tourism to Timor-Leste.

Lastly, I thank you, the Honourable Members of Parliament, for your cooperation and determination to debate and improve the 9th Constitutional Government strategic agenda.

Tomorrow begins today, here and now. Let us be worthy of the mandates - of Parliament and Government - that we have received from the Timorese. It is our duty. It is our responsibility.

I am counting on your vote of confidence so that, together, we create opportunities for our people!

Thank you very much.

Top: Prime Minister Gusmão delivers his Special Remarks at the
ASEAN Business Summit, Plenary Session, September 2023

Above: The 26th ASEAN Plus Three Summit.

Top: With the new President of Indonesian H.E Prabowo Prabowo Subianto at the Joint Leaders Session, Indonesia-Africa Forum (IAF), Bali-Indonesia, 2024.

Above: Prime Minister Gusmão at the Plenary Session of the 44th ASEAN Summit, October 2024.

At the 18th East Asia Summit.

Top: Delegates at the Opening Ceremony 43rd ASEAN Summit and related Summits.
Above: The 43rd ASEAN Summit, Plenary Session.

43RD ASEAN SUMMIT PLENARY SESSION
5 SEPTEMBER 2023, JAKARTA - INDONESIA

ASEAN
INDONESIA
2023

Both images above: The 43rd ASEAN Summit, Retreat Session.

Top: Bilateral meeting with the Prime Minister of Australia, H.E. Anthony Albanese.

Above: Bilateral meeting with the Prime Minister of the Kingdom of Cambodia, H.E. Samdech Moha Borvor Thipadei Manet Hun

Top: Bilateral meeting with the Sultan of Brunei Darussalam and the Prime Minister of Brunei, H.E. Hassanal Bolkiah Muiz'zaddin Wad'daulah.

Above: Bilateral meeting with the former Prime Minister of Singapore, H.E Lee Hsien Loong.

Top: Bilateral meeting with the Prime Minister of Malaysia, H.E. Dato Seri Anwar Bin Ibrahim.

Above: Bilateral meeting with the Prime Minister of Vietnam, H.E. Phạm Minh Chính.

Top: With the former President of Indonesia, Joko Widodo, and his wife, Ms Irina Joko Widodo.

Above: Launch of the Timor-Leste's Future Leaders for ASEAN Program, April 2024.

Top: Launch of the Timor-Leste's Future Leaders for ASEAN Program, April 2024.

Above: First High Level meeting Archipelagic and Island State Forum Bali–Indonesia 2023.

Top: The 9th Our Ocean Conference: An Ocean of Potential, April 2024.

Above: Inauguration of the 9th Constitucional Government, July 2023, at President Nicolau Lobato Palace, Dili, Timor-Leste.

Official Dinner in Honour of His Excellency The Prime Minister of The Portuguese Republic and His Delegation

Noble Palace of Lahane, Palácio do Governo, Díli
25 July 2023

Your Excellency the President of the Republic,
Your Excellency the Speaker of Parliament,
Your Excellency the Prime Minister of Portugal and my dear friend, Mr António Costa,
Your Excellency, the President of the Court of Appeal,
Distinguished Members of Parliament,
Your Excellency the Minister for Foreign Affairs of Portugal and my dear friend, Mr João Gomes Cravinho,
Your Excellency the Minister for Labor, Solidarity and Social Security of Portugal, Ms Ana Mendes Godinho,
Dearest members of the Portuguese Delegation Members of the Timorese Government, Distinguished members of the Diplomatic Corps,
Excellencies,
Ladies and Gentlemen,

It gives me great pleasure to welcome Your Excellency Mr Prime Minister and your distinguished delegation to Timor-Leste.

The 9th Constitutional Government entered into office only 25 days ago, and this is the first official visit of a head of government to our country since then.

I could say that I feel honoured, and even privileged, but I choose the word 'emotional' to describe today's meeting with Your Excellency, my dear friend, in the capital of my country.

For me, for the government of Timor-Leste and also for the Timorese people, this visit represents the confirmation of something that we feel with emotion: our friendship, affection, and mutual respect, particularly for those who share profound feelings of unity.

The Portuguese government has delivered a clear message today as to its determination to strengthen friendship and cooperation between our two countries, which are fundamental for this new political cycle we are experiencing, one that aims for transformation and progress for the Timorese people.

There are few who know our history as well as the Portuguese. It is a history of struggle and sacrifice, of conquest and freedom, of rebuilding and consolidating the state, with ups and downs, crises, and even setbacks – but always a history of ambition, the ambition of a people dreaming of a dignified life and opportunities for development.

The electoral process of last May once again demonstrated that the Timorese people have a democratic culture and exercise their legitimate right to decide their future. Indeed, the Timorese want to consolidate a Democratic Rule of Law that is credible, independent, and responsible, a state that promotes tolerance, human rights, social justice, and international solidarity, a state that leads to development and progress.

Still, we all recognise with humility that we are still a young and fragile country, and we must therefore strive harder, work harder, to find solutions and create opportunities that will lift us out of poverty.

This was precisely the commitment of the government upon taking office and presenting its program to the National Parliament last week. Unprecedentedly, this program was approved unanimously, demonstrating the collective will of all major political forces in the country to work for the well-being of the people.

And, as I mentioned before, there are few who understand the challenges and needs of the Timorese people as well as Your Excellency, Prime Minister, and the members of your Government.

Mr Prime Minister,

The relationship between our two countries is truly special. In addition to sharing a language and a common identity, we also share common sufferings and hopes. And I do not mean only when the Portuguese national squad takes to the pitch!

The Portuguese in Timor are our allies and mentors, and the Timorese in Portugal are welcomed into your families, supported, cared for, and encouraged to progress and prosper.

In a world filled with turmoil, wars, power struggles, greed, and challenges that threaten the very survival of humanity, we should rejoice in this special relationship, our shared past, the dynamism and partnership of our present, and the future we can still build together.

I would say that Portugal is like our older brother. Not only for the crucial role played in our struggle for sovereignty, which I can never forget and will never stop thanking, but also for the continuous bilateral cooperation and Portuguese investment in practically all crucial sectors for our development.

While I cannot list here the extensive range of all areas of cooperation where Portugal is an unparalleled partner (otherwise, we would never get to our dinner!), I must emphasise crucial areas that we would like to see strengthened, such as education and training, justice, public finance, healthcare, defence, social security, tourism, and the development of basic infrastructure.

I would like to seize the moment to share the challenge I made to Your Excellency Prime Minister during our bilateral meeting for greater cooperation in projects that are part of the new momentum of this Government. We believe these projects can be drivers for our country's economic development and an opportunity to generate employment for our youth, who, as you know, are growing in numbers and are vulnerable.

I refer, firstly, to our goal of decentralisation, knowing that Portugal's experience in public administration and municipalities is a source of knowledge and excellence that we want to learn from, to advance with this priority.

Secondly, 'Portugal is Sea,' 'Timor is Tasi'. While our countries may be small, they grow exponentially when we look to the sea. It was the sea that united us, and it was with Portuguese 'sailors' that we learned the language of Camões.

From the sea, there is a whole range of sectors that present themselves as potential drivers of sustainable development. From traditional to more recent sectors, we want to build a sustainable blue economy. And I know that Portugal is also investing in the blue economy, not only to generate wealth for its people but also to strengthen the climate and the ocean.

Therefore, we would like our strategy in defining a national policy for the blue economy to benefit from the experience, knowledge, and innovation of the Portuguese. Let us sail together in establishing a sustainable blue economy in Timor-Leste.

Your Excellencies, Mr Prime Minister,

Portugal is also an unparalleled partner in the values we uphold in the multilateral sphere, promoting peace, justice, and combating poverty and inequalities.

Our cooperation and common vision for the global future, based on the commitments of the United Nations charter, mobilise us in the fight against climate change, defending international law, promoting territorial integrity and security among states, strengthening democracies, and advancing social and economic development for all, so as to leave no one behind.

Within the framework of the CPLP [Community of Portuguese Language Countries], the strategic value of friendly nations that share principles, values, and affections should converge towards new ambitions that elevate the living conditions of our citizens, particularly for our young Portuguese speakers. The CPLP can and should benefit more from economic cooperation in strategic sectors for the development of our societies. And just as Portugal connects our community to Europe, so too can Timor-Leste be a gateway to Southeast Asia and the Pacific.

Mr Prime Minister and dear friend, António Costa,

I believe that, as a result of this visit, we have established a new milestone in the history of our diplomatic relations. The willingness of both our countries to reaffirm the commitment to cooperation for the development of our peoples and communities in Portugal and Timor-Leste has never been so evident.

During your last visit to this country, in 2006, at a bitter moment in our still young independence, in your capacity as Minister of Internal Administration, you said that 'a friend in need is a friend indeed' and that 'Portugal is a friendly country'. It has not just been through words but through concrete actions – from the Portuguese government, public and private institutions, and Portuguese individuals who visit or reside in Timor-Leste – that the Timorese people witness this friendship daily.

We are aware of the challenges that Portugal also faces, after the pandemic and now the war in Europe. This war brings uncertainties when we least need them and poses new challenges to the world, including inflationary pressures and increased living costs, also making the daily life of the Portuguese more difficult.

As you said, Mr Prime Minister, a friend in need is a friend indeed. Besides having a fraternal relationship with Portugal, Timor-Leste also wants to strengthen its solidarity and commitment to ensure that our bilateral cooperation takes on a form that benefits both our countries, with partnerships, projects, and investments that yield tangible benefits, not only to the Timorese but to the Portuguese as well.

I sincerely hope, Mr Prime Minister, that you and your delegation feel at home during this visit and that you enjoy our culture and affection.

In Timor, true friends are like our brothers and sisters. Therefore, this is the visit of a close family member, whom we want to have always close by.

Finally, I wish every success for the World Youth Day, which will be attended by Pope Francis, also a great friend of Timor-Leste.

Thank you very much.

Presentation of the 2023 Amending Budget Law Proposal

National Parliament, Díli
22 August 2023

Your Excellency Madam President of the National Parliament,
Your Excellencies Vice Presidents of the National Parliament,
Your Excellencies Honourable Members of the Parliament,
Ladies and Gentlemen, Members of the Government,
Dear Timorese,

First of all, I would like to present the greetings of the members of the 9th Constitutional Government, thanking you for the opportunity to present, in this Parliament, our law proposal for the amending budget for the year 2023.

We were here just last month to present the five-year Government programme, through which we will seek to improve and force ourselves to strengthen the development of our beloved land, Timor-Leste.

We apologise for taking a while to make the right decisions about this budget, which will only be used until December 31st.

Honourable Members of the Parliament,
Dear Timorese,

There's no need to remind this National Parliament why the people chose the 9th Constitutional Government. The answer is straightforward: Because in recent years, people felt something was going wrong.

It was with great sadness that I, as Chairman of the Committee for the Preparation and Review of the Budget, could observe, with my own eyes, what the beloved Timorese have been experiencing daily over the last few years.

I have to say that I'm sad, because the financial system that existed, previously established during the mandate of the 4th Constitutional Government, which the international financial institutions held in high esteem and asked to be strengthened a little more, this financial system has undergone significant changes, thus violating the sound principles of public finance management. What was good was spoilt.

During the week we worked on the budget review, I could see the violations that had taken place over the last five years, which happened because deviations originated from the changes made to the national financial system.

As an outsider, I was always surprised by the billions of dollars that went into the state budget, yearly. The people also heard this information. And because people didn't see results showing they could finally hope to improve their lives, they chose the 9th Constitutional Government.

Honourable Members of the Parliament,
Dear Timorese,

I need to make these initial remarks so that the Honourable Members of the Parliament can understand better why we are bringing in this amending budget and the proposed amendments.

The transparency portal doesn't provide complete information on the budget and planning, and often doesn't work.

The programme budgeting principle was eliminated to create the Major Planning Options, with their implementation failing to follow the programme budgeting principle. This allowed all the institutions to act randomly and at will, and to act outside their competences.

The principle of the annual nature of the budget, which regulates expenditure until December 31st of each year, is no longer valid and has given way to a new 'disease', called 'income' for the institutions, no longer called the management balance, which, correctly, should return to the state coffers.

The principle governing transfers of funds from one category to another was eliminated, allowing Ministries and other Institutions to freely make transfers between categories ('*viroment*'), from the 'Salaries' category to the 'Goods and Services' category and the 'Minor Capital' category, and from the 'Minor Capital' category back to the 'Salaries and Wages' category.

The principle of transparency can manifest itself in practice in situations where an institution depends on other institutions, so that it can be demanded that everything follows the norms and rules that are established in the system. However, the powers of the CNA and ADN have been eliminated, and many projects that were simply handed over did not follow the procurement or tenderisation procedures, leading to the fact that we now do not have correct data on the cost of each of the projects that are still in progress or those that have already finished.

In light of all this, the 9th Constitutional Government decided to suspend the contracts that the previous Government signed close to the end of its term in office, above all because we realised that there was no detailed analysis of the actual cost of these projects, which are very expensive and which did not follow procurement procedures.

Due to the emergence of this type of environment, violations of the civil service rules have also taken place, with the merit and experience of employees no longer being taken into account, resulting in uncritical dismissals and the hiring of people with no experience whatsoever.

Due to the Civil Service Commission's failure to act, a policy of recruiting thousands of casual workers, who had no work to do because there was nothing for them to do, also emerged in election years.

Honourable Members of the Parliament,
Dear Timorese,

Based on all these facts, the 9th Constitutional Government decided to correct the situation by returning to the old rules, with only five categories: Wages and Salaries, Goods and Services, Minor Capital, Public Transfers, and Development Capital.

Despite this, and even starting with this amending budget, the 9th Constitutional Government will continue implementing the already underway sub-programmes, as it is very difficult to change everything simultaneously.

Next year, through the 2024 General State Budget, the Government will be able to restore the old financial system, which is very good.

Honourable Members of the Parliament,
Dear Timorese,

So, Honourable Members of the Parliament, I would now like to present what will be included in this amending budget, based on the following five aspects:

Firstly, to make the new government structure viable, with the creation or change of some ministries. For this reason, some adjustments will be made to the titles of the organisational classification of the 2023 General State Budget.

This includes the creation of the Ministry of Tourism and Environment; the Ministry of Rural Development and Community Housing; the Ministry of Youth, Sports, Art and Culture; and the Ministry of Planning and Strategic Investment, which replaces the Ministry of Planning and Territory.

Still on this subject, I would like to clarify that the 9th Constitutional Government will begin a policy of reducing the public institutes created by the previous government, which are only used to house party members, without any administrative or economic rationality. The approach I have just mentioned will continue in future budgets, with the aim of extinguishing (or eliminating) the National Agency for Planning, Monitoring and Evaluation (ANAPMA), as well as the National Authority for Water and Sanitation (ANAS, I.P.) and the National Authority for Electricity (ANE, I.P.).

Secondly, we all want public accounts to be contained. That's why, having analysed the execution of the budget to date, the 9th Constitutional Government is proposing a reduction in the expenditure provided for in the general state budget, and thus also a reduction in the amount of transfers from the Petroleum Fund.

This reduction can be achieved because it results from an already carried out evaluation, which has identified savings in a group of services and various entities of the public administrative sector. A review of expenditure and responsible management, which can constantly (or frequently) correct deviations and superfluous spending, will not just be a method (or a good way) but will effectively be the philosophy of this Government.

Thirdly, the high inflation rate in Timor-Leste has caused significant difficulties in the living conditions of our people, punishing mainly disadvantaged families. The 9th Constitutional Government is committed to reducing this inflationary pressure, and we propose, in this amending budget, to reduce the rates of excise duty on sugar and customs duties on imports that will apply in 2023.

Fourthly, since good governance requires rigour and transparency in the execution of the general state budget and the management of public accounts, we also propose amending the law no. 2/2022, of February 10th, on the framework of the general state budget and public financial management, to allow the 2024 budget to be prepared following the new rules.

Still on this subject, we believe that what has been called 'presentation by programmes' in the state budgets since 2017 has caused a lack of control and transparency in public accounts. Therefore, we will gradually return to the organisation of the state budget into five categories (wages and salaries, goods and services, public transfers, minor capital, and development capital) to increase the level of detail in the information that will be presented to the National Parliament, increasing its comprehensibility and facilitating future scrutiny.

I say 'gradually', because we must wait for the 2024 general state budget.

Furthermore, to guarantee greater stability in the approved general state budget, we will repeal the Major Planning Options law and create an annual strategic investment plan to pave the way for a multi-annual vision of the budget in line with international best practice.

All these changes will guarantee sustainability, rigour, and transparency in public accounts.

Fifthly, and lastly, we propose an amendment to law no. 8/2008, of June 30th, the tax law as amended by law no. 5/2019, of August 27th, so that we can have adequate clarification on the concept of permanent establishment, provided for in the tax law, and thus put an end to doubts about the tax regime applicable to these situations, giving greater legal certainty and fiscal stability to foreign investment in Timor-Leste.

Madam President of the Parliament,
Vice Presidents,
Honourable Members of the Parliament,
Dear Timorese people,

With this amending budget law proposal, total consolidated expenditure will be US$1,771,867,112, financed by domestic revenues, the estimated sustainable income (ESI), and withdrawals in addition to the ESI. In this way, we have also reduced the amount of authorised transfers from the Petroleum Fund from US$1,346,090,000 to US$1,208,194,889.

The central administration now has an estimated expenditure of US$1,633,000,000. Social Security, not including the Social Security Reserve Fund, is increased to US$130,965,306 (the total consolidated figure does not include US$75,860,306 from central government transfers to avoid double counting). The special administrative region of Oe-Cússe Ambeno (RAEOA) will receive an estimated figure of US$83,762,112.

From a technical point of view, Your Excellencies can already see changes to the structure of the general state budget tables. These changes are aimed at greater transparency and better understanding of the information. In particular, tables I and II of the general state budget also show which revenues and expenditures are financed by the Central Administration, including transfers from the Central Administration to the Social Security budget and the budget of the special administrative region of Oe-Cússe Ambeno and others that are financed by each subsector's revenues, so that they do not become a burden for the Central Administration or the Petroleum Fund.

We present the totals in three different ways: with and without income and expenditure from the Social Security Reserve Fund and the total consolidated, so that it became clearer which expenditure will actually be realised this year so that there is no duplication, and also which expenditure is not real, since it is invested from this reserve fund.

On the other hand, tables V, VI, VIII, IX, XI, and XII will be presented as part of the economic classification, already with the five new categories mentioned, so that the 19 previous categories will become second-level subcategories, thus increasing the level of detail of the information we present to the National Parliament.

The 9th Constitutional Government is firmly committed to a fiscal policy that will lead to the country's economic development and will manage our expenditure and revenue scrupulously and efficiently, once again fostering the confidence of citizens and investors.

We hope that with the approval of this amending budget law proposal, as well as the amendments to the laws mentioned above, we will not only be able to guarantee more outstanding and better execution of the 2023 budget to tackle the inflation that is currently affecting the living conditions of the Timorese but also to immediately start preparing the 2024 general state budget, whose budgetary process will already follow the philosophy of the 9th Constitutional Government.

The approval of this budget will also allow the new government structure to fulfil its mission, namely in implementing the measures we committed to for the first 120 days of our term.

For this reason, and because our people cannot wait any longer to be able to feel the benefits of the policies that the Government intends to implement, we have presented this law proposal with a request for priority and urgency. Therefore, I would like to thank the President of the National Parliament and all of the honourable Members of Parliament for listening to our request and scheduling this debate at such short notice.

The 9th Constitutional Government is fully aware of the significant challenges, and realises that implementing a sustainable fiscal policy and rational public spending in response to planning will only be the first important step towards consolidating and transforming the provision of services, by improving the management system and through investment strategies.

And this Government, as we all know, will not travel this road alone. The constructive and democratic debate we will be engaged in over the next few days will be the key to achieving the sustainable and inclusive national development we all want.

Thank you very much, and my compliments to all of the honourable Members of the Parliament.

On the Occasion of the Budgetary Days on the General State Budget for 2024

Ministry of Finance, Díli
12 September 2023

Ladies and Gentlemen,
Honoured guests,

Good morning.

Today, I come here before Your Excellencies as the representative of all the people of Timor-Leste, responsible for presenting an amended budget for our country. It is a great honour to address Your Excellencies to discuss the financial plan that will shape our beloved country for the future.

Firstly, I would like to thank all the citizens of Timor-Leste for their continued support and resilience. Our nation has come a long way since its independence, and it is the unity and determination of all of us that has allowed us to get this far.

As we delve into the details of our budget, we must rethink the guiding principles that should shape our financial decisions: transparency, accountability, inclusiveness, and sustainability. These principles are at the core of our Government's efforts to create a prosperous and harmonious Timor-Leste.

The main objective of our budget is to increase economic growth, prioritising the well-being and development of our people. We aim to foster an environment that attracts foreign investment and creates opportunities for local entrepreneurs and small businesses. By supporting these sectors, we can unleash the full potential of our people and drive sustainable economic growth. This means fostering growth, and not just through public spending.

Infrastructure development is very important for developing countries like ours. For this reason, a significant part of this budget will be allocated to transport, water and sanitation, energy, and telecommunications projects. Improving our road and transport networks will connect isolated communities, promote trade, and facilitate the movement of goods and services. In addition, we will continue to invest in renewable energies and improve access to electricity, trying to use our natural resources in an environmentally friendly way.

Education remains a priority for our entire Government. The future of Timor-Leste is in the hands of our youth, so it is our responsibility to provide them with the skills and knowledge they need to succeed.

Investing in education and increasing human capital will also contribute to reducing unemployment and poverty rates. We will focus on improving the quality of education, promoting vocational training, and ensuring equal opportunities for all, regardless of origin or geographical location.

Health care is a crucial aspect of our citizens' well-being. Our new budget includes provisions for the expansion and improvement of health facilities, as well as for the recruitment and training of doctors and other health professionals. We are committed to building a robust health system that guarantees universal access to quality health services for everyone in Timor-Leste.

Agriculture, our traditional sector, continues to play a crucial role in our economy. Ensuring food security and supporting farmers will remain a top priority. We will encourage modern farming techniques, support agricultural cooperatives, and invest in research and development to increase farm productivity and competitiveness.

Furthermore, as a country rich in natural resources, we must manage them responsibly. The budget includes measures to improve resource management, promote sustainable practices, and invest in renewable energy projects. We must protect our environment for future generations and ensure that our natural resources can be used in an economically beneficial and ecologically sustainable way.

In conclusion, this new budget for Timor-Leste reflects our commitment to the well-being and development of our country.

With a strong focus on economic growth, infrastructure development, education, health, agriculture, and resource management, we are confident that we can build a prosperous and sustainable future for all of our citizens.

Successfully implementing this budget requires the collaboration and involvement of all stakeholders, including the Government, the private sector, civil society organisations, and our citizens.

Together, we can tackle the challenges and fulfil our vision of a prosperous Timor-Leste. And we can all continue to work together, hand in hand, towards a brighter future.

Swearing-in of the New Governor of the Central Bank of Timor-Leste

Central Bank of Timor-Leste, Díli
13 September 2023

Excellencies,
Ladies and Gentlemen,

I am delighted to participate in the swearing-in ceremony of the new Governor of the Central Bank, Dr Hélder Lopes.

This is another crucial step for the country, since the BCTL, our financial regulator, is fundamental to consolidating the national economic sector. Consolidating the rule of law is only possible with a credible institution that holds the financial system accountable and manages the oil fund, our national wealth, with transparency and independence.

I would like to express my complete confidence in the new Governor of the Central Bank. I believe that Dr Hélder Lopes, who is taking on the leadership of this institution today, will act with the responsibility of someone who has made a public service commitment to the state and the people of Timor-Leste.

I would also like to express a word of gratitude and appreciation to Dr Abrão de Vasconcelos, who has led this institution with commitment, professionalism, and integrity over the last 12 years.

A long road has been travelled since the establishment of the Banking and Payments Authority and its transformation into the Central Bank of Timor-Leste in 2011. It has been a democratic maturing of the state itself, where accountability, transparency, and independence, critical factors of a democratic rule of law, have accompanied the national objectives of developing the economic and social sectors.

National interests cannot be defended without an efficient and effective financial sector. The outgoing Governor of the Central Bank understood this responsibility, and I am convinced that the new Governor will continue this legacy.

For the relationship between the Government of Timor-Leste and the

Central Bank, I have two concrete aspirations that can be summarised in two words: independence and cooperation. The prestige of the Timorese state, the nation's success, and the future of the Timorese depend on this healthy relationship between these two institutions.

Perhaps we should remember the fundamental role that the Central Bank plays for the country since it is a discreet institution that may go unnoticed by Timorese society – until the day it stops fulfilling its role with efficiency and professionalism. We could even say that the importance of the Central Bank would only really become visible the day it failed miserably to fulfil its mission.

The financial sector is crucial in contributing to Timor-Leste's economic development. The Central Bank is responsible for mobilising the country's savings resources effectively and efficiently, and managing foreign investment capital resources. On the other hand, the Central Bank plays a fundamental role in the execution of payments, which are inherent to economic dynamics and commercial development, drivers of economic growth and, consequently, the well-being of citizens.

This naturally includes the development of the private sector, the job creation that goes with it, and the regulatory action it takes towards Timor's existing commercial banks, which support the country's economic development.

For these reasons, I hope that the Central Bank, with this new leadership, will be able to fulfil its role as a partner of the Government in facing the country's challenges. And that it can advise the Government of Timor-Leste to maintain the stability of the national financial system.

I wish the new Governor success in his term so that he maintains the independence of the Central Bank. But this independence does not mean alienation, in the sense that its presence and advice are of the utmost importance for national development through its technical capacities, which must be continually improved and modernised, and active but conscious and impartial participation in the fulfilment of national development objectives.

I believe that the Central Bank can be an essential partner for the Government as a solid and independent institution in defining national policies that lead the country towards progress, prosperity, and the well-being of all Timorese.

Thank you very much.

Presentation of the 2024 General State Budget Law Proposal

National Parliament, Díli
12 December 2023

Your Excellency Madam President of the National Parliament,
Your Excellencies Vice Presidents of the National Parliament,
Your Excellencies Honourable Members of the National Parliament,
Members of the Government,
Ladies and gentlemen,

It is a privilege to address you, Madam President, Vice Presidents, and Honourable Members of the Parliament, to present the 2024 General State Budget Law Proposal.

With all due respect, I thank you for considering this law proposal as a matter of urgency, and allowing the legislative process to be finalised this year. This will enable the 2023 General State Budget to end on December 31st and a new budget to begin in 2024.

This is not only desirable but also most beneficial for the country. However, it represents a substantial effort on the part of the National Parliament and the Government itself, which, in six months, have worked and debated on a new government programme, an amending budget, and a general state budget.

The Timorese deserve their leaders and public institutions to work quickly, efficiently, and responsibly. They also deserve that the priorities set for the coming year be implemented on the first day of the year without uncertainties or delays.

This is only possible when the democratic institutions of the state cooperate to defend the people's interests.

I am also pleased that we are returning to the right track of consolidating democratic exercise through dialogue, cooperation, and institutional interaction, which are fundamental principles for achieving the common project of promoting Timor-Leste's economic and social development.

Alongside good governance, transparency, and the financial and administrative responsibility that this Government instils in the budgetary process, institutional cooperation between the sovereign bodies also contributes to reaffirming the Democratic Rule of Law, a commitment of the 9th Constitutional Government.

Ladies and Gentlemen, Members of the National Parliament,

The project that the Government is presenting today for the year 2024 is entitled 'Building a Bridge to Tomorrow: Investing in the Productive Sector and Social Capital'.

In this budget, we have summarised the strategic objectives of the 9th Constitutional Government's programme in two fundamental pillars: the productive sector and social capital.

This budget, the first of this new Government, lays the foundations for what we want to achieve over the next five years. And in what way?

It promotes priority investments that contribute to building a prosperous and sustainable future.

Investments in public infrastructure, production capacity, job creation, and diversified economic sectors will boost economic growth.

From a social point of view, investments in education, health, inclusion, the fight against poverty, and the protection of the land and maritime environment – in short, investments in sectors with a direct impact on improving the quality of life of the Timorese, and with long-term results.

Madam President of the Parliament,
Vice-Presidents of the Parliament,
Honourable Members of the Parliament,

The proposed 2024 General State Budget presents a consolidated figure of US$1.95 billion for the Central Administration, Special Administrative Region of Oe-Cússe Ambeno (RAEOA), and Social Security, excluding the Social Security Reserve Fund.

This includes an allocation of US$1.83 billion for the Central Administration, US$60 million reserved for the RAEOA, and US$347.6 million for Social Security.

State revenues are balanced with state expenditure for the Public Administrative Sector, Central Administration, and the Social Security and RAEOA sub-sectors.

A transfer from the Petroleum Fund above the estimated sustainable income is necessary to implement the strategic measures to leverage the productive sector and social capital.

As you know, this fund is totally transparent and professionally managed. Every dollar of revenue from our oil resources goes into the fund, guaranteeing sustainability for future generations.

As such, the estimated sustainable income will be transferred to invest in economic diversification, rather than to feed the state's current expenditures.

We realise that withdrawals from the Petroleum Fund, above the estimated sustainable income, are the primary funding source for the budget deficit, as has been the case for the last decade, and this trend needs to be strongly counteracted.

The only solution for the country is to invest these resources wisely, to end this dependence on a fund which, as I said, should be invested as a guarantee for future generations, for the country's sustainable future.

So, to protect it, we must invest it. Without investment, there is no growth and no economic and social development. Without investment, it is not possible to energise the productive sectors that generate employment or to develop healthy, qualified citizens who can contribute to the diversification of the economy, which is necessary to avoid the depletion of the Petroleum Fund.

Therefore, we are applying the withdrawal from the Petroleum Fund with rigour and responsibility to allow for greater economic stability, the generation of income and employment, and the economic transformation that will promote the economy's sustainability.

The 2024 Draft General State Budget proposes a transfer from the Petroleum Fund of US$1.38 billion. This transfer corresponds to US$522.1 million of the estimated sustainable income and US$855.54 million above it.

We are talking about investments in agriculture, fisheries and livestock, tourism, small- and medium-sized industries and companies, and support for private initiatives. In other words, we are talking about everything that promotes the creation of livelihoods and incomes for families while strengthening sovereignty and independence by replacing imported goods with domestic production.

For 2024, we will focus on three crucial areas for substantial investment in productive infrastructure.

Firstly, the electricity sector, with an allocation of US$165.6 million, reflects the strategic importance of guaranteeing a reliable and accessible energy supply to the population and businesses. This investment will benefit the 20% of the population who still don't have access to the national electricity grid.

The infrastructure construction sector came in second place, with an allocation of US$153.5 million, reaffirming the urgency of developing essential infrastructure to promote economic growth.

Second, we will rehabilitate and build basic infrastructure and modernise the water, sanitation, and drainage systems, especially in Díli. We will also complete the installation of fibre optic cable to guarantee quality internet access for all citizens and, simultaneously, facilitate the growth of businesses and entrepreneurship.

Thirdly, with an investment of US$104.2 million, the oil and natural gas sector emphasises the government's vision to harness and optimise the country's natural resources to promote sustainable economic development.

The Government is committed to establishing a supply base and refinery on the South Coast to connect to the Greater Sunrise pipeline. The goal is to develop a national oil industry that, among other things, provides employment for the Timorese.

I would remind you that the Tasi Mane project aims to contribute not only to the development of the South Coast, and the petroleum industry in particular, but also to provide direct and indirect economic impacts throughout the country, capitalising on the economic benefits derived from the exploitation of Timor-Leste's natural resources.

The previous Government stalled efforts to reach and draft a development agreement for Greater Sunrise. The 9th Government resumed these efforts to bring the pipeline to Timor-Leste.

In a young and fragile country like ours, where around 60% of the population is under 25, we must have the courage to invest in projects that will transform the economy and consolidate national stability.

Let me remind you of an example of the development we want for Timor-Leste, which can be witnessed in Darwin, Australia. I was in Darwin in 1974, and returned in 1999. Years later, when I returned, I was impressed by the rapid development of the Northern Territory of Australia at the expense of exploiting Timor-Leste's Bayu Undan field.

We also want to use our resources to develop our South Coast, including constructing new towns and supporting infrastructure. During the construction and operation phase of this project's infrastructure and support services, we want to create around 50,000 direct and indirect jobs.

Madam President of the Parliament,
Vice-Presidents of the Parliament,

Honourable Members of the Parliament,

As you will see from the budget documents you have analysed, the 2024 budget includes other necessary strategic measures for the country's long-term economic growth and development, allowing it to meet current needs and the needs of future generations.

To ration my time, I will list a few that are more relevant and cut across governance.

I want to start by saying that, in 2024, we will review the *Strategic Development Plan 2011-2030* to adapt it to the nation's current state and the global dynamics experienced in recent years.

The COVID-19 pandemic, the worsening climate emergency, the war in Europe, the conflict in the Middle East, and recent technological developments represent new challenges that Timor-Leste must meet.

I am not just talking about the negative impacts, such as rising inflation and interest rates, fluctuations in the price of oil, and the slowdown in the global economy but also the possible opportunities created by global dynamics, such as the commitment to the green and blue economies and the innovation provided by the latest technologies.

To this end, at the beginning of next year the Government will approve the Blue Economy Action Plan as a strategic approach aimed at promoting a sustainable economy linked to the ocean and marine resources, where there is a balance between the economic activities developed and the long-term capacity of marine ecosystems to support these activities.

We will finalise land borders and accelerate maritime border negotiations with Indonesia, reaffirming our national sovereignty and boosting the economic potential of border regions.

I am pleased to say that the technical teams negotiating the land border have finally managed to close the unresolved Noel-Besi-Citran border segment at Oe-Cússe Ambeno. With the completion of this final segment, we will proceed with maritime border negotiations with Indonesia next year.

I have mentioned border regions because we believe it's necessary to ensure that the specific potential of each region, of each municipality, is valued and promoted. The fundamental instrument for this to happen is the process of decentralisation through local government.

Over the last six months, the Government has been working hard to draft the legislative framework that supports the local government process and the phased decentralisation. The 2024 budget envisages initiating local governance by creating the necessary infrastructure and technical conditions, with the involvement of local stakeholders.

In line with this desire to bring citizens closer to the state and enable access to public services throughout the country, we will open one-stop shops in all municipal centres next year.

The Balcão Único programme, also called one-stop shop, is being developed with the support of the UNDP. This programme is part of the policy of administrative decentralisation and local power, intending to simplify and modernise local administration.

In the health sector, we are committed to implementing the National Health Policy and the National Strategic Plan for the Health Sector 2011–2030, maximising efforts to guarantee better service provision and general access to quality health care.

We will invest in combating malnutrition in the country, in ambulances and specialised equipment to support the provision of health care, in doctor residences, and in recruiting more doctors and health workers.

Regarding the education sector, I would highlight the establishment of a Commission for the Coordination of Universities and Higher Education Institutes to develop a collective strategy for strengthening state support and improving the academic quality of these institutions. Subsidising private universities to promote education and qualifications for the professional sector and continuing to make the necessary efforts to implement CAFE schools in each administrative post is also planned.

Another commitment made in the government programme was to create and support a Timorese Art and Culture Association to train and encourage talented young people in arts and culture, thus promoting Timorese identity on international platforms. To this end, funds have also been allocated in this state budget to realise this objective.

We will also, as committed to in the government programme, reform the justice sector by creating the Supreme Court of Justice and providing comprehensive training for judges and prosecutors.

Regarding international relations and foreign policy, I would highlight the investment of a new embassy in India, one of the world's largest economies and democracies, and a consulate in Northern Ireland to protect and provide consular services to Timorese living in this region.

I also highlight the critical role of diplomacy in attracting job-creating foreign investment and continuing to develop programmes for seasonal workers in friendly countries.

As part of the development of traditional economic sectors, I would highlight investment in agriculture and the fisheries sector, including the purchase of improved boats and equipment for deep-sea fishing, and more significant support for the private sector to enable local businesses to start up and grow, as provided for in the National Industry Policy recently approved by the Government.

We will also establish the Development Bank of Timor-Leste to facilitate access to long-term financing at affordable interest rates. Associated with this measure, we will combat the bureaucratisation of processes and create a more favourable environment for investors, facilitating the commercial activities of the banking sector, insurance institutions, microcredit institutions, and the financial market in Timor-Leste.

Lastly, this Government will contribute to a fair nation that fights inequalities and promotes inclusion, creating opportunities for everyone, regardless of gender, age, place of residence, religion, social or economic status, or sexual orientation.

To promote inclusion, we will develop the Voice of the Voiceless programme, invest in women and children, pay social pensions, and support the elderly and disabled by increasing social pensions to ensure a decent income for all those who need it.

Madam President of the Parliament,
Vice-Presidents of the Parliament,
Honourable Members of the Parliament,

For the sake of transparency, we cannot present a state budget without talking about public-spending figures.

The total amount of expenditure planned for the Central Administration and the Special Administrative Region of Oe-Cússe Ambeno is broken down as follows:

- US$468.8 million for wages and salaries
- US$386.3 million for goods and services
- US$589.7 million for public transfers
- US$34.2 million for minor capital
- US$411 million for development capital

The Social Security budget, including the Social Security Reserve Fund, has an allocation of US$347.6 million.

If we prefer to look at the distribution of the General State Budget in sectoral terms, we have:

- US$788.2 million for economic affairs
- US$389.6 million for environmental protection

- US$467.1 million for social protection
- US$140.9 million for education
- US$66.2 million for health
- US$45.2 million for housing and collective infrastructures
- US$55.3 million for security and public order
- US$34.9 million for defence

We still must talk about figures in terms of budget execution.

Because of the transition from the 8th to the 9th Governments, in 2023, we have two different periods for budget execution: the first between January 1st and June 30th, and the second between July 1st and December 31st. As of November 15th, the 9th Government's total budget execution was 34%, compared to 29% for the previous Government over six months.

In general terms, we estimate a budget execution of 85% by the end of the year, compared to 79% for 2022.

Regarding the implementation of the 9th Government's budget, I can't help but mention that in these first few months, the Government teams dedicated themselves to exhaustively mapping all the corrections that need to be made to governance, including the processes, systems, and methodologies that have been holding back economic growth and sustainable development.

This included preparing the organic structure of each ministerial line, renewing the legal-administrative framework of national structures and policies, and defining objectives and priorities for the next five years.

Finally, I'd like to talk briefly about the national macroeconomic scenario.

As I said, this budget lays the foundations for the country's development between 2024 and 2028, with a target of reducing poverty by 10%, an average annual economic growth rate of 5%, improvements in the management and sustainability of public finances, and, intrinsically related to this, the creation of at least 50,000 jobs.

The real non-oil GDP is expected to have slowed to 2.2% in 2023 due to a drop in public spending after the elections. However, expenditures are expected to increase in 2024, and, consequently, GDP growth will rise to 4.1%. The aim is to maintain an annual non-oil GDP growth rate of 5% in the coming years.

The budget allocation for the year 2024 decreases by 8.3% compared to the 2023 budget, even though the Government identified efficiency savings in the 2023 amending budget.

The increase in the 2024 budget corresponds to capital development expenditure of US$144 million to boost economic growth. Even applying a lower budget limit than in the original 2022 GSB and 2023 GSB for the

Central Administration and RAEOA, capital investment was offset.

I must remind you that the previous Government's budget limits were set well above the highest value of executed expenditure in the country's history. So, to guarantee budgetary sustainability, the budget ceiling for 2024 is closer to absorption and execution capacity, also allowing for more effective and efficient investment.

In simpler terms, from a macroeconomic point of view, by the end of its mandate, this Government intends to more than double real non-oil GDP, increase household consumption growth, drastically reduce the growth of imports, and exponentially increase investment and exports.

Inflation has increased in recent months due to the rise in the price of rice and oil, which is unrelated to the national situation.

Although this situation is expected to continue in the first few months of 2024, the repeal of the sugar tax and the reversal of the increase in import duties implemented by the 9th Government in the 2023 Amending Budget should lead to a reduction in inflationary pressures in the medium term (after the markets have had time to readjust). In this case, we are talking about an inflation rate (CPI, annual average) of 7% in 2022, to a forecast of 8.3% in 2023 and a rate of 2.5% in 2024.

This Government does not want to be populist but, rather, transparent and upright. As such, I want to clarify that to achieve the desired 5% non-oil economic growth, we need to invest wisely and with quality over the next five years.

To do this, let me reiterate: We will have to double agricultural growth while also reducing imports; improve internet connectivity to improve productivity and grow companies and businesses; invest in tourism, for which the blue economy could bring great returns; become members of ASEAN and the WTO to capitalise on new opportunities and open up new markets; and support the growth of the private sector, which should help reduce public spending.

Madam President of the Parliament,
Vice-Presidents of the Parliament,
Honourable Members of the Parliament,

Having presented, in general terms, the 2024 General State Budget, which aims to implement strategic and indispensable measures to meet the needs of the current generation and give tools to future generations, promoting the well-being of all Timorese citizens, I would like to put before you, Honourable Members of Parliament, what I have presented here.

I am humbled to say that all considerations for using this budget to serve the Timorese people are welcome.

Our commitment is to the Timorese, not our ego, or personal or political vanity.

In this sense, we believe that the debate that will follow in the coming days, a debate that we want to be constructive and responsible, is essential to serving the nation, following our commitment to defend the national interest and honour the sacrifices of those who perished so that we can exercise our rights and duties in freedom.

For the well-being of all the women, men, and children of our beloved country, we are all, once again, called upon to put all our commitment, integrity, and professionalism into analysing this budgetary instrument that reflects the Government's priorities and policies for the coming year, making rational use of the state's limited financial resources.

For the well-being and sustainable development of Timor-Leste's future, I thank you in advance for your contributions and demand that the bridge we are building today for tomorrow be solid and resilient in the face of the challenges we foresee, and those we cannot foresee.

Thank you very much, and my respect to everyone.

National Seminar:
Rules and Procedures in the Development of Timor-Leste's Infrastructure

Auditorium Hall of the Ministry of Finance, Dîli
15 February 2024

Your Excellencies,

Vice-Prime Minister and Minister Coordinator for Economic Affairs and Minister of Tourism and Environment, Mr Francisco Kalbuadi Lay,

Vice-Prime Minister and Minister Coordinator for Rural Development and Community Housing, Mr Mariano 'Assanami' Sabino Lopes

Distinguished Members of Government,

Your Excellencies,

President of the FRETILIN Bench in the National Parliament, Mr Aniceto Longuinhos Guterres Lopes,

President of Commission E of the National Parliament, Mr Marcos Xavier,

President of Commission C of the National Parliament, Ms Cidelizia Faria dos Santos,

Ambassador of Australia to Timor-Leste, Ms Caitlin Wilson, Ambassador of Japan to Timor-Leste, Mr Kimura Tetsuya,

President of the Chamber of Commerce and Industry of Timor-Leste, Mr Jorge Serrano,

World Bank Representative for Timor-Leste, Mr Bernard Harborne,

Asian Development Bank Representative for Timor-Leste, Ms Stefania Dina,

Chief Representative of JICA in Timor-Leste, Mr ITO Mimpei, UNDP Resident Representative in Timor-Leste, Ms Katyna Argueta,

Distinguished Rector of the National University of Timor Lorosa'e, Professor João Soares Martins,

Representative of the University for Peace, Esteemed Director of the Faculty of Engineering, Mr José Manuel Maniquim,

President of the NGO Forum of Timor-Leste – FONGTIL, Mr Valentim da Costa,

Dear Guests,

Ladies and Gentlemen,

I am pleased to participate in this national seminar on 'Rules and Procedures in the Development of Timor-Leste's Infrastructure'.

Between 2007 and 2017, infrastructure development was undoubtedly a major engine of national progress, and supported the leveraging of social capital, economic growth, job creation, and the consolidation of institutions.

The Government is committed to resuming these efforts and to move forward with an integrated infrastructure plan, with the best possible value, to support sustainable development in Timor- Leste.

I thank the Ministry of Planning and Strategic Investment for organising this seminar. To the Minister, Mr Gastão de Sousa, and his team, my congratulations on the initiative, which will surely bring important lessons and recommendations for the sector.

And with the results of today's dialogue, with the sharing of experiences and lessons learned, with all these distinguished participants here today, I can only say, 'Let's get to work!'

The development of infrastructure is vital to national development. Infrastructure is the backbone of all the country's productive sectors.

It is not news that if we want economic and social development for the Timorese, we must build and maintain a wide range of basic infrastructure that supports health, education, agriculture, people's mobility, industry, the growth of the private sector, and the general well-being of the people.

Investing in infrastructure is also about creating conditions for job creation and income generation, which are essential for national stability.

And if we talk about rules and procedures, and lessons learned, it is essential that we apply the utmost rigour and professionalism throughout the infrastructure development process, from the planning phase to budgeting, procurement, monitoring, supervision, and evaluation of projects with transparency and absolute compliance with legislation and the rules in force.

Our country has many infrastructure needs, but it also has opportunities.

Let me make a special reference to our development partners represented here today, most of which have been present since our independence 22 years ago. You have been extraordinary in providing us with support, funding, and the transfer of skills and knowledge, so that we, the Timorese, can realise our projects and ambitions. As such, I take this opportunity to thank you for your dedication, generosity, and patience.

As you must understand, a country rising from the ashes must necessarily have its own idiosyncrasies, priorities, and circumstances, which are not always fully appreciated by individuals, organisations, or governments outside our reality and experience. A fragile state, as Timor-Leste continues to be, will always have more obstacles and challenges than easy roads and triumphs.

And yet, I know that the challenges Timor-Leste faces as a young country are already known to all. We have many institutional, infrastructure, and human resource weaknesses, as well as challenges in access to knowledge and technology.

However, we also have opportunities. Timor-Leste is creating conditions to be a more active and dynamic economic partner in the region, including the accession process to ASEAN and the joining of the World Trade Organization on 26 February.

I believe that full membership in these international organisations will also provide foreign companies and investors with the confidence and security to invest in our country, which, in turn, will necessarily require infrastructure to support these investments. As such, public investment in infrastructure continues to be a national priority.

For this reason, it is now more important than ever to talk about rules and procedures in the context of infrastructure development.

Rules and procedures bring certainty and security, including the protection of people and goods.

Rules and procedures instil greater effectiveness and efficiency in construction processes and projects, allowing for better time management and better management of financial and human resources.

Rules and procedures instil quality and sustainability on infrastructure construction, as well as safeguard impacts on social life and the environment.

Lastly, rules and procedures make the country more credible and qualified as a partner or recipient of development assistance or investment.

Compliance with rules and procedures ensures conformity with legislation and regulations in force, which is a key factor for a rule of law that operates with transparency, integrity, and professionalism, preventing disputes and litigation, and promoting the needs of every part of society, and with consideration to the inequalities in our country.

Your Excellencies,
Ladies and Gentlemen,

The goals of the *Strategic Development Plan 2011–2030* (SDP), to develop social capital, the economy, and infrastructure, and strengthen good governance, were reinforced in the programme of the 9th Constitutional Government.

The Government, however, plans to revise the SDP to update it in light of current national and global circumstances.

Diversifying the economy remains one of the main goals to be achieved by this Government. This will go hand in hand with creating fiscal, legal, and bureaucratic conditions, enabling greater confidence for national and international investors to take a chance on Timor-Leste, and for development partners to continue to trust our institutions.

We aim to diversify the economy through the development of productive sectors (agriculture, forestry, livestock, fishing, tourism, petroleum and minerals, and manufacturing), and we wish to promote the growth of the private sector, which will gradually lead to substituting imported products with those that can be produced locally. Further, we want to invest more in the sectors of transportation, energy, and telecommunications.

Infrastructure and a comprehensive and transparent financial market facilitate investment in strategic sectors and drive economic growth within a sustainable and diversified non-oil economy.

We also believe that the creation of a Timor-Leste Development Bank will facilitate access to long-term financing, with affordable interest rates, including for the development of our infrastructure.

And we want to keep up with current global trends by launching energy efficiency and waste management projects, as well as a more sustainable agricultural, fisheries, and livestock sectors. This will require integrated planning of basic infrastructure.

As you are probably aware, Timor-Leste is in the initial stages of the blue economy development programme, which will include not only economic diversification and income generation but also the protection and conservation of ecosystems, protecting biodiversity and marine habitats.

Yet, we know that basic sanitation is essential for human health, for the environment, and for the sustainability of water resources, including the ocean and seas. The lack of adequate basic sanitation can lead to water contamination and the emergence of diseases, affecting the health of coastal communities and populations that depend on the sea for their subsistence.

Pollution caused by the lack of basic sanitation also harms marine ecosystems, leading to the loss of biodiversity, and compromising fishing and aquaculture activities, as well as other economic activities related to the sea.

As such, developing basic sanitation infrastructure is also essential for the development of the blue economy, ensuring the protection of the ocean and the quality of life of Timorese communities.

In short, from the blue economy to the country's electrification, from renewable energy to the building of ports and airports, from roads, bridges, and riverbank containment to access to health, education, and leisure centres, and to primary economic activities, infrastructure is the backbone of our country's socioeconomic development.

It is in this sense that rules and procedures are fundamental to the nation's development, especially where it concerns infrastructure.

A healthy administration of processes and systems provides guidance, consistency, and security to infrastructure development. Over these last 22 years, we can say that we already have a wealth of experience in learning and correcting mistakes in order to set the country on the right course.

I believe, ladies and gentlemen, that your contributions today will reinforce this Government's commitment to managing public investment projects transparently and in accordance with approved legislation and procedures, because on this rests the credibility, well-being, and future of the country.

If we all contribute to solving problems, and if we all meet challenges with efficiency and rigour, we can do more, and better, for the Timorese people.

Thank you very much.

GOVERNMENT

Peace & Human Rights

Accelerating progress towards SDG 16: *Access to Justice for All in conflict-affected states*

United Nations, New York
20 September 2017

Your Excellencies,
Ladies and Gentlemen,

It is almost precisely two years[2] since the transforming 2030 Agenda for Sustainable Development was unanimously approved by world leaders at a historical summit held at these United Nations Headquarters.

This global commitment conveys the needs and aspirations of humankind in a broad and thorough manner; it has been informed by the lessons we have learned from the past, including from the implementation of the Millennium Development Goals, to ensure that people are at the centre of our actions, both in developed and developing countries. Indeed, this new Global Agenda states that *no one should be left behind*.

It should be noted that the process for setting the ambitious 17 Sustainable Development Goals (SDGs) included inputs from fragile and conflict-affected states. This has allowed a more considered and effective approach to the various aspects of sustainable development and its challenges at a global level, as well as to the vital role that peace and stability play in achieving this development vision.

The g7+, and the New Deal, which advocates for the need to adopt proper peacebuilding and statebuilding processes, have enabled more collaborative actions to create a new development paradigm, as well as new forms of engagement in fragile and conflict-affected states. The difficulties experienced in these countries, which often include widespread and extreme poverty, require cautious international intervention in which all parties are both students and teachers, as we know that all situations and contexts are unique and therefore do not allow for a one-size-fits-all approach.

We, the members of the g7+ group, are aware that our countries present

2 The United Nations Resolution was approved on 25 September 2015 and entered into force on 1 January 2016.

very particular development challenges. As such, we have assumed the political commitment to adopt the 2030 Agenda, in which we advocated the inclusion of Goal 16, *Peace, Justice and Strong Institutions*, since we know that without peace, justice, and sound and efficient institutions, it would be very hard for us to implement any of the other 16 SDGs.

We must acknowledge that our agenda will fail to achieve its goals if it does not start by improving the living conditions of the people in countries plagued by wars and conflict, particularly as we expect extreme poverty in 2030 to be concentrated in those countries.

> *Giving back hope to men, women, and children who have been left behind in the progress of humanity is more than a moral duty — it is also a global responsibility and a matter of justice.*

> *Poverty and conflict are man-made. As such, I believe they can be stopped by all of us who share the values of freedom and human dignity.*

Nothing is impossible as long as the promotion of democracy and human rights replaces the rhetoric espoused by the great powers, those proud pioneers of freedom and democracy, with pragmatic actions towards peace and the protection of collective interests instead of the interests of a mighty few who pretend, because it is to their benefit, to be oblivious to the true causes of inequalities and injustice throughout the world.

Indeed, while we are debating issues of justice and promotion of human rights, we look numbly at the plight of millions of displaced people, many of whom try to reach the 'lands of freedom' only to become hostages to that pipe dream and put in refugee camps throughout the Pacific and Europe, as if this were not another global problem caused by international policies.

> *Thus I say that there will not be sustainable development for all unless we all make a sustainable change in the way we engage fragile and conflict-affected states.*

In order to do this, we must start by putting human dignity above any other political, economic, or strategic interest or consideration. We also must not impose patronising values and presumptions, as if seeking to civilise countries. In other words, we must replace an engagement model that is corrupted by interests with a true model of justice that promotes inclusive and sustainable development for all.

If we want justice for all, we must free all peoples living in conflict.

These countries did not achieve even a single Millennium Development Goal. They face unsurmountable obstacles when trying to escape from a situation of fragility without the effective support of the international community.

International assistance is essential to the sustainability of these nations. However, the approach adopted by development partners must be suitable to the real needs of these countries, and the engagement must be restricted to the specific circumstances and challenges of each nation. On the other hand, one cannot make the mistake of trying to solve the problems of these peoples, much less trying to impose solutions, without their direct involvement.

The experience in transitioning from conflict to stability in Timor-Leste taught us that the only path, even if it is a painful one, is to search for the root causes of our problems within our own societies. If we are part of the problem, we must necessarily be an even bigger part of the solution.

Your Excellencies,
Ladies and Gentlemen,

Promoting the Rule of Law and ensuring equal access to justice for all in fragile and conflict-affected states are extremely complex tasks that are often poorly understood by international assistance.

It is firmly agreed by the g7+ that consolidating the sector of justice is of paramount importance for peacebuilding and statebuilding. It is also vital for conveying trust and attracting the necessary investment to develop the economy. We face several common challenges that include legal frameworks that are weak or inadequate to our realities, poor and limited infrastructure, and, of course, difficulties in capacity building and training of human resources. These are vital requirements for enabling access to justice for all.

Although these shortcomings can be explained by the historical context, we cannot stop advancing and investing in our institutions. In the case of Timor-Leste, we lived for hundreds of years under a Portuguese administration that did not invest in the higher education of the Timorese so as to keep power and justice in the hands of the European, or at most a few assimilated Timorese. During the period of Indonesian occupation, our people were subjected to all kinds of deprivations and atrocities, and the few that had the chance to study in Indonesia were never allowed to work as prosecutors, public defenders, or judges.

All of our experience in the area of justice during that dark period of injustice comes from the Resistance movement, in which we ran a sort of traditional court, so as to take action against some offences and crimes within a context of popular justice.

Already in 1999, on the path towards independence, the Indonesians who ensured the operation of the justice sector were replaced by international legal staff and a few dozen Timorese trainees who had studied in Indonesia. It was only in the year 2000 that the first Timorese judges started to hear cases at formal courts, although they were always underrepresented in the international legal panels. Regrettably, this approach option ended up not being effective.

A hybrid system was then established, in which neither the Timorese nor the internationals were given full control over the administration of justice. As a result, no one took responsibility for the failures and ambiguities deriving from the sharing of responsibilities. Another consequence of this approach was that a blind eye was turned to situations where people proved not to have the minimum competence required for holding such complex responsibilities, therefore weakening the overall system.

In 2002, after achieving formal independence, the Timorese Government started to gradually change the system left by the United Nations in favour of one more inspired by the Portuguese model. This created a new challenge, as most Timorese staff in the justice sector were not familiar with the Portuguese legal system, and even less so with the Portuguese language, essential for the proper interpretation and application of laws.

The justice sector is unequivocally a key sector for development. A fragile sector of justice may jeopardise the very state, as well as the economic and social development of the nation. No one will invest in the economy if there is not a legal system that ensures that the law is upheld. And without investment, there is no employment, and without employment, there is no peace.

While it is important that we provide the institutions of justice the appropriate and necessary respect, we are agreed that this is an issue that must be addressed with the urgency and seriousness that the humane and humanitarian demands of justice requires from us, lest we risk a justice system that is inflexible or even, without intention, one that neglects respect for the rights and guarantees of victims, witnesses, and, as importantly, the accused.

Although Timor-Leste has relied on international assistance for these past 15 years, or maybe because of the way in which this international assistance was led, we must now invest more so that we may have an efficient justice system where cases are processed in a prompt, balanced, independent, and efficient manner.

A thorough reform of the justice sector is still to be undertaken in Timor-Leste. This task will surely take years, in view of its complexity and starting position. I believe that this reform is very important. Indeed, while acknowledging the meritorious effort made by the Timorese magistracy to improve its operation, the fact is that there is a long way ahead of us in order to prevent perceptions of injustice that might undermine the very rule of law and the trust of citizens and investors. International cooperation, through a process that is responsible, humane, inclusive, and owned by national decision makers, will surely be part of the solution to this challenge.

Your Excellencies,
Ladies and Gentlemen,

Timor-Leste is truly committed to accelerating the issues listed in the new agenda. To this end, the Government held an international conference last May [2017] on the 'Roadmap for Implementing the 2030 Agenda and the Sustainable Development Goals'. Our country has set a clear path for progressing towards the SDGs, and we have aligned these goals with our Strategic Development Plan, giving proper consideration to our national context.

Our commitment to promoting the g7+ is also based on our strong desire to share experiences, strengthen fragile-to-fragile cooperation, implement the SDGs, and, naturally, strive to live up to the motto:

'Leave no one behind and reach the furthest behind first'.

Consequently, SDG 17, seeking to strengthen the means of implementation and breathe new life into the global partnership for sustainable development, splits up into several important goals that are valid instruments for the transformation we seek to achieve. In order to be successful, we must maintain a critical view of the process and make monitoring a key part, to ensure we remain on the right track.

This requires both sound cooperation with our developed partners and a careful and inclusive internal process that involves not only Governments and public agencies but also civil society and the community.

In short, we want to see an actual impact on the lives of the people, instead of mere statistical results. Consequently, we must at all times place people at the centre of our actions. This is as valid for the partner that receives assistance as it is for the partner that provides it. Humanising partnerships is a vital precondition for everyone's success.

Development partners on the ground must step out from their comfort zone. One cannot have their 'homework' already prepared by copying what was done in other countries over the years.

We need more creativity, more sensitivity to the specific intricacies of each mission, more consultation, and even more evidence-based decision making, so that we may identify constraints and propose partnership solutions.

Last, but not least, we need time. Sustainable reforms, good practices, and strong institutions cannot be built in a day.

Thank you very much.

The Pursuit of Peace Through Nationally Owned Mechanisms: Learning From Countries' Experiences

United Nations, New York
20 September 2017

Your Excellency Mr António Guterres, UN Secretary-General,

Your Excellency Mr Ernest Bai Koroma, President of the Republic of Sierra Leone,

Your Excellency Mr Francisco Guterres Lú-Olo, President of the Democratic Republic of Timor-Leste,

Your Excellency Mr Faustin-Archange Touadéra, President of the Central African Republic,

Your Excellency Mr Momodu Kargbo, Minister of Finance and Economic Development of Sierra Leone

Your Excellencies,

Ladies and Gentlemen,

It is an honour for me to take part in this high-level meeting and to see such a distinguished audience from the various corners of the world, sharing experiences and challenges in seeking to eradicate conflict and build sustainable peace in the world.

While we take part in this 72nd session of the UN General Assembly, tens of millions of people are suffering directly from wars and conflicts. An even greater number suffer indirectly. Around the world, over 65 million people are currently displaced due to internal conflicts and violence.

Most of these conflicts have been going on for decades. The causes of most of them are well known. Most make us question ourselves about the values of humanity and civilisation, in a world that is supposed to be developed and technologically advanced.

Today we are so globally interconnected that an event in one part of the world may soon affect the lives of common citizens, institutions, and states in any other part of the world. The physical distance separating local from global events is often minimised by technology. Because of this, the wealth of a few clashes shamefully with the extreme poverty of many, leading to generalised feelings of revolt and intolerance.

We cannot remain indifferent to the tragedy faced by some of the peoples of the world, unless human solidarity is on the wane and we all are becoming inured to the suffering of others. Such problems are the responsibility of us all, even if some of us are mired in our own internal problems. We cannot interfere in international matters only when we have national interests and strategies to defend.

Ultimately, peace depends on every one of us, through small decisions, actions, and initiatives that we can make and adopt in order to change the world. It is urgent that we understand that peace inside each of us depends upon peace between all of us, regardless of ethnicity, religion, ideology, or culture.

One of the reasons why the United Nations was created was precisely to keep alive the spirit of cooperation and the feeling of common responsibility in the pursuit of peace, safety, human rights, economic development, and social progress in all nations of the world.

Whether rich or poor, large or small, no country can reach these goals by themselves. We must work together as a community in order to find solutions to our common problems and to prevent tragedies and suffering now, as well as in the future.

We have endured two World Wars and a period of Cold War. If we can learn something from our recent history and from the tragic consequences of these conflicts, it is that we cannot put an end to war by waging war: we cannot stop violence with further violence. We cannot wash off blood with blood!

We cannot repeat the errors of the past. We must face the causes of problems, read their signs, and anticipate and foresee the future. I refuse to accept that one can talk about war from a perspective of defence or attack while mechanisms of dialogue and diplomacy are still available to us which might build tolerance and trust between countries. Which might build peace.

We already know the results of interventions that use force - they end up leading to even bloodier conflicts. We see tensions continue to rise until they even become nuclear threats. We witness ethnic rivalries, religious rivalries, and various types of extremism. We witness an increasing number of acts of terrorism and an increase in the number of refugees who, instead of being celebrated for their sacrifice and for the courage they display in surviving, are instead shunned! And, still, we continue to be unable to find proper international solutions to problems that plague humankind?

We are living in a world disorder that requires the rebuilding of the international system – a system that establishes long-term partnerships between countries, without hidden agendas, towards common goals of stability, development, and human dignity.

The key questions in today's world are knowing how much longer major powers will continue promoting and funding wars and conflicts, and how much longer international organisations will continue to react to problems instead of trying to prevent them.

The 2030 Agenda for Sustainable Development was unanimously approved by the 193 UN member states. Are these world leaders truly committed to goals that seek to make the world a better place?

I am speaking of fragile and conflict-affected states which, by advocating the inclusion of the promotion of peace in this global agenda, have the moral obligation to do all they can so that peace and stability are realities in their own countries, so that their various institutions can manage development assistance effectively and transparently, and so that wealth is distributed fairly and equitably among their citizens.

I am also speaking of rich and developed countries, which must make sure that the commitments they make are more than short-term displays for public relations purposes within an intricate juggling of meetings and negotiations, and where unconditional support to peace and sustainable development is declared in the morning and billion-dollar weapon sales deals are made in the afternoon!

Your Excellencies,
Ladies and Gentlemen,

I represent a country that lived under colonial administration for hundreds of years, that was violently occupied for over two decades, and that, already as an independent nation, had some very difficult periods of internal instability. I spent a good part of my life fighting for freedom, which unfortunately also entailed leading an armed resistance struggle.

Despite all we endured — including torture, deprivations, and death — we were not able to put an end to violence in our society and live in freedom until we finally settled on the path of dialogue, tolerance, and reconciliation.

We understood, including from the experience of other countries in conflict, that without a strategy of internal reconciliation, we would not be able to build our nation, since peace is a requirement for development. In 2000, we established the Commission for Reception, Truth and Reconciliation (known by its Portuguese acronym CAVR), the first reconciliation commission ever created in Asia. This was a pioneering model that enabled us to dig up the truth on the injustices that had been committed, and to help the people deal with that truth.

Still, our fragility led us into a vicious cycle of conflict every two years (which peaked in 2006), that caused more death and destruction, in addition to thousands of internally displaced persons.

It was only in 2009 that we managed to close our chapter of suffering for good, under the motto of 'Goodbye conflict, welcome development', by committing as a nation to beginning a new journey, one where we all put the national interests above any grievances and political convictions dividing us, so that the next generations might grow within an atmosphere of peace and trust. This had to include an intense process of dialogue and reconciliation, where forgiveness overcame hatred, and where tolerance overcame revenge. Thus, we were freed from painful memories and corrosive feelings. This was indeed the true liberation of the Timorese people.

So, too, with Indonesia, we put the past in the past and enabled reconciliation between our two countries. We created a joint Commission for Truth and Friendship, and now our countries, in addition to having strong ties of friendship and mutual respect, are cooperating in all areas of diplomacy, and have become role models of peace in Southeast Asia.

I would ask that you kindly also allow me to discuss the historical agreement reached only very recently between Timor-Leste and Australia on our long-standing dispute on our maritime boundaries. Timor-Leste has always advocated the international rule-based system for regulating relations between states and for contributing to the resolution of international disputes in a constructive and peaceful manner, so that it is not always the law of the strongest that prevails. As such, Timor-Leste was the first country ever to initiate the Conciliation Commission mechanism under the United Nations Convention on the Law of the Sea (UNCLOS) in order to find a fair and peaceful solution for its dispute with Australia.

I believe that the agreement reached between the two nations may serve as an example for the international community, showing that neighbours can work together in peace and friendship and settle their differences under international law, proving that the authority of a State is not determined by the size of its territory, its wealth or its military or economic power.

Your Excellencies
Ladies and Gentlemen,

The g7+ member countries are united by a common cause of peacebuilding and statebuilding, sharing their experiences with each other. We are monitoring closely the challenges faced by countries such as the Central African Republic, South Sudan, and Guinea-Bissau, and we want to promote a culture of solidarity under the banner of 'Fragile-to-Fragile Cooperation'. We are also interested in drawing important lessons from experiences in other countries outside the group, such as Rwanda and South Africa, which is why we would like to invite them to join us in promoting this culture of dialogue and reconciliation within a true experience of peer-to-peer learning.

As a group, we must congratulate the UN Secretary-General for launching the agenda on sustaining peace, and pledge all our support to the promotion of this important initiative. Although the g7+ is, overall, a relatively small group, each of its members has direct experience in handling conflicts and violence. Unfortunately, some of these countries continue to live in these same troubled situations of conflict and violence, which is why we must have direct participation and added responsibility in contributing to build and maintain peace in each of these countries.

Being home to around 300 million people, most of us have become a playground for regional and global politics, an experimental lab for peacekeeping, humanitarian and development approaches, and a breeding ground for multi-billion-dollar corporations seeking to exploit our resources.

Some of us have been taking steps to escape the trap of permanent instability and conflict by making use of national mechanisms with wisdom and courage. We believe that our experience enables us to contribute so that the community of nations may achieve sustainable and lasting peace. This requires national leadership and ownership of decisions, programs, and mechanisms, supported by flexible and efficient international intervention.

The g7+ established a council of eminent persons, to which I have the privilege of belonging. I would like to use this opportunity to invite other citizens who advocate peace and development to join this noble cause.

The g7+ is a group that does not impose values or doctrines, and that does not preach. On the contrary, we want to provide support while respecting the timings and processes of all peoples and countries.

Thus, we want to encourage the necessary transformations so that the processes for escaping conflict and achieving sustainable peace are owned collectively and internally by each country.

I conclude my address by pledging the collective support of the g7+ to the agenda on sustaining peace by the UN Secretary General.

Thank you very much.

What we have Learned and how it Links to Actual Successful Transitions: Supporting Core Government Functions to Address Fragility and Sustain Peace. Keynote Remarks.

Blavatnik School of Government
Oxford, England
28 February – 1 March 2018

Your Excellencies,
Distinguished Delegates,
Ladies and Gentlemen,

First of all, please accept my apologies for not being present in person at this important event. My absence is a result of the ongoing representation of Timor-Leste in the fight to defend the rights and interests of the people of my young nation against the greed of the so-called multinational companies, whose only purpose is to plunder as much as possible from small, weak, and fragile countries, as is our case.

This said, I would like to thank the organiser (Blavatnik School of Government, LSE Commission on State Fragility, Growth and Development, and the UNDP) for organising such a useful conversation on the issue that we grapple with on a daily basis.

Over the course of the past one and a half days, we have benefitted a lot from the insights shared by the distinguished guests and, in particular, officials from my fellow g7+ countries.

I'm here also to share with you the insights of fragile in- or post-conflict countries, called the g7+, ranging from Africa to the Caribbean, from the Middle East to the Pacific.

The g7+ is a voluntary association of 20 countries that are, or have been, affected by conflict and/or are now in transition to the next stage of development.

The main objective of the g7+ is to share experiences and learn from one another, and to advocate for reforms to the way the international community engages in conflict-affected states.

The g7+ was formed to work in concert with international actors, the private sector, civil society, the media, and the people across countries, borders, and regions to reform and reinvent a new paradigm for international engagement.

The goal of the g7+ is to stop conflict, build nations and eradicate poverty through innovative development strategies, harmonised to the country context, aligned to the national agenda, and led by the states and its people.

Your Excellencies,
Ladies and Gentlemen,

As a citizen of a post-conflict country, Timor-Leste, where I was born and raised under a colony, lived with struggles to get rid of occupation, and are now trying to consolidate our territorial boundaries, I would like to share some insights and perspectives of what it looks like to live in and lead a country going through such transition.

This is just an example from one country, but as a group of 20 countries, we have had a similar fate. That is the reason we have come together in solidarity, as we feel each other's situation better.

Timor-Leste is a young country and, consequently, its state is considered fragile. There are many challenges inherent to the construction of such a state and to the achievement of sustainable political, social, and economic development.

We have been investing in a democratic and effective model of a justice system, strengthening institutions that ensure equal access, and delivering services to the people. Still, I must acknowledge that the application of justice in fragile states and consolidation of state institutions affected by conflict entails great complexity.

Fragile countries typically have serious institutional, procedural, and operational weaknesses.

The theme of the meeting, 'Supporting Core Government Functions to Address Fragility and Sustain Peace', reminds us that every citizen has a fundamental right: the right to live – most importantly, to live in peace and access services by the Government of the day.

We are called fragile, or sometimes failed states. 'Illegitimate governments', 'weak states', 'hostile situations', to name but a few, are the stigmas attached to our countries. Such descriptions of our situation sometimes over-cloud the mindset of development and humanitarian experts and policy makers. This is something I am personally dealing with at this moment, where the mindset of our neighboring super-rich and super-developed country, working hand in hand with the oil companies, is centered exclusively on the amount of money they can reap from the natural gas reserves that legitimately belong to the people of Timor-Leste.

Hence, our states and the indigenous potential and capacity of our institutions are undermined globally. Such stigmas have even scared away investors in the private sector, which is a backbone for employment and livelihood generation.

Your Excellencies,
Ladies and Gentlemen,

Fostering and sustaining peace is at the centre of the agenda of the g7+. Most of our member countries have been mired in decades of suffering caused by conflicts, violence, terrorism, etc. Some of these countries have been able to break the torturous cycle of suffering, and have pursued peace and stability. At the core of such successful transitions towards peacefulness lies the strong will of the leaders and people of these countries. The causes of violence can be external or internal.

But fostering peace and stability requires the nation to own the pathway of the transition. This is evidenced from the trajectory of my own country, Timor-Leste, and our giant neighbour, Indonesia. The peaceful co-existence of both countries in the coming decades would require us to forget the bitter past at the cost of brighter future characterised by friendly relations, mutual trade, and cooperation.

With this note, let me outline three main lessons that characterise our trajectory of development in g7+ countries:

First, despite the fact that our nations are fragile, our people are resilient, as they have survived and still survive colonisation, foreign aggression, civil war, terrorism, and natural disasters. They have lived through decades of troubles with a belief in peace and resilience.

Look at Afghanistan, which has been circus ground for regional and international interests for the last four decades. The price is paid by Afghan men and women and children.

See Somalia, which has been struggling to maintain a minimum standard of livelihood for its people amidst extremism, famine, and internal conflicts.

Think about Sierra-Leone, Liberia, and Guinea, which had just started consolidating their institutions after years of civil wars, when their strengths and development gains were, once again, tested by an outbreak of Ebola.

The list of such countries goes on. However, in all of these countries, people still dare to hope for a better tomorrow. They still aspire to leave a better legacy for the generations to come. They never give up while fragile; if they did, they would fail.

In addition, state institutions such as security, justice, health, and education contain challenges that are much bigger than the resources available to them. Incapacitated these institutions may be, but they are not failed. They are capable of providing core services, if they are led by committed leadership, and sufficient resources are put at their disposal.

My own country, Timor-Leste, started from the ashes of 24 years of brutal occupation, which was supported by a western country that proclaimed every year at the United Nations General Assembly the right of all territories to self-determination and independence, but in practice stepped all over these universal principles to steal our oil and gas, signing with our occupier an exploitation treaty in exchange for 50% of the resulting revenue, and turning a blind eye and thus allowing for the loss of more than 200,000 Timorese lives during our resistance war. Today, with just 16 years of existence, Timor-Leste is among the group of resilient nations. The credit goes to the leadership equipped with sufficient revenues from its own natural resources. But not all countries are bestowed with natural resources, but instead have to rely on external aid.

Despite their dependency, these countries need to win the trust of their citizens to prove their legitimacy. Such efforts are sometimes hindered by the fact that they also have to win over the parallel mechanisms, institutions, and systems that are put in place by development partners.

Each development and humanitarian intervention leaves behind a legacy of distorted salaries, complicated frameworks, and parallel units that the countries have to deal with in the aftermath. Therefore, our people and our states are not fragile, nor are they failed. They are just in need of the right support that is sufficient to bring about self-reliance.

Second, the delivery of core services is the ultimate responsibility of the state. There is no doubt that we need to build our institutions so that they are capable of serving our people's contemporary needs.

However, there are countless priorities that we need to sequence and address:

- The first and foremost is durable peace, and stopping the suffering of human beings. Unless we have peace, our efforts of statebuilding will all be in vain.
- Peace should be the number one priority upon which all actors have to be united. We need to foster country-led dialogue and reconciliation that bring about peace.
- The political leadership should put aside all differences and aim to make and build peace.
- Foreign actors should mobilise all tracks of diplomacy to make this possible.

All of this might seem like inspirational talk in the world of politics and technocracy, but we have learned it from our own trajectory of development.

Without making peace with our neighbour, Indonesia, which occupied us for 24 years, we would have never been able to stand on our own feet as a nation. Without having put our national interest above all, we would not have been able to prevent conflict in 2006. Instead, we would have been pushed into perpetual dependency.

It is important to recognize and understand that peace needs to be actively maintained; peace cannot just be taken for granted. This requires recognising the centrality of compromise when in the presence of different perspectives, diverging interests, and conflicting views.

Sometimes there may be a need to buy peace, if needed for the greater common good. During phases of special fragility, such as in the immediate aftermath of a conflict, reconciliation is the number one priority.

Third, state institutions evolve over time, given political leadership and sufficient resources. This process of evolution, which is intrinsic in nature, takes place in a given context and culture of the country.

The mindset of rich and developed countries and their agents, including diplomats and experts, is to maintain dependence in all aspects. They maintain that the people of poor and underdeveloped countries cannot think, and do not have the right to make decisions for themselves, and they proclaim their right to determine the future of these people. The fight against this mindset is what, unfortunately, keeps me from being with you today.

There is a need of support to nurture that evolution instead of imposing imported solutions. Academics know this fact very well, that the transformation of the institutions is a long-time phenomenon.

Attempting to transform state institutions overnight, based on external and irrelevant assumption, has always ended in frustration.

Every year, billions of dollars are spent in the form of technical assistance to fix the targeted institutions in these countries. However, there is very little or no attention paid to investing in higher education in these countries, which can have a lasting impact on the capability of generations to come.

Similarly, billions of dollars are spent to react to incidents of famine and drought, such as those in Somalia, Yemen, South Sudan, and other countries.

The impact of such interventions tends to be short-lived, despite being expensive. Even if a portion of such investment were diverted to the potential, such as construction of dams, roads, and irrigation, it would wield huge impact and tend to produce durable results.

Your Excellencies,
Ladies and Gentlemen,

To conclude, I want to reiterate that the g7+ members are committed to accelerating the issues listed in the new Agenda 2030, in particular Goal 16, which is dealing with peace, justice, and effective institutions. And member states have begun to set a clear path for progressing towards the SDGs, giving proper consideration to the national context.

As we embark to implement SDG 16, we must maintain a critical view of the process and make monitoring a key part to ensure we remain on the right track. This requires both sound cooperation with our developed partners and a careful and inclusive internal process that involves not only Governments and public agencies but also civil society and the community.

Our commitment to promoting the g7+ is also based on our strong desire to share experiences, strengthen fragile-to-fragile cooperation, implement the SDGs, and, naturally, strive to live up to the motto 'Leave no one behind, and reach the furthest behind first'.

So, let's embrace shared prosperity, peace, and development for all of us. Thank you.

High-Level Roundtable on Security Sector Reform and Sustaining Peace. Keynote Remarks.

United Nations, New York
23 April 2018

Your Excellency, Miroslav Lajčák, President of the General Assembly,

Excellencies,

Ladies and Gentlemen,

Allow me to express, on behalf of the g7+, my sincere gratitude for having invited me to this high-level roundtable on security sector reform, which is central to sustaining peace, particularly in conflict-affected countries. I thank the UN group of friends of security sector reform for speaking up in support of such an important matter.

Traumatised by conflict, our people know that security is the most fundamental commodity their state can provide; this is not exaggeration, but a fact. Provision of security is one of the primary pillars of the social contract between citizens and the state. As a citizen of Timor-Leste, a country that I led in a struggle for freedom and peace, I am not here to present a scientific analysis on how important a capable security sector is. But I would like to share with you some of the realities and negative results, the lessons of which can help to guide in the undertaking of security sector reform.

Generally, the man-made wraths such as aggression, conflict, and civil war leave our societies torn apart. People get divided into warring factions which keep struggling for control over others and the country. In pursuit of power, each faction gets armed and well equipped. An atmosphere of mistrust takes over the bonds which used to connect them. Ethnic and tribal tensions lead to long-term blood feuds and vendettas, which make even families so fragmented that achieving social harmony seems next to impossible.

In the initial years after achieving freedom and seeking peace, the societal division and mistrust remain visible. Usually, a country becomes overwhelmed with the priorities of protecting the borders and maintaining internal security. The deployment of peacekeeping missions is viewed as an immediate and necessary international intervention. A country would be considered fortunate to receive such missions in an effective and timely manner; otherwise, we must cling to the hope of international diplomatic bureaucracy trying to become involved. Attempting to achieve and maintain the minimum peace through back-breaking efforts, the country becomes an experimental lab for different, if not competing, theories on how to stabilise the country. When this fails, it can lead to societal fragmentation, which will require continuous assistance, funded by the taxpayers of the international community.

Excellencies,
Ladies and Gentlemen,

In Timor-Leste, since our independence in 2002, and starting from zero, with little experience, we recognised that we made mistakes and endured cyclical periods of instability. Notwithstanding our setbacks as apprentices of a true democratic experience, we relied on our social infrastructure to bring about peace and stability in such a short period. We have been humble, to learn from the errors we made and move forward to try to put an end to a mentality of conflict.

However, around every two years, Timor-Leste became trapped in a vicious cycle of disorder that resulted in civil unrest. In 2006, this included conflict between our police and our army, which led to killing, and around 150,000 people being internally displaced.

As a natural consequence, we asked for the intervention of peacekeepers and UN police. After being deployed in Timor-Leste, the United Nations demanded that the National Police and defence forces not carry arms and remain confined in their respective barracks. However, in 2008, the President of the Republic was shot and it took more than two months to see the UN peacekeepers and the UN police do something concrete to try to solve the problems. We had to take action, and the government told the peacekeepers and UN police to return to their barracks. As a state, we had to take charge of our trajectory. We had to address our fragility in our own way, and on our own terms, and in accordance with our context. For that we undertook a genuine and inclusive dialogue, between state institutions as well as with our communities. Through this process, we solved our problems in two years. This was contrary to what the UN agencies had advised us: that it would take between 10 and 15 years, which was consistent with their experiences in other countries.

We also recognised that we had to address the root causes of our problems to achieve permanent solutions. Those solutions had to be rooted in our national context, rather than international theories and solutions that are imposed from outside.

Excellencies, and Ladies and Gentlemen,

We have shared our lived experiences with other g7+ countries, not to teach them to do exactly what we did; instead, by sharing our lessons, we warned them against the failure of a one-size-fits-all approach imposed from the outside.

We promoted the superiority of national interest over the interest of the individual. Under the spirit of solidarity, and brotherhood, the principle that is embedded in g7+ fragile-to-fragile cooperation, Timor-Leste extended financial support to countries like Guinea-Bissau, Central African Republic (CAR), Sao Tome Principe, and nations affected by Ebola. This support was provided directly through state institutions and their national budget. All we required of them was to submit a report of the output of the support. The underlying principle for such support was our TRUST in their leadership.

I led a mission to Guinea-Bissau in 2015, where the conflict was not civil but political. Guinea-Bissau needed to hold elections; however, the international community was not ready to help, because it was under international embargo due to repeated coups.

The Government of Guinea-Bissau asked us for 19 million US dollars to conduct their elections. (According to estimates by the UN and EU, the election would cost more than 30 million dollars.) However, we undertook a re-evaluation of the country's election needs and the cost came to less than 6 million US dollars, which my Government committed to provide. We approached the UNDP to ask them to manage the money provided by Timor-Leste, but in response they required an 18% commission.

With less than 6 million US dollars, Guinea Bissau was able to hold peaceful and democratic elections.

With this fact, I can complain that international aid is ineffective and inefficient. With our practical experience, I am confident in saying that international assistance, that taxpayers in donor countries, can work to address our challenges, if we reform the system. This ranges from humanitarian and peacekeeping operations to development assistance.

On my visit to Central African Republic, Haiti, and the Democratic Republic of the Congo (DRC), I observed peacekeeping troops being deployed for years, with very little impact on peace. Yes, these missions have been helpful in containing the impact of conflict on human lives, but they have failed to deliver sustainable results. Billions of dollars are spent to deploy these missions, yet we see little progress. If you walk along the roads in Bangui, you see peacekeeping troops with their tanks and armours protecting their own selves. On the other hand, when you walk through a Government Ministry, you see poorly equipped offices deprived of even the most basic tools, such as computers or fans, needed by the officials to perform their duties. Yet, when you meet donor officials, you hear them complain of the non-functionality of Government institutions. How can state institutions become functional if they are under-resourced and have to compete with parallel institutions and systems which are well equipped and resourced by donors?

How can you build a justice system, when the Government's annual budget for justice and rule of law is less than one tenth of what donors and UN missions spend on the so called justice, rule of law, and governance on parallel programs?

I met with youth and women's organizations in Bangui who were passionate and committed to work to stabilise their country, asking me for some assistance and telling me that the UN mission there had more than 500 million [TBC] doing very little and not involving them in the disarmament, demobilisation, and reintegration. I met groups of former rebels who wanted to be reintegrated into society and serve their country. I asked myself: Will donors be humble to invest in the local economy so that these young men and women have employment opportunities? Will the international community trust the Government and support it to implement its DDR program as they committed to, under the peace agreement?

For international support to be effective in making reforms in state institutions such as security, justice, and rule of law, there is need of local ownership and leadership. This helps to make sure everyone becomes an agent of peace and development.

Excellencies,

I believe it is urgent to think profoundly about the root causes of the problems throughout the world which appear to be insoluble. To solve them, we should not rely on a scientific approach; rather, we need to find a humane solution. The United Nations needs to promote the culture of accountability for all actors. Recently, I was invited to speak at a conference on oil and gas in Abu Dhabi. I told the audience that our countries are so rich in natural resources, yet they are so poor. Their resources are exploited by multi-national corporations which have no sense of social responsibility to these countries. Even worse is the case where these multi-nationals fuel the conflict, so they can benefit from signing dubious deals while the country is in chaos and has no capacity to realize the faults in those contracts.

The g7+ member countries have had these experiences of dealing with UN peacekeeping troops, with international troops, with multi-national companies, and with donor organisations while addressing the repeated cycles of conflict and violence. Our experiences and perspectives can be helpful in reforming the international efforts to change the approach to cooperation. We just want to make sure that the innocent citizens of these countries do not become the victim of bad policies that emanate from the international community. Hence, I would like to leave you with these key messages:

First: Reconciliation within societies with a bitter past to reach a brighter future has been the only viable option to maintain peace and order in a country.

Fostering peace through promoting tolerance, forgiveness, and a sense of prioritising the greater good over personal prejudice should be the basic principle of any type of national and international intervention. This is a matter of belief which should take place in people's minds and hearts. Forgetting the traumatic past may seem difficult, but it is never impossible. Today, I am proud to say that my country has proved, in reality, that the past, however terrifying it might have been, can be overcome with a sense of humility and forgiveness. We reconciled our enmity with Indonesia which occupied us for 24 years and, today, our two countries live in peace and harmony.

I led a g7+ mission to South Sudan in 2011 where we had a ministerial meeting. I made a plea to the South Sudanese leaders not to fall into conflict. I warned them that a conflict in such a populous country would take a long time. Today, it is sad to see that they can't seem to overcome their differences in a peaceful way. Why don't they take pity on their own people and set the national interest above their personal differences? It is sad to see why the South Sudanese can't reap the benefit of their own natural resources.

Second: National ownership of the process of the reforms has proven to be central to success. Ownership doesn't only mean control over the resources but entails the owning of challenges,

and the solution thereto. Recognition of the unique context and trust in national leadership are the preconditions to realising this principle.

We had the fourth ministerial meeting of g7+ in Afghanistan. I was surprised to see, with my own eyes, how the international community has undermined national ownership by imposing external solutions, ignoring the potential and capacity of Afghans to build their own country. The international media always speak of billions of dollars being spent on Afghanistan since 2001. These billions of dollars are registered as 'assistance to Afghanistan'. However, in reality, a larger portion of this assistance has gone into the accounts of international consultancies, and multi-national construction companies outside Afghanistan, while the blame of failure of impact is put on Afghans. This has been the case in several aid-dependent countries where the country leadership is overloaded with imposed solutions which look good only in theory. Their reliance on international support weakens their voice while pursuing such reforms. My only plea to our international partners is that you please help us achieve what we believe is good for us, not what you think is workable. Our institutions need to win the trust of our people. The deployment of international troops and programs cannot and will not suffice or replace the role of the national institutions. Our partners, thus, have to show humility and respect for the national context.

Third, and finally: The provision of security, justice, and rule of law has been the most expensive commodity. This continues to be the case, particularly in the initial years of our journey from conflict to resilience.

While building resilience in these institutions is a long-term task, it also needs resources at the discretion of the leadership of these countries. The countries face several priorities in the immediate aftermath of conflict. Quick and time-bound solutions without consideration of national context and ownership lead to failure in building and sustaining peace. The taxpayer money of donor countries is too valuable to be wasted in failure. Only we, the citizens who have suffered conflict, know the consequences of the failure of peace which could be avoided with a minor but right investment.

Two years ago, I was invited by a commission of the European Union at Expo Milano with the theme 'Human Right, Right to Food; what is missing?' I told the conference that what was missing was PEACE, because the international community thinks that to impose peace is to participate in war.

I reminded everybody that the hundreds of thousands of immigrants to Europe will not return home unless they have peace in their countries. When the UN talks about reforming the security sector, I hope that the first efforts will be to put an end to the wars and conflicts around the world.

I would like to conclude by reiterating that the g7+ ask for a change of mind-set in the international support system to build peace and resilience in conflict-affected countries. We need to start working on that change of mind-set from right here, from the headquarters of the UN. As the UN Secretary-General says, we need to make the UN fit for results. In order to do so, we need to be humble and accept the faults in the existing systems and policies, and thus reform them for the betterment of all of us.

Thank you.

WTO Public Forum 2018, Keynote Speech:
Trade For Peace: Integration of Fragile States into the Global Economy as a Pathway Towards Peace and Resilience

Geneva, Switzerland
4 October 2018

Excellency Ministers,
Ambassadors,
Distinguished Guests,
Ladies and Gentlemen,

Good afternoon.

I am honoured to be with you, and I thank you for the opportunity to address you today on a matter that is impactful on the lives of 1.4 billion of people who have suffered decades of wars and conflicts. Unfortunately, some still suffer from wars, conflict, and violent extremism.

These countries are sometime referred to as failed, failing, or fragile states in the global discourse, and have been the focus of humanitarian, charity, and development organizations for decades now.

The g7+ (with the little 'g' to avoid confusion) constitute 20 of those so called 'failed', 'failing' or 'fragile' states. While the world has been increasingly integrated and connected through trade, cooperation, and technology, these countries are left out or are 'farthest left behind', as they say, nowadays.

Yet, these countries have been providing, or have the potential to provide, the fuel for the economic prosperity of the developed and developing hemisphere of the world. Let me mention some of them.

Afghanistan lies across the Silk Road that connects civilisations and has the potential to become a regional development hub. Instead, it has been the contesting ground for hegemony in the region, at the cost of millions of Afghans who have been the victim of this circus.

Somalia has one of the longest coastlines in Africa that could be a tourism destination and a producer of fisheries and trade. Instead, wars inherited from colonisation have made it so impoverished, despite its wealth, that its own kids are dying of hunger.

South Sudan is one of the oil-richest countries in the region and lies on the bank of the Nil River, which has the potential to lift the whole region out of poverty. Yet, its civil war has made the country one of the poorest in the world.

Democratic Republic of Congo (DRC) has, underneath it, minerals worth more than 23 trillion US dollars, yet colonisation, dictatorship, and civil war have deprived millions of its people of even the most basic resources for decades now.

Look at **Sierra-Leone, Liberia, Guinea, Burundi, Central African Republic, and Chad**. All of them possess precious natural resources and arable land that can produce food enough for the entire continent, yet conflicts and civil war have made these countries dependent on foreign aid.

The list goes on, if I speak of my own country, **Timor-Leste,** along with **Solomon Island, Haiti,** and others.

Despite the natural richness and potential of these countries, it is extremely saddening to see that these countries are home to the poorest people living in the most miserable conditions. It makes us think, why? Why are these countries deprived of peace and prosperity for generations, now?

Absence of peace is the common feature in all these countries. The peace in these countries has been hijacked and subdued by the greed for hegemony, power, and financial gain. It is not that people in these countries embrace wars and crisis. It is not that people in these countries would not love to live a prosperous life. It is because people are kept so overwhelmed with the daily hardships and miseries inflicted on them that they are unable to think logically as to who gains and who loses in war.

Excellencies, Ladies and Gentlemen,

Trade, investment, and cooperation among the countries in the world bring about prosperity and development.

However, we need to share that prosperity, and it is only possible if we are fair in distributing the gains of global trade. It is the universal and moral right of countries which contribute to global trade to gain equitable share from such a prosperity. Hence, in the global conversation about trade and global economic integration, it is crucial that perspectives and contexts of conflict-affected countries are heard and taken into consideration.

For us the g7+, fragility is not an essential characteristic of our countries but a temporary phase in our trajectory, which requires

special care and attention to peacebuilding, statebuilding, and, hence, development.

This further requires special attention to building solid economic foundations on which these countries can grow economically and socially.

For that to happen, the first and most important condition is peace. Without peace at home, these countries will remain as providers of raw materials and recipients of charity and aid.

To sustain the painstakingly achieved peace, our people need basic services such as livelihood, jobs, education, health, etc. States need to be able to maintain providing such services as their ultimate responsibility. This responsibility cannot and should not be assumed by humanitarian and development partners. Their role, instead, is to help our state institutions to be able to serve their citizens by aligning and harmonising their assistance behind our national priorities to attain self-reliance in agriculture and food production.

They need to invest in necessary infrastructure and building state capacity to nurture endogenously, rather than being duplicated and overwhelmed by imposed prescriptions. This is the best lesson we can learn from countries like that of 'Asian tigers' as they are so called.

Only then will these countries be ready to participate in global trade. Only then can they contribute on a fairer basis to global prosperity. We need to be able to walk on our own two feet before we can participate in the global game that can bring us so many gains.

Excellencies,
Ladies and Gentlemen,

The second most important condition for the fair participation of our countries in global trade is the need to introduce ethical codes of conduct in global integration of the global economy. Our citizens should be allowed to gain their fair share from investment, as their right. Our limited capacity, our insufficient infrastructure that need resources to develop, does not mean we have to be deprived of the gains of our resources.

Our oceans and our lands are the providers of the raw materials, the processing of which takes place outside our countries' borders, where most of the subsequent benefits flow. Investors in minerals and gas evade the tax we deserve by looping us into complex contracts, taking advantage of our weak capacity to negotiate those contracts.

The richer countries, such as those of the G20, can do a lot more to help change this state of affairs, not only by helping us increase our capacity but also by taking greater responsibility for monitoring and tackling illicit outflows and international tax evasion.

The multilaterals, such as the World Bank, IMF, and others, can help us build physical and soft infrastructure.

Our countries can only attract investment and leverage participation in international trade for economic progress if adequate transport, energy, and communications infrastructure is in place. However, most of our countries lack the financial resources to put in place the infrastructure required to lift up the economy. Unfortunately, the donors' assistance in this regard has often been insufficient and ineffective, targeting sectors that are dear to the donors, rather than to the recipient countries.

Excellencies,
Ladies and Gentlemen,

The international debate on extreme poverty, which affects over 1.5 billion people who are forced to beg for humanitarian assistance, is centred on the transfer of aid, including its rules and compensations, rather than the fact that an enormous amount of wealth is accumulated by a small few. The global development agenda must discuss seriously not just the extreme poverty of some but also the extreme wealth of others. We need to ask ourselves: Who profits from conflict? Who monitors the large corporations that manufacture and sell weapons, and the governments that export them?

Every international report and evaluation does a fantastic job in pointing out the ambition for economic and political power, the corruption and greed of the leaders and agencies of fragile and conflict-affected countries, holding them responsible for the failings in their nations. Still, those same reports invariably lack the courage to identify those who continue profiting from other people's misery. And this goes without mentioning the recent arms business, which amounts to 100 billion US dollars.

We need peace! We need an inclusive, fair and developed world.

However, we know that one cannot install universal values, consolidate peace, or build democracies by way of military means. Ill-guided approaches that fail to observe the multiple and diverse factors of fragility, or, worse still, are supported by contradictions or conflicts of interest, only contribute to fuelling inequality, radicalism, and extremist acts.

We cannot continue to ignore the complexity of today's world and the way in which crises and their impacts are interconnected and affect every corner of the globe. In an age where crises gain expansive media coverage, one cannot claim ignorance of the true cost of conflicts and the tragic effects they have on the lives of millions of people.

We cannot continue to ignore the lessons of history and refuse to learn from the errors of the past. After World War II, the number of states unable to stand on their own feet tripled. The lack of strong and consolidated institutions, and the endemic poverty resulting from the lack of resources – or sometimes bad governance in managing those resources – quickly led to rampant imbalances and differentiation between countries, with the markets dictating the fates of fragile peoples left without any help.

Then, as now, solidarity between north and south continues to be a mirage. The focus on certain nations continues to be driven by greed and an unbridled desire for energy and resources. It is this asymmetrical relation between rich states and poor regions that radicalises speeches of hate and vengeance, which can lead to extreme barbarity. The increasing northbound migratory movements by people who are hungry and tired of violence are the most evident and public effect of this lack of truth when responding to poverty.

In view of this, failing to seriously reflect on the root causes of the problems we face today is a risk that may have a high cost and that history would have never imagined us being obliged to pay.

In today's modern world, having even just one people or one country suffering should be considered a tragedy for every country in the world – for the whole of humankind. We must all be held accountable for these problems; at least then we all become responsible for mankind's failure.

Excellencies,
Ladies and Gentlemen,

To conclude, we all have much to gain from a global system of open and fair trade, but our countries need to be nurtured, prepared, and supported. This is likely true for all developing countries, but it is especially important for countries recovering from fragility and conflict.

Thank you very much.

Ninth International Conference on Human Rights Education: 'Unleashing the Full Potential of Civil Society'. Plenary Session 1: The Foundation – UN Universal Declaration of Human Rights: *Harvesting Human Rights for Independence and Democracy*

Sydney, Australia
27 November 2018

Excellencies,

Ladies and Gentlemen,

It gives me great pleasure to take part in this 9th International Conference on Human Rights Education, at Western Sydney University.

I would like to start by thanking the organisers for their kindness in inviting me to address such an illustrious audience. I would like to thank in particular my dear friend Dr Sev Ozdowski, who is both a remarkable philanthropist and an exceptional host.

The topic that brings us here today is vital to the healthy development of our societies.

As you know, I represent a country that had to endure serious human rights violations and that is presently one of the world's youngest and poorest democracies. As such, we are still building and consolidating our state while keeping a close eye on everything going on around the world. And we find what we see quite puzzling.

We are living in troubled times, with real threats to global stability and even a certain mistrust in the political and democratic institutions. I find this worrying.

Much of what we are asked to contribute towards a better world, such as safeguarding and promoting human rights in favour of democracy, justice, and tolerant and peaceful societies is considerably dependant on human nature.

And what is going on in today's world? Are human rights on the wane? If so, are our democracies in crisis? What can we do to educate our societies, particularly our younger citizens, so as to have a culture based on human rights? What can we do to improve the very human beings who betray their own nature?

In today's globalised world, we often hear speeches spewing hatred and instigating violence. We see and feel increasing contempt for others, for those who are different. For minorities. Even countries that appear to have the most consolidated democracies in the world are growing in a manner that is frighteningly unequal, leaving behind those who need help the most. In these countries, which are the main exporters of 'expertise on human rights', we also witness a dangerous increase in the number of cases of human rights violations: corruption, discrimination, racism, xenophobia, hatred, violence, and many other deadly passions.

The messages by political leaders increasingly nurture feelings of mistrust and discredit in an international order that provides security and safety to the people: economic security, food security, environmental security, and physical safety.

While living in safety and with dignity is unquestionably the cornerstone of core human rights, our time is, instead, dominated by fear and hatred. Increasing social conflicts make societies enter crisis mode. Faced with instability, unemployment, violence, and fear of others, human beings defend themselves as they can and become withdrawn. Solidarity, cooperation, and the very bastion of human rights falter. The influx of millions of migrants into Europe, looking for security and dignity, is one of the more recent and obvious examples of this reality. This is a challenge that must involve each and every one.

In my opinion, state of the art technology is also yet to show that it is here to have a positive impact on humanity. The services, benefits, and knowledge provided must be put to the service of everyone in a careful and democratised manner, so that it becomes possible to make the world a better place. Technological power entails risks that, when associated with military might, may have dramatic consequences on human beings.

Additionally, the generalised access to social media is increasingly contributing to disinformation and misunderstandings. With or without fake news, we are witnessing the extrapolation of the same hate speeches that make people even more disillusioned with the political elites and with democracy itself.

[I]t is urgent to have more historical education on internal and external political systems, particularly for young people who

have never experienced contempt for their rights, who have not known autocratic contexts, and who have not lived under antidemocratic regimes.

It is important to call upon young people to have greater political participation, greater knowledge, and greater engagement in democratic processes. It is essential to instil in everyone, from a young age, that each and every one of us has a vital role to play in promoting individual and collective rights and liberties and, more importantly, has duties to those same collective rights and liberties. President John F. Kennedy famously said: 'Ask not what your country can do for you – ask what you can do for your country.' I would add that you ask what you can do for *humanity*.

As such, our new common goal is to educate. I am talking about education that is humanistic and focused on acceptance, equality in difference, and respect. Education that goes well beyond formal education and that is adjusted to reality. Education that seeks freedom and justice for everyone, rather than being manipulated in such a way as to protect the interests of a few.

Your Excellencies,
Ladies and Gentlemen,

My people learned about oppression for 24 long years. We learned about how the rights of expression and assembly can be repressed. We learned about torture and impunity, about arbitrary arrests and forced disappearances, about violence and sexual abuse against our women and children. We learned about hunger, disease, and death throughout endless days and nights. What was it that kept us going? It was the collective dream by an entire people of independence, freedom, and democratic ideals.

When at last the international community came to our aid, a third of our population had already perished. At that time, we also received visits from many international organisations that came to teach us what human rights were all about, bringing with them concepts and realities that seemed alien to us, as all we wanted was to heal our wounds and regain some dignity after years of sacrifice and all sorts of humiliation. At that time, we knew that it would not be easy to recover from yet another serious violation of international law.

Consequently, when the international community tried to teach us the concept of 'no to impunity', it was *we* who said no. The only way we could accept such lessons from the international community were if all those who sold, and still sell, weapons that kill human beings, including civilians and the innocent, were also brought to justice. Accordingly, we chose the path of reconciliation, peace, and friendship.

As we began reconstructing a country from the ashes, we met an even greater challenge: creating democratic institutions that would correspond to the true aspirations of our people: food, housing, health, education, and the construction of a series of basic infrastructures that had been completely destroyed.

The sad fact is, ladies and gentlemen, that democratic principles, by themselves, do not feed or heal anyone. Democracy is but the means through which we can realise the aspiration of every human being, namely to live in safety and with dignity. This realisation cannot be imposed – it needs to be adapted to each context and reality, while trusting the judgement of the population. As such, we have been building our own democratic experience, learning from our own mistakes and moving forward, doing our best to put an end to a mindset of conflict.

During this journey, we understood that we were but one million among hundreds of millions of people all over the world who yearn for peace, stability, and dignity, but whose intrinsic fragility not always allows that to happen.

I represent a group of countries called g7+, a voluntary association of countries affected by conflict and fragility that, today, encompasses 20 member states from Africa, Asia, the Pacific, and the Caribbean.

The g7+ was created in 2010, in Díli, to serve as a platform for its member states to achieve lasting peace and stability by promoting dialogue and reconciliation, advocating solutions adjusted to the reality of each country, and facilitating the sharing of experiences among ourselves. Voluntarism, solidarity, and cooperation are the three key commitments that keep us united, despite our singularities.

We are aware that peace and the protection of human rights are not feasible in these countries until their leaders lead by example and with accountability, and until their people demand placing national interest above each and every private interest. Still, conflicts in many of our countries are also due to struggles for power and hegemony by more powerful nations. And they are due to the invested interests of large multinational corporations, which completely ignore the rights and liberties of the voiceless.

The trajectory of some of the countries in our group speaks for itself. Afghanistan has been the victim of an endless cold war between the powers in the region, preventing it from exploring its potential resources and causing great loss of human lives. In Yemen, global indignation is not enough to save millions of children from dying of hunger, victims of the struggle for hegemony by great powers. This country, holding important deposits of oil and gas, and known for its important coffee and honey plantations, is at the mercy of war while waiting for goodwill and charity to finally arrive.

I could also mention the cases of Somalia, Southern Sudan, the Democratic Republic of Congo, the Central African Republic… a list that is too long and painful, of countries where colonisation, civil war, dictatorships, and external greed and interests led the populations into misery and dependence, despite the high untapped potential in their soils and subsoils.

Timor-Leste was blessed as well with important oil and gas reserves, not to mention our world-class coffee. However, centuries of colonialism and a quarter century of occupation castrated our ability to exploit this wealth. Instead, at a time when we were still fragile and faced with the colossal task of rebuilding a country from the ashes, we were forced to start a new fight with Australia in order to achieve the final delimitation of our maritime boundaries.

Affirming our full sovereign rights is more than the obvious concretisation of our political and economic independence. It also means ensuring that the sacrifices made by our people were not in vain and that future generations will have the dignity and development they deserve.

As such, after exhausting every attempt to bring Australia to the negotiating table, Timor-Leste initiated the first ever United Nations conciliation commission, under the United Nations Convention on the Law of the Sea (UNCLOS), seeking to help us to solve our lengthy dispute with Australia concerning our maritime boundaries.

Although it was not an easy process, on 6 March 2018 we signed the historical Maritime Boundary Treaty with Australia to enable us to consolidate our nation's sovereignty and contribute to setting an important template for the peaceful solution of international disputes.

This template is particularly important at a time when geopolitical tensions concerning maritime disputes are on the rise, worldwide. The experience of Timor-Leste as a small, fragile, and developing country that faced a large and powerful maritime neighbour shows the need for and the potential of a trust fund that will support developing countries and promote equal access to the international legal mechanisms for solving maritime disputes.

We are discussing this with several countries that share our vision and we are planning to formally launch this trust fund next year, around the 25th anniversary of UNCLOS. Timor-Leste has already made a symbolic commitment of AU$250,000 for this initiative.

As you know, even though every nation is equal before the law, not every nation has access to the international legal system.

We believe that when one acts with solidarity, it is always possible to do better, helping those who need it and thus bringing justice to every corner of the world. This is what defending and preserving the highest paradigm of human rights means.

Seeking to exercise our right to stability and prosperity, two months ago we completed an agreement with ConocoPhillips, an important investor in our Greater Sunrise oil and gas reserves. We will be buying a 30% interest in the joint venture currently owned by ConocoPhillips. This is a landmark event that will enable us to bring the pipeline to Timor-Leste and ensure that our people benefit from the exploration of our natural resources while we continue developing the country.

Ladies and Gentlemen,

Timor-Leste still has many challenges ahead in terms of consolidating itself as a democratic state.

With more than half of the population being younger than 20 years old, finding employment for all these youngsters – who often lack the necessary skills – is no easy task. These young people are the future of our nation, which is why their training and education are both our main focus and our main challenge.

This is why it is so urgent for us to implement our 2011-2030 Strategic Development Plan, which seeks to diversify the economy, develop our human capital, and make our country grown sustainably.

Step by step, we must also invest in the fight against political and civil illiteracy by our youngsters. We want to build a critical and responsible civil society that will monitor our democratic institutions and help them to perform better. This role does not belong to the state alone. The state must guide its agencies, but it is for the political and social groups of the nation to guide their children and to instil in them an ethic of hard work, a more solidary social behaviour, a participative and responsible attitude, and an inclusive and democratic mindset.

Education in the area of human rights starts at home, in our schools, in our workplaces — in other words, in every sphere of public and private life. This is the hope that democracy gives us: that it is possible to educate in true freedom and a pluralism of ideas.

An independent assessment conducted by *The Economist* in 2017 considered Timor-Leste the most democratic country in Southeast Asia. This assessment took into account electoral processes, pluralism, freedoms and guarantees, political participation and culture, and the manner in which agencies operate.

While this mention does Timor-Leste credit, on second thought it could not have been any other way. Indeed, we earned independence, democracy, and peace with great effort and sacrifice, and not too long ago.

Less than two decades ago, the vast majority of our people, in a magnificent display of democratic awareness, endured an atmosphere of intimidation and violence and marched to the polling booths to vote for independence. And yet, our youngsters are already starting to forget the sacrifices their parents and grandparents made so that Timor-Leste could be independent. They are starting to forget that living in a democracy does not replace the duty that each and every citizen has to their country. Indeed, voter abstention has been rising over the last few elections, particularly by those who have only known an independent Timor-Leste.

Ladies and Gentlemen,

> Democracy feeds on human rights. Human rights feed on acceptance and inclusion of those who are different or think differently. It is education that can enable every nation and people in the world to be, and to think, in freedom, in justice, and in peace.

Such an education must take into account the global changes over the last few decades and be two-pronged: Internally, it must renew institutions and political mindsets, so as to make people trust their institutions again; externally, it must renew the way we see and implement international law.

> If perceiving the transformation of politics into a business kills democracy, then economic and military supremacy threatens the rights and the very existence of human beings.

To act positively towards a better future for everyone is the common challenge that will decide the fate of humanity. It is possible to do better, both for others and ourselves.

Each of us has an important individual and collective role to play towards the 'advent of a world in which human beings shall enjoy freedom of speech and belief, and freedom from fear and want', which was proclaimed as the highest aspiration of the common people.

Only thus can we realise an old dream that, 70 years ago, united the post-war nations around a universal declaration of human rights, and aspire to a fair, peaceful, and humanising world.

I trust that we will not have to meet again in another post-war scenario in order for peace and human rights to once more receive the attention and devotion they so thoroughly deserve.

Thank you very much.

The 5th Ministerial Meeting of the g7+.
Keynote Speech

Lisbon, Portugal
26-27 July 2019

Your Excellency Teresa Ribeiro, Secretary of State for Foreign Affairs and Cooperation,
Your Excellencies the Ministers and Representatives from g7+Countries,
Ms Asako Okai, Assistant Secretary General and Director, United Nations,
Distinguished Members of Parliament of Timor-Leste,
Development Partners and Representatives from Civil Society Organisations,
Honourable Guests,
Ladies and Gentlemen,

I must start by thanking the Portuguese Government and the people of Portugal for welcoming our g7+ delegation to the beautiful city of Lisbon with such warmth, kindness, and friendship.

It is always a pleasure for me to be with my brothers and sisters from the g7+ countries. The g7+ is a platform that brings us together under pillars of fraternity, empathy, and solidarity – some of humanity's dearest and most blessed characteristics.

Three years ago we met in Kabul, Afghanistan, for the 4th Inter-ministerial Meeting of the g7+. Since then, we have made it our mission to spare no effort in promoting peace, stability, and prosperity. At the end of our Kabul meeting, I was hopeful that the next time we met, we would see conflict and war abating in our countries, so that the suffering of so many men, women, and children could somehow be alleviated.

I believe that everyone here shares this feeling. We all want more peace and harmony in our lives and in the hearts of our people.

At that time, I was feeling optimistic and encouraged, since a few months before our meeting in Kabul, the United Nations had agreed on the 2030 Agenda, which has peace as one of its five cornerstones. And my optimism only grew when, just a few weeks after our meeting, the UN Security Council and the UN General Assembly adopted key resolutions on sustaining peace.

However, my dreams of a more peaceful world would be unconstrained if I were to believe every red-letter global resolution, agreement, and report drafted and socialised with such sophistication.

The truth is that I find myself shocked and saddened every time I read about new wars, conflicts, and acts of violence that result in the sacrifice of innocent lives. My heart bleeds each time I learn about men, women, and children suffering in Yemen, Afghanistan, South Sudan, Somalia, the Central African Republic, and other places throughout the world. It has been terrible to witness the continued pain and suffering of so many human beings over these past few decades. Entire generations are growing up in places of war and conflict, knowing nothing of the so called sustained and lasting peace that seems to exist only in international resolutions and reports.

Why is it that there must be so much death and suffering, both within and between countries? Why can't we simply live in peace with each other?

These are the questions that the innocent people who suffer under these conflicts keep asking us. Questions which, I believe, deserve honest answers.

Your Excellencies,
Ladies and Gentlemen,

Only this month the world celebrated the 75th anniversary of D-Day, which marked the start of the final stage of World War II. At that time, the dream was that the victory of the Allied forces might bring peace to Europe and the world.

This lofty goal was reflected in the creation of the United Nations, which seeks to uphold the spirit of better understanding between countries, and joint responsibility in promoting harmony and cooperation, human rights, and social and economic development in every nation of the world, so as to meet the intrinsic need of human beings to live in peace and safety.

However, it was not long after World War II that wars of national liberation spread across Asia and Africa. These wars of independence were given legitimacy by the universal principle of the right to self-determination of all peoples, as set out in the Charter of the United Nations. Ironically, most of these wars came to an end in the 1970s, just as Timor-Leste was starting its long, tragedy-filled path towards independence. The end of this path was not reached until 1999, when our people bravely voted for independence.

During much of this important period of anti-colonialism, the world was divided into two blocks and lived under a climate of Cold War. This was a difficult time for humanity and it led people to yearn for a new world order.

Sadly, today we see that this hope of a new world order has led to a new world disorder. One needs only look at the interventions in Iraq and Afghanistan, where wars were started in the name of democracy and human rights – wars that are still being waged today, and whose end results are becoming increasingly difficult to predict.

This new world order has created a new, perhaps even more complex phenomenon, in which the psychological effects of conflict, and tactics similar to those employed in guerrilla wars, are used to create unpredictability and fear. This leads to mistrust and uncertainty, which undermine the relationships among people, between people and states, and even between states. Meanwhile, we will continue to witness extremist actions, including in places where we would least expect them, because world leaders refuse to change their perceptions of this complex new reality.

Internal crises and ethnic rivalries are taking root and extending their branches across borders, aided by a lack of capacity and leadership within countries, which is worsened by multinationals and the economic and strategic interests of foreign powers. In a way, this is leading to a globalisation of instability.

Europe and the West are feeling insecure, because of sporadic acts of terrorism. Meanwhile, conflicts in the horn of Africa and the Middle East go unresolved, because international powers want to perpetuate their ascendency, indifferent to the flight of millions of people into Europe.

The primitive policies of 'An eye for an eye, a tooth for a tooth' by the world's key decision-makers only lead to greater distance and a desire for vengeance and destruction, when what we really need is the creation of the necessary space for dialogue in support of peace.

We must accept that the growing extremism and fanaticism, with its violence and cruelty, are but responses to the cynicism and supremacy of the large powers.

If the West refuses to heed the consequences of its own policies, the horrors of violence against innocent civilians will no longer be confined to television programmes reporting from faraway countries. Instead, attacks will strike increasingly close to home.

As fear and mistrust grow, solidarity and cooperation between people diminish. The flight of millions of migrants into Europe, looking for safety and dignity, is the most current and obvious example of this sad reality. Tragically, we are seeing many people – including children – die as they try to cross the Mediterranean. Surprisingly, however, we continue to fail to address the root causes of this crisis.

In 2015 I was invited by a European Union Commission to address Expo Milan on the subject of 'Human rights, right to food and land rights... what is missing?' In my address I mentioned the people migrating to Europe, who at the time were still in the tens of thousands, and said that the thing missing was peace. These migrants had plenty of land; they were merely fleeing from the wars promoted by world leaders – ironically, under the guise of installing democracy and human rights.

My question is this: Are we to continue responding to the consequences of global policies, as if lulled by impressive but superfluous statements, or are we to change those policies – and change them now?

Your Excellencies
Ladies and Gentlemen,

The subject of this Ministerial Meeting is leading change in order to consolidate peace and development. We, the leaders of our countries, need to display strong leadership and fight for peace and development in our countries.

From the perspective of the g7+, and not without much sadness and disappointment, I congratulate the President and the former Vice-President of South Sudan for concluding the peace agreement. I hope that both leaders will finally honour that peace for which their people have suffered for so long. The people of this young nation fought for freedom in order to live in peace and prosperity, not to suffer at the hands of their own leaders.

I commend the President of Afghanistan for his courage in making an unconditional offer of peace to the Taliban. I am also pleased to see the United States of America working to start talks with the Taliban and to see the regional powers promise to support the peace process. It is vital that peace be promoted by and between the Afghan people, so that it can be sustained for the prosperity of this nation that has suffered for decades now. Indeed, the history of Afghanistan shows that peace and prosperity in the country depends on the Afghans themselves.

I am happy to learn that the Government of Yemen and the Houthi leadership are committed to implementing the Stockholm Agreement, which I trust will be the basis for a sustainable peace. The citizens of this beautiful country have endured one of the worst humanitarian crises. I urge my Yemeni brothers and sisters to acknowledge that they have no choice but to live in peace and harmony among themselves in their own country.

I was also very happy to learn of the conclusion of the peace agreement between the government and the warring factions of the Central African Republic. I thank the regional organisations, such as the African Union, for their support. Having visited the country twice, I have witnessed the untapped potential of this war-torn country.

Making, building, and maintaining peace requires sacrifice and much dedication. It is necessary to make a serious commitment to put the wellbeing of our nations and our future generations above egos and personal interests.

In order to be prosperous, a nation must have the courage to accept difference and diversity. We need the courage to walk this path, knowing that no one can walk it for us. It is the people of each country who must take control over their destinies and be accountable for their failures. We need to think and act as nations, rather than as individuals or as ethnic, political, or religious groups. This is the only way one can develop a true sense of state and nation. It is also the only way one can fight violence, foreign interference, extremism, and terrorism.

Even the current glaring threats of climate change may be mitigated if we come together as nations in our respective countries.

Your Excellencies,
Ladies and Gentlemen,

As you know, Timor-Leste remains strongly committed to consolidating peace and implementing our Strategic Development Plan, so as to realise the aspirations of people who fought tirelessly to become independent.

Later this year, on 30 August, we will be celebrating the 20th anniversary of the Popular Consultation. Needless to say, this date holds great symbolism to all Timorese, since we will be celebrating the anniversary of the historic vote by our people who, bravely and in the face of increasing violence by our opponents, expressed their unequivocal will for Timor-Leste to be an independent and sovereign nation.

To mark this occasion, we will be hosting a series of events both to celebrate this historic landmark and to remind the Timorese, particularly the younger generations, of the sacrifices the Timorese had to make on this path towards national liberation. We must also remind the Timorese of the fragility we still feel and, most importantly, the obligation of each Timorese citizen to look after the stability of our nation and our people, so that we may all contribute to the promotion of peace, progress, and development for future generations.

If we fail to do this, all the sacrifices made by our people will have been for nothing. If our veterans and national heroes shouldered the enormous task of leading us to freedom, it does not seem excessive to ask our young people today to fight to preserve this freedom and to build their own nation. To fight for peace and development in Timor-Leste.

I hope that we may have representatives from the g7+ countries in attendance on this joyous occasion.

Ladies and Gentlemen,

Most of the countries affected by conflict, including those in the g7+, are endowed with an abundance of natural wealth that can be a source of prosperity and resilience. On the other hand, some g7+ countries are located in regions of geo-strategic importance. And yet, they are at the bottom of social and development ladder. We have to ask why.

I told the attendees of the WTO public forum, during the Trade for Peace session, that while the world has become increasingly integrated and connected through trade, cooperation, and technology, our countries have been left behind or are 'farthest left behind'. Our countries have the potential to fuel the economic prosperity of the world. Why, then, are our children suffering from malnutrition? Beneath many of our countries lie millions of tons of precious commodities. Why, then, are we still dependent on foreign aid and humanitarian assistance? What are we missing that holds us from prosperity?

My answer, and I believe your answer, brothers and sisters from the g7+, is that *peace* is missing. We believe that there can be no development without peace, and there can be no peace without sustained development.

Our peace has been supressed by the greed for power, and for the financial gains of a very few who are already rich and powerful who seek even more wealth and more power. They gain from our suffering, and from war. Wars and conflicts in our countries fuel manufacturers of arms and weapons. Division among us gives better deals to multi-national corporations who exploit the resources from our lands.

So, who can bring us peace? The right answer is... NO ONE, BUT OURSELVES. This is what we endeavour to remind ourselves: that peace starts within our home, our community, our neighbourhood, up to and including the level of our nation.

We cannot achieve peace unless all of us in our societies take charge of our national destiny and resolve to make peace among ourselves. We may fight with each other in our countries in the pursuit of any cause, any ideology, and any interest, but we all lose in wars. Wars among ourselves have no winner. We have no option but to live in the same territory, to share the same land, the same resources and the same destiny. So why not live in peace and shared prosperity?

Excellencies,
Distinguished Members of g7+,
Ladies and Gentlemen,

We, the g7+, comprise countries that come from diverse backgrounds and yet share common experiences of periodic war and peace. We are united by the solidarity between us, a solidarity that is both priceless and unprecedented in today's polarised world. We represent the voice of hundreds of millions of the world's poorest people who live in our countries. We, as a group, are expected to lead change in the world by setting an example. We are recognised for our ability to influence reforms in the global peace and development architectures.

Therefore, I have a strong hope that this meeting will be an opportunity to consolidate the group, and our efforts to seek observatory status at the UN. I would like to call upon my brothers and sisters from the g7+ to use this opportunity to define a vision for peace and prosperity. I have a strong hope that we will conclude this two-day meeting with a resolve to spare no effort for peace and development.

Thank you very much.

Kim Dae-jung Peace Forum 2021:
Envisioning the World beyond COVID-19: A New Basis for World Peace.
Keynote Speech on Reconciliation and Solidarity

Kim Dae-jung Nobel Peace Prize Memorial
Mokpo, Republic of Korea
27–28 October 2021

Your Excellencies,
Ladies and Gentlemen,

I am deeply honoured to take part in the Kim Dae-jung Peace Forum. Thank you for your kind invitation.

Allow me to start by acknowledging the Kim Dae-jung Peace Centre and Jeollanamdo Province for enabling this forum on world peace to take place.

In a world that reels with division, conflict, and suffering, I bow to the memory of Kim Dae-jung. President Kim Dae-jung was an inspirational leader, whose steadfast values and faith nurtured democratisation, peace, and human rights both in the Korean Peninsula and throughout Asia.

As well as these reasons for honouring Kim Dae-jung's memory, his resilience and political courage, which shined through when promoting peace and reconciliation with North Korea, is also a reminder to the international community of the importance of 'conscience in action' and the value of persisting with dialogue, forgiveness, and reconciliation.

The more daunting the challenges, the more pressing is the need for all people to be peacemakers. The current orchestra of the new world order (or perhaps world disorder) needs to be fine-tuned so as to play music that conveys hope. This is the only way we can achieve an environment of stability and peace.

And yet we continue to meet hatred with hatred, and division with further division. We respond to chaos and war by waging even more war, often under the banner of a 'civilising mission'.

Reconciliation may well be the only way to restore peace. Democracy, when desired by the people, may also be the only way to achieve balanced and inclusive development. And in this regard, we must look to the exemplary lessons taught to us by Kim Dae-jung, and his ability to forgive and move forward towards a democratic transformation that understands that the process can be long and difficult and that the very individuals who are destabilising peace must necessarily be the ones who contribute to peacebuilding.

And peace is just what the world needs!

This century is being marked by growing unrest. International relations are confusing, and appear to be governed by an unquenchable thirst for resources and power, rather than guided by a moral imperative to shape peace.

This became very clear with the global pandemic, which is perhaps the most serious crisis the world has faced since World War II. The pandemic hit both the rich and the poor, and in both the global North and South.

COVID-19 exposed many of the weaknesses of the international order. Borders were closed and economic, social, and institutional crises spawned all over the world, leading to the inevitable increase in poverty in the poorest countries.

Global inequality is a historical and structural problem that concerns us all.

Ensuring equitable access to vaccines all over the world is everyone's responsibility. And yet we see some countries preparing to administer third doses, while other countries still wait for their first, with limited access to supplies. These circumstances reveal a great international selfishness.

The situation in Africa, where only a marginal percentage of people have been vaccinated, is a flagrant example of how international society is failing. It is failing because we continue to lack the ability to help those who need it the most, and because our selfishness makes us blind to the risk of having the virus mutate into new variants that lead to new public health crises.

Global threats require global responses. In our time, no one is safe until everyone is safe.

The manner in which we handle COVID-19 is a generational test for the international community.

This is the time for everyone to practice 'conscience in action', so as to leave no one behind. It is urgent to facilitate access and administration of vaccines to the most vulnerable populations, lest we fail our test of moral solidarity precisely as we begin to envision a new age, the post-virus age.

And the first step towards 'Envisioning the World beyond COVID-19: A New Basis for World Peace' is to revise engagement paradigms that contribute to peace, as well as to jointly reflect on how international solidarity can work faster when responding to and preventing crises.

Your Excellencies,

At the start of the pandemic, many believed that this was a unique opportunity to build a better world. However, this requires global cooperation like never before.

Such cooperation goes well beyond public health. There are shocking disparities in terms of human development within and across borders. I would point to the disparities in terms of access to education and modern technologies, which became even clearer during this crisis. To provide children and young people with the tools for their development is to invest in the peacekeepers.

On the other hand, unless we reduce economic inequalities between countries, we are not working towards global sustainable recovery and growth.

While 'without peace there is no development', it is no less true that 'without development there is no peace'.

Notwithstanding these concerns, this crisis has shown that people can respond collectively, including with social distancing and isolation requirements. From this we can draw a fundamental lesson: the importance of collective action.

We need to take action for the common good. We need solidarity in action. We must not create a new generation of inequalities! We cannot exclude development from any place, no matter how small it may be.

We must reflect on what it is that divides humankind in such a way that peace can be so difficult to obtain.

The Afghan tragedy can leave no one indifferent.

No one may feel reconciled with themselves knowing that Afghan people are enduring hell on earth. It is obscene to think that those, such as Afghan girls and women, who already lack so much are about to lose the very last thing onto which they were holding: Hope.

It was not surprising to witness the chaos and despair caused by the withdrawal of those who proclaimed 'Mission accomplished' in Kabul. Even before that, I could no longer contain my indignation at the suffering occurring in Yemen, Libya, and Syria.

So too is Africa deeply wounded. South Sudan, the Central African Republic, Mozambique, Ethiopia, and other Sahel countries, along with so many others. People like us, with faces, names, families, and hopes …

In Palestine and Israel, conflict and violence have been the reality for generations. It is imperative that we spare no effort to promote dialogue between their leaders. Even though division runs deep, we need to test the power of reconciliation.

Nature's fury has brought additional pain to people who have been suffering for so long. Haiti is one of the most recent examples. While it is urgent to provide humanitarian relief, the people of Haiti require long-term solidarity.

During the pandemic we watched democracy weaken in many parts of the world. In more fragile democracies, the pandemic brought the temptation to cross thresholds, some of which are unacceptable. How much longer will democracy in Myanmar continue to be but a pipe dream?

Democracy and peace cannot be attained by people who are not willing to earn them and to take responsibility for their own fate. Still, although the international community cannot do everything for a country, it should take care not to harm it due to lack of unity and consistency.

Your Excellencies,
Ladies and Gentlemen,

As someone who led people who were the victims of illegitimate occupation within a Cold War context, and who hoped for a new world order, I am saddened to see that what we now have is a new world disorder.

The interventions in Iraq and Afghanistan were carried out in the name of democracy and human rights. Still, after decades of investment to establish order and progress, legitimated by the concepts of 'capacity building' and 'state building' that adopted foreign models, doctrines and experts, the results are plain to see.

Not only did situations deteriorate for those people, we now have thousands joining the ever-growing list of refugees, for which the international community is yet to find an answer.

I believe that the primitive policies of 'An eye for an eye, a tooth for a tooth' followed by key world leaders only lead to further antagonism and thirst for revenge and destruction, instead of creating the necessary space for dialogue on peace and cooperation towards regional safety.

I am afraid that if world leaders fail to respond to the consequences of their own policies by investing in reconciliation and processes of dialogue, they will have to deal with the horrors of violence against innocent civilians increasingly close to home, rather than just continue to watch from a distance within the comfort of their homes.

Last month it was the 20th anniversary of the 9/11 attacks, following which 'hard power' was used to fight a global threat. The world declared war on terrorism.

We have not won this war, and we never will until we address the root causes of the problem. Terrorism is a strategy that adapts to circumstances.

In order for the international community to defeat terrorism, it must adopt a long-term strategy, rather than simply responding to arising circumstances. This strategy must not be constrained by the need for economic and geostrategic supremacy but, rather, be guided by the need for serious investments in societies and people, taking account of the realities in which they live.

I admit that obstacles on the path to peace are hugely complex. Nevertheless, we must stop to consider whether the lens through which we see them is the most adequate one. The Western lens does not apply to every idiosyncrasy. The international community is too myopic to restore the trust required to overcome the problems ahead.

We must acknowledge the mistakes of the past and let go of pent-up tensions and hatred. This is what a reconciliation process is all about.

Throughout this process, to find intelligent policies for a peaceful world, we cannot ignore the dark clouds hovering above our common future: environmental catastrophe and nuclear weapons.

With the former, we must all do our part. Still, let us be realistic. It is the strongest economies that benefit from pollution, while the weaker economies suffer the most.

We are putting our final hopes in the commitments to be made at the COP26. Mitigating the effects of climate change also means preventing tensions, conflict, and even further pandemics. If there is a will, we are still in time to reconcile ourselves with nature.

As for the latter,

it is inconceivable to me that we can think of establishing approaches towards world peace without greater collective effort to ensure nuclear disarmament. To free ourselves from the nuclear threat, we must first free ourselves from pride and hubris.

We must continue insisting on communication, dialogue, and diplomacy. We need brave 'sunshiners'[3] in this mission to ensure peace both in the Korean Peninsula and throughout the world.

Your Excellencies,
Ladies and Gentlemen,

To make peace in the world is no easy task. Still, we can start by making a difference in our own societies, with our neighbours, and in our region.

For over 20 years, Timor-Leste endured the cruelty of illegal occupation by a giant neighbour that did not act alone. In addition to enormous resources, Indonesia also relied on a geopolitical alliance, as well as international hypocrisy.

Still, the Timorese were steadfast in refusing to permit their fates to rest in the hands of the superpowers that had decided we were not suited to be an independent state.

We resisted, not by waging war, since we could never compete with the heavy weaponry and thousands of soldiers supported by the regional players, but, rather, by using guerrilla tactics and with the heavy sacrifices of the Timorese people.

We resisted and we put our faith in the central role that legitimacy plays in international relations, urging the international community to find a peaceful solution for the political status of Timor-Leste.

Together we realised international law, with unique examples of international diplomacy and solidarity. Through the 1999 Referendum, held under the UN banner, our people voted overwhelmingly for independence.

Although Indonesia ultimately accepted the outcome of the referendum, it left behind a country in chaos that needed to be rebuilt from scratch.

Fortunately, we were able once more to rely on the amazing solidarity of the international community. We established development partnerships that enabled us to take our first steps to build our country.

I would like to recall that President Kim Dae-jung was always an important supporter of the Timorese cause, even going as far as making the South Korean army available to the international community in order to protect human rights in Timor-Leste.

---

3. Kim Dae-jung introduced the 'Sunshine' policy to engage with North Korea in 1998, seeking lasting peace for the Korean Peninsula.

I can honestly say that the first years of independence were not much easier than the years of occupation and conflict. Not only did our state have to learn how to be a state, so too did our people — wounded and scarred by decades of occupation — have to learn how to be a nation. Thus, we endured cyclical crises of violence.

The good news is that we learned important lessons from this and were able to choose peace.

We started by investing in reconciliation between the Timorese, who had become polarised as a result of the difficult and complex struggle leading to independence. This polarisation was affecting the process of building the new country.

We also sought reconciliation with our Indonesian neighbours, since we soon realised that we could not move forward with building our country if we still harboured feelings of hatred, mistrust, and vengeance towards our closest neighbour, with which we ultimately share so much.

The people of Timor-Leste and Indonesia chose to walk together the path towards democratic transition and economic growth. We currently enjoy an excellent relationship of friendship and cooperation with Indonesia, enabling stability in the region and development in both our countries.

We learned to address our state's key weakness, which was the inability to address the real causes of problems in a sustainable manner.

We appeared before the institutions of state with a new political stance, searching together for inclusive and lasting solutions, and putting collective interests above all other interests.

Throughout this process it was also important to restore dignity to those who made countless sacrifices to the cause of independence.

We invested in the demobilisation and reintegration of veterans, created measures of welfare protection and justice for the most vulnerable groups, and reformed our law enforcement and our military, so as to reconcile the differences that kept them apart and to correct the mistakes made during their capacity building and training.

Some of our development partners frowned upon our decisions. It seemed to them that we were buying peace. But I say that no one knew our nature and our reality better than us. In order to walk the path towards peace, all those who are part of the problem must be involved and feel part of the solution.

Solidarity is more than just being ready to help. It also means wanting to learn about and to understand the reality and suffering of those who need help. Timor-Leste is forever thankful for the international solidarity that has seen us through our most difficult times.

Your Excellencies,
Ladies and Gentlemen,

My country is testament to the success of multilateralism.

Timor-Leste relied on international law and international organisations to achieve its independence.

Recently, Timor-Leste relied once more on international law and international organisations to achieve its full maritime sovereignty.

After years of disputes on where a maritime boundary between Timor-Leste and Australia should lie, both countries managed to reach a mutually satisfactory outcome through a compulsive conciliation process held under the United Nations Convention on the Law of the Sea.

We are currently holding consultations with Indonesia seeking final delimitation of our shared maritime boundaries. It has been agreed that negotiations will be held in good faith and in accordance with international law, particularly UNCLOS.

These are good examples of how it is possible to rely on the legal order and on international relationships to solve disputes peacefully.

Recently the Secretary-General of the United Nations, António Guterres, launched the 'Our Common Agenda' report at the United Nations General Assembly.

I believe that this may be an important roadmap to guide our future actions. In today's multipolar world, no nation – no matter how powerful – can meet global threats by itself. If a threat can cross a border, then it can also dilute that border.

We need to come together around an agenda that is centred on people. We need a truly shared agenda in which people can have trust and have hope.

It is unquestionable that the United Nations and the Security Council are in need of major reform.

Still, it is no less unquestionable that giving up on multilateralism and on a rule-based international order would mean giving up on children, men, and women who suffer from violence, conflict, disease, and hunger. It would also mean giving up on refugees, the underprivileged, and even Nature herself.

Giving in to chaos and uncertainty will not lead us to peace. However, if every one of us, whether individually or in a group, whether informally or formally, displays greater solidarity and is able to come together around a common agenda, we can still hope for a world of peace.

Before I conclude, I would like to convey to you a story about unity.

Timor-Leste is part of a group of fragile and conflict-affected states called the g7+, where around 20 countries share their experiences on peacebuilding and statebuilding. Through the 'Fragile-to-Fragile Cooperation' (F2F) Programme, we promote peace, reconciliation, and sustainable prosperity.

As a result of this unity and commitment, we became part of the global discussion on sustainable development in fragile states, while seeking a new world order. If a global partnership on our development is being discussed, we say, 'Nothing about us without us'.

Our member states, which hail from various parts of the world, could not be any more different in terms of geography, history, culture, and even ideology. Nevertheless, we all share the suffering of our people and the dream of a world of peace.

We cannot stop daring to dream, because where there is a will, there is a way.

We can and must do everything in our means to make peace – everything except giving up the fight or silencing our voice.

Thank you very much.

International Peacebuilding Forum 2021: Japan Commission on Global Governance. The Parliamentary Committee of the Diet of Japan for World Federation:
How Timor-Leste Achieved Reconciliation and Good Relationship with Indonesia and Australia after its Independence

Tokyo, Japan
25 November 2021

Excellencies,
Distinguished Guests,
Ladies and Gentlemen,

Ohayo gozaimasu. (Good morning).

I want to start by thanking you for inviting me to take part in this session. It is a pleasure to address such a distinguished audience.

Japan has an active voice when it comes to peacebuilding. This is demonstrated both within the country as well as through consistent deliberations in favour of world peace in the international arena.

Japan's story of reconstruction is a source of inspiration for the world in general, and for Timor-Leste in particular. Seventy-six years after the end of the Second World War, Japan is an example of how a country can move on from a troubled period to build a harmonious and prosperous society that promotes global peace.

And while the role played by the National Diet of Japan towards supporting a better and more inclusive system of global governance has always been important, it has never been more urgent than it is today.

I am honoured to join my voice to that of the National Diet of Japan in advocating for greater cooperation between all nations of the world, so that we may look forward to a future of stability, harmony, and prosperity for all people.

We are living in uncertain times, where global challenges require global responses.

In order to overcome humanitarian and security crises, the climate emergency, and the global pandemic, as well as put a stop to increasing social and economic disparities, we need a true alliance between nations, based on collaboration, trust, and mutual respect. This is the only way we can have hope for the future.

And while this is true for every nation, it becomes imperative for neighbouring countries.

It is plain to see that there is insufficient economic growth and unfair social development in many parts of the world, which weakens resilience against crises. And yet we do very little – if, in fact, we do anything at all – to prevent those crises, even when we can see them coming.

The first time there was talk about preventive diplomacy within the United Nations was in the 1950s, when the UN Secretary-General advocated crisis prevention. This means we should have already started to act over six decades ago.

Armed intervention, with the loss of human lives, continues to be the instrument that is used, rather than dialogue and diplomacy.

With goodwill and joint diplomacy between nations, it is possible to prevent conflicts, or at least mitigate their spread and consequences, which can make a dramatic difference to the lives of men, women, and children.

And so I ask: What are we waiting for?

We cannot continue to ignore that most conflicts in fragile countries are the result of the self-interested policies by powerful nations and/or their multinationals. Nor can we continue ignoring that these fragile countries are often used as battlegrounds in which others fight their wars.

I insist that we must address the true root causes of the problems. We must act pre-emptively in order to minimise any situation of conflict, engaging the entire international community in attempting to reconcile the parties in question.

Throughout the world we are witnessing the rise of ethnic and religious extremism, with growing nationalism and populism filled with prejudice and hatred for those who are different. This leads to millions of people living in poverty and misery, which, in turn is made worse by environmental disasters.

As such, we have the current humanitarian crises, where thousands of migrants flee their countries in search of safe haven, only to be turned back everywhere they go. This causes increasing despair and suffering, and, in some cases, even death.

While I was already troubled by the issue of refugees, I cannot but comment with one word on the situation on the European Union's eastern border: Unacceptable!

The world must put an end to this cycle of contradictions and conflicts. All problems that are caused by human beings can be solved by human action.

There will always be different perspectives and conceptions of reality. Still, with respect and common sense, it should always be possible to overcome divergences, provided that there is a willingness to build bridges between people and responsibility by individuals and societies to make peace.

Your Excellencies,
Ladies and Gentlemen,

I believe it is time for repentance and forgiveness. This is what the beauty of humankind is all about. We are all human beings, and as such, we have flaws. We make mistakes and we err due to ambition, hubris, and an indiscriminate thirst for economic, financial, political, and ideological power. And yet we are also capable of repentance, forgiveness, and atonement.

I would like to recall the recently deceased Frederik de Klerk. After having spent much of his political life defending racism, segregation, and violence in South Africa, it was he who put an end to that very regime and who freed Nelson Mandela.

He came to acknowledge the damage he had caused and the pain, suffering, and indignity that he had inflicted on other human beings. He corrected the terrible error of apartheid and he ultimately died on the right side of history.

This is an example for every individual living in the realm of indifference, hubris, intolerance, racism, xenophobia, and misogyny.

Everyone is different and everyone is the same. There is no one more equal than others, and there are no differences that cannot be reconciled.

This brings us to the importance of reconciliation.

We must be aware that hatred cannot be fought with hatred, in the same way that wounds cannot be healed by inflicting more wounds.

As difficult as it may be for any people or nation to look back on the darkest pages of their own history, having the courage and the commitment to do so is the first step towards peace.

Further, in world history, no one is completely innocent. I can think of the tragic colonisation by Europe, expansionist ambitions, blind nationalism, the evils perpetrated on indigenous populations, and even catastrophic interventions disguised as 'civilising missions' in the name of human rights and democracy.

Up until now, the story of humankind has been one of suffering.

Nevertheless, we cannot be stuck in the past. We have to move forward. Since we are no longer living in the past, we need genuine reconciliation between people, between people and states, and between states.

Of course, this is no easy task. It is a long process that is full of setbacks. There are always two sides to every issue, and these issues may take several generations to resolve.

Resolving long conflicts requires more than internal investment by the governments and the peoples of the countries in question. It also requires favourable international circumstances.

This is why I say that the international community has collective responsibility for reconciliation processes. We cannot just stand by and say that it is the parties' fault that they cannot reconcile.

Only tolerance, friendship, and trust allow us to understand common values, and to apply them towards honest reconciliation that enables common development.

Leaving the past behind means that if we move towards peace today, we will have a peaceful future.

This is not just a responsibility of all the people who are in disagreement. It is also a responsibility of and for all people in the world.

Your Excellencies,
Ladies and Gentlemen,

Forty-six years ago, we in Timor-Leste declared our independence. Nine days later, we were invaded and annexed by Indonesia. This was a brutal invasion by tens of thousands of soldiers, armed with heavy equipment, against people who were helpless and unprepared to deal with a war.

Still, faced with extermination or total domination by a foreign power, we chose to fight to the best of our ability.

For 24 years the small Timorese guerrilla army fought against its powerful neighbour, which was receiving weapons, ammunition, and military training from Western countries.

It should be said that this new war in Southeast Asia started a short time after the US lost the war in Vietnam. The spectre of the Cold War loomed over the world and the West was afraid of the possibility of having new countries adopt socialism.

Furthermore, Timor had rich resources, including oil, which had been discovered one decade before the Indonesian invasion. In a world where greed prevails, this undoubtedly played a part in the Western support to Indonesia.

While the world turned a blind eye to a war that the Timorese were waging with great sacrifice, Australia — the only Western country to acknowledge our illegal annexation — started negotiations with Indonesia in order to delimit our maritime boundaries.

As you know, in post-war Asia, there was more division than integration. The Cold War forced countries to enter into geopolitical alliances that conformed to the international hypocrisy of the time, which argued that our annexation into Indonesia was the best solution for world peace.

Thus, Australia and Indonesia signed an agreement in 1989 splitting in half the revenue from the exploration of the valuable resources in the Timor Sea. This was known as the Timor Gap Treaty.

Yet, these resources belonged to Timor-Leste. These resources could have enabled an independent state, despite all who claimed that we would never be able to succeed as a democratic state.

This meant we had to continue fighting for our self-rule. And so, we reorganised the struggle into three fronts: the armed front, the political/clandestine front, and the diplomatic front.

This allowed every Timorese citizen, both inside or outside of Timor-Leste, to take part in the liberation effort. This included demonstrations abroad and pressuring foreign governments that were complicit with the serious breaches of international law and human rights being perpetrated against the Timorese population.

We managed to attract the attention of many solidarity groups the world over, and they started advocating for the Timorese cause. Subsequently, we were able to carry out more promising diplomatic actions.

This long process, filled with blood and tears, culminated with a UN referendum on 30 August 1999. Here, despite an atmosphere of violence and intimidation, our people voted overwhelmingly for independence.

In 2002, our country began a new challenge, that of building a state/nation literally from the ashes.

After years of subservience, colonisation, and occupation, it seemed almost impossible to survive without external aid. Here, I must confess that there were times when we wondered how much of that aid was truly humanitarian aid, and how much was back payment for past exploitation or, worse still, an attempt to hold on to political and economic control over us.

Indeed, the myth that we lacked the ability to rule ourselves benefited not just the Indonesian occupiers but also the Australian interests in the Timor Sea.

For decades we suffered from deceitful diplomacy that claimed that oil and gas on our side of the median line belonged to others.

For years the Australian government and multinationals turned a blind eye to the tragedy taking place in my country, because having control over our resources was more important to them than human suffering.

Just two months prior to Timor-Leste regaining its independence, Australia withdrew from all international law maritime boundary dispute resolution procedures, thus preventing Timor-Leste from requesting an international tribunal to rule on permanent maritime boundaries with Australia.

On the first day of our independence, we were induced to sign a treaty that re-established the agreements Australia had made with our previous occupier, so that Australia could hold on to its rights and benefits in the Timor Sea.

At the time, Timor-Leste was a young and inexperienced country, in dire need of revenue to lift its people from poverty. What could we have done but sign that treaty?

Two years after our independence, at a time when we were negotiating how resources should be shared, the Australian government bugged the Timorese government's office. By the time we learned of this, we had already signed a new treaty setting a 50-year moratorium on maritime boundary negotiations.

Despite continuing to refuse our attempts to hold dialogue on the permanent delimitation of maritime boundaries, Australia was one of the key donors and partners in the stability and development of Timor-Leste.

Your Excellencies,

Ladies and Gentlemen,

When we became an independent nation and the 191st state to enter the United Nations, we were a country which was small, poor, and traumatised by war. And we were located between two giants: Australia and Indonesia.

We relied on the support of the international community and international organisations when taking our first steps.

I must take this opportunity to, once again, highlight and thank the magnificent support provided by Japan, through Friends of Timor, as well as the financial support and the deployment of Japanese military engineering units to take part in the peacekeeping operations in Timor-Leste. This was Japan's first international mission since World War II.

It was also here in Tokyo, in 1999, immediately after our referendum, that the first Development Partners meeting was held. This was evidence of the key role that Japan would play in our nationbuilding.

Throughout this process, we wanted to believe that the strong do not always prevail over the weak. Still, in order not to be weak, we required one last act of courage: to forgive, to let go of past grievances, and to move forward towards a reconciliation process.

This was both reconciliation between the Timorese, who were the victims of a campaign designed to divide us, as well as with the occupying power, realising that both Timorese and Indonesians had been the victims of the same regime. This way, we were able to walk together on the path towards democratic transition.

Working alongside Indonesia, we established the Commission for Truth and Friendship. The purpose of this commission was to listen to testimonies of human rights abuses. As a nation, we acknowledged that we could not build a state without making peace between ourselves and with our neighbours.

We went to the roots of our problems, we faced our victims and our bitter memories, and we focused on national unity. Although this was a collective process, it was also an individual process. Indeed, all it would take to jeopardise the entire process was for one individual to refuse reconciliation.

This was the mindset of Timor-Leste when taking its first steps as an independent nation. Speaking as the first elected President of the Republic in the history of my country, I can tell you that the challenges we faced were enormous.

I recall that, back then, the Japanese Prime Minister, Junichiro Koizumi, 'forced' me to run for President of the Republic for at least five years, in order to improve relations with Indonesia.

While it is true that wartime requires people to make huge sacrifices for a common ideal, it is no less true that reconstruction in peacetime also entails considerable effort, including to maintain that unity.

Throughout this process, the international community insisted that reconciliation could not replace accountability. This meant that human rights crimes would have to be tried in accordance with international law.

We refused to do this, for two main reasons. Firstly, we did not want to be burdened by our bitter past. Secondly, several Western countries had been complicit with the atrocities carried out in Timor-Leste, by training and selling weapons to the occupying force, and by silencing our voices in the international arena. Who, then, would be held accountable for all the atrocities that had been perpetrated? Would it be just the Indonesians?

And so we sat with our former occupiers and we embraced those who had deprived us of freedom and dignity for a quarter of a century. We also brought together brothers and sisters, cousins, and sometimes even parents and children, who had gone in opposite directions during that dark time in our history.

Today, Timor-Leste and Indonesia are a positive example of cooperation between the Muslim and the non-Muslim worlds. Both countries provide an example of friendship, trust, and common development.

Today, our countries are committed to setting our maritime boundaries in accordance with international law. Although it is expected that such a negotiation process will necessarily entail some tension, we know that nothing can jeopardise the peace and stability we sacrificed so much to achieve.

This is a powerful example of where the path towards reconciliation can lead you.

Your Excellencies,
Ladies and Gentlemen,

Timor-Leste and Australia are friends and neighbours.

Nevertheless, this relationship has always had a 'pebble in the shoe'.

By 'relationship', I mean our relationship with the successive *governments* of Australia, since the people of Australia have always made it clear that they did not support the illegal occupation of Timor-Leste.

Reconciliation with Australia made use of the international law created by the Community of Nations to regulate relations between states, and to contribute towards the constructive and peaceful resolution of international disputes.

Timor-Leste is a steadfast defender of the international system and international law.

The final delimitation of maritime boundaries is a national priority for us and the final step in our long struggle for full sovereignty.

Consequently, instead of giving up in our efforts regarding Australia, we decided to make use of the compulsory conciliation mechanism under the United Nations Convention on the Law of the Sea. It was the first time ever that this mechanism had been used.

The Conciliation Commission established under the compulsory conciliation helped Timor-Leste and Australia reach an agreement on maritime boundaries. Today, this agreement is a reality, thanks to the Australian government, which finally acquiesced to take part in this process, and thanks to the work of the Conciliation Commission.

The conclusion of this treaty clarifies the rights and responsibilities of Timor-Leste and Australia concerning the resources and activities located within our respective sovereign territories.

And this is an important new start.

Timor-Leste and Australia set a good example of how it is possible to overcome differences peacefully, while at the same time strengthening friendship and cooperation between both countries. This was achieved by realising that every state is equal before international law, regardless of whether they are large or small, rich or poor.

I am certain that our countries will continue to work together in the future, bringing development and prosperity to our nations and to our region.

Your Excellencies,
Ladies and Gentlemen,

In conclusion, I can say that we kept the promise we made to the West during the years of occupation, namely that we would never jeopardise stability in the region.

Not only did we keep our word, but we advocated dialogue and peaceful political actions in the region and in the world.

We are a founding member of the g7+, a group of about 20 fragile and conflict-affected states throughout the world that share their experiences and promote peacebuilding and statebuilding, reconciliation, and sustainable prosperity.

Among other things, this group made us realise that, regardless of our disparate historical, cultural, and ideological backgrounds, we all want the same things: peace and development, which are inseparable.

We also acknowledge that reconciliation is vital for preventing recurring conflict and for building peaceful and prosperous societies. This reconciliation must come from within, and must include everyone's participation: political and religious leaders, the private sector, and civil society, particularly women and young people.

Furthermore,

reconciliation must be able to rely on the international community's genuine and active participation, putting the interest of world peace above any other interests.

The world needs to feel peace and to have hope that humankind will move into a new stage: the stage of reconciliation, cooperation, and mutual trust. The stage where all individuals, peoples, and states contribute to a world of peace.

'Under the almond trees in bloom. Humanity swirls and boils'
— *'Hanasaku amondo no konoshita. Jinrui o yusaburi, futto sa seru.'*
– Matsuo Bashô.

Domo arigato gozaimasu.
Thank you very much.

Ukraine Peace Summit: Intervention at the Plenary Session

Bürgenstock, Switzerland
15 June 2024

Excellencies,

Thank you for giving Timor-Leste the opportunity to share our perspective. I would like to thank Her Excellency Viola Amherd, President of the Swiss Confederation, for inviting me to this peace summit.

I will keep my intervention brief, focusing on a message that I humbly ask you to bear in mind as we discuss the pathways forward to bring peace to Ukraine and its people.

Timor-Leste profoundly understands the suffering faced by the Ukrainian people as a result of the ongoing conflict.

We also experienced invasion and occupation, and our people still carry the haunting memories of the war, which still remain all too vivid for us.

From our experience, we learned that we could not put an end to a war which was being supported by Western nations, the same countries that used to speak of the importance of international law and rules-based order.

What kept us determined to continue to fight and risk death, was the hope that, after the war, we would live in a new world order that was being promoted at the time. But, unfortunately, after 24 years of war, and now being independent, what we see is a world of disorder with even more conflict than before.

Excellencies,

International law is the foundation of global peace and order. However, it must be applied uniformly to every nation, and all states must abide by it.

Today, we continue to see the selective application of international law. We see some nations oppose occupation in one country, but not in another. Too often, the very nations that proclaim the sanctity of international law are the ones that violate it.

If we are committed to maintaining international peace and security, we must apply international law consistently, without selective enforcement, and treat all conflicts with equal importance.

We have a moral obligation to address and be concerned about all conflicts equally. Currently, around 65 wars continue worldwide. Even if they seem distant from our own countries, we must not dismiss them.

We must hold on to international law's promise of justice and reach for peace.

Excellencies, I will conclude my message by once again appealing to you to remember these points as we move forward in our discussions, and, more importantly, after we return to our respective countries.

Thank you.

Resources

Atlantic Council Global Energy Forum, Plenary Session.
Meeting East Asian Gas Demand

Abu Dhabi, United Arab Emirates
12 January 2019

Distinguished Guests,
Ladies and Gentlemen,

I am very pleased to be back in Abu Dhabi for the Global Energy Forum. This is the ideal place for us to come together to discuss our global energy challenges, as well as our future opportunities.

It also provides our country, Timor-Leste, with the chance to present our petroleum development plans and learn from the experience of the UAE. With its vision and leadership, the UAE can provide great insights for the Asian region in building a sustainable future.

Across East Asia, we see increasing demand for energy, when the type of energy we use will determine whether the world meets a different challenge: climate change.

These two connected challenges will be the story of East Asia in this new century.

With its growing economies and fast-rising population, Asia continues to be the engine room of global economic growth. We have already seen hundreds of millions of people lifted out of poverty, urbanisation on a massive scale, and the rise of global powers, including China, India, and South Korea. In Southeast Asia the population increased by 23 percent between 2000 and 2017, and continues to rise strongly. This is leading to the emergence of such countries of the future as Indonesia, Vietnam, and the Philippines.

All of this development, and these people, and these industries bring with them an enormous demand for energy. In Southeast Asia alone, demand is up more than 60% in the last 15 years and is currently growing at twice the pace of China. Southeast Asia's energy demand is predicted to grow by almost two thirds by 2040.

The countries that grasp these trends – and the opportunities they provide – will shape our global future. The UAE knows this well – after all, 73% of Persian Gulf energy exports go to the Asia Pacific, meeting almost half of the region's demands.

However, much of Asia's rising energy demands are being met by coal. The Asia Pacific produces 70% of the world's coal and is also its biggest user. This equates to greater global emissions of carbon dioxide and climate change.

I come from a country that is a half island nation, and from a region of many island states. Climate change and rising sea levels pose an existential threat to countries in our neighbourhood.

So, what should we do?

Natural gas provides a bridge to a lower carbon future, and across East Asia, the demand for gas will continue to rise. In Timor-Leste, we can see this future and we know that we can help contribute to the solution and respond to the rising demand for gas.

The good news is that developing our petroleum industry will also transform our economy, create jobs, and build a foundation for our long-term future. And so this is not only good energy policy, but it is good economic and social policy.

Following our historic Maritime Boundary Treaty with Australia, we have now secured a majority of one of the largest gas fields in Southeast Asia, Greater Sunrise. And so, we are planning for the exploitation of Greater Sunrise to become an anchor for the opening up of other known fields and potential new fields in the region, and for it to underpin the development of a regional petroleum hub on the south coast of our country.

The Tasi Mane project, as we call it, will establish a 100-mile corridor along our southern coast, that includes the construction and operation of a refinery, a petrochemical plant, an LNG plant, a linking highway, plus seaports and airports.

Experts project that the total revenue from the development of Greater Sunrise — including LNG production — will reach over $58 billion US dollars and create 38,000 jobs for the Timorese people, all because we want to ensure that the jobs and the industries that come from our resources stay in Timor-Leste — on our shores, and for our people.

We are also looking to develop our immediate region, and have established a tri-lateral initiative to promote Timor-Leste, East Indonesian, and Northern Australian social and economic integration, including in fisheries, transportation, tourism, and marine security, as well as our petroleum industries, to respond to growing East Asian gas demand.

While we are just starting, we know that we can learn from others who have travelled the same path – countries like the UAE that possess the experience and leadership to build the foundation for a positive future. This includes the need for economic diversification and long-term sustainability.

We have already made a good start. From the very beginning, we have viewed our natural resource wealth as the foundation of a diversified economy. We also put every dollar from our petroleum resources into our fully transparent petroleum fund, which has now grown to over $17 billion US dollars today.

Ladies and Gentlemen,

I am confident that, by working together, we can achieve the global, low-carbon economy we need. I am also confident that we can meet Southeast Asia's energy demands.

Timor-Leste can be a part of the solution to these challenges. And in working to respond to East Asia's demand for gas, we can build our petroleum industry, and a diversified economy, to meet the dreams and aspirations of Timor-Leste's next generation.

And so, I look forward to our panel discussion, and to learning more from all the distinguished leaders and experts here today.

Thank you very much.

Timor-Leste Oil and Gas Summit Keynote Speech.

Díli Convention Centre, Timor-Leste
3-4 October 2019

His Excellency Taur Matan Ruak, Prime Minister of the Democratic Republic of
   Timor-Leste,
His Excellency Dr Jose Ramos Horta,
Members of Parliament,
Members of the Government,
Ambassadors and Diplomats,
Distinguished Delegates,
Ladies and Gentlemen,

It is a great pleasure to welcome you to this Timor-Leste Oil and Gas Summit and speak about the potential of our country and our plans for the future.

I therefore want to thank you for your presence and reinforce its importance to us as Timorese.

On 30 August we celebrated the 20th anniversary of our Independence Referendum, in which our people bravely exercised their right to self-determination. It was an occasion when we reflected on the heavy sacrifices that were made in the struggle for freedom and celebrated the future promise of our nation.

As part of the celebrations, on 30 August, Timor-Leste and Australia exchanged diplomatic notes to bring into force the Treaty Between Australia and the Democratic Republic of Timor-Leste Establishing Maritime Boundaries in the Timor Sea. This was an historic step to achieve sovereignty over our seas and maritime rights in accordance with international law.

An important part of these rights relates to the seabed and its exploitation. In preparation for the signing of the treaty, it was necessary to agree on transitional arrangements for the production-sharing contracts in the Timor Sea.

And so, on 28 August, after 18 months of negotiations, six new production-sharing contracts with 10 oil and gas companies were signed, nine of which were international companies. These contracts allow for the continued development of our petroleum industry under the new maritime boundary treaty.

Ladies and Gentlemen,

The petroleum sector is a key pillar in the development of our country. Along with tourism and agriculture, Timor-Leste's Strategic Development Plan, 2011–2030 designates petroleum as a strategic industry designed to underpin our economic growth, job creation, and our future progress as a successful and stable nation.

The Strategic Development Plan aims to secure the opportunities of the petroleum sector for our people through employment and training, building our national petroleum company Timor Gap, delivering the Tasi Mane project on our south coast, and developing petroleum-related industries across our country.

This first ever International Oil and Gas Summit held in Timor-Leste provides the opportunity to discuss these plans, engage with participants in the industry, talk to potential investors, and move forward together to develop our nation.

We have already come a long way. We have established the petroleum fund to provide full transparency and proper management of our petroleum revenue for current and future generations. We were only the third nation in the world, and the first in Asia, to sign and fully comply with the Extractive Industries Transparency Index.

We have built our national oil company, Timor Gap, and, importantly, we are training the Timorese people so that they can make the most of the opportunities provided by our development. So far, we have supported over 200 Master's graduates and over 2000 undergraduates in the petroleum industry.

As you know, we are now working on the Tasi Mane Project to build our petroleum industry on our south coast. This project includes the Suai Supply base, a refinery at Betano, and the Beaco LNG Plant so that we can exploit the Greater Sunrise field and the opportunities provided by oil and gas in our region.

Timor-Leste, through Timor Gap E.P., now owns the majority share in Greater Sunrise and looks forward to working closely with industry partners to ensure its development in the next few years.

Ladies and Gentlemen,

Our Prime Minister, His Excellency Taur Matan Ruak, will shortly launch an international licensing round for petroleum exploration and exploitation in our country. This round will provide excellent opportunities to invest in the oil and gas potential of our country and to work together with us to develop our country.

Before I finish, I would also like to thank Ms Chryssa Tsouraki and the IN-VR team for the partnership they have established with the ANPM, and their hard work to organise this oil and gas summit.

I wish you all the best for this summit, and trust it will provide many opportunities to discuss the development of the petroleum industry in Timor-Leste and its potential to transform our country for the benefit of our people.

Thank you very much.

To Our Youth

Upon receiving an Honorary Degree in International Relations from Hunan University

Changsha, Hunan Province, China
12 May 2017

Mr Duan Xianzhong, President
Rector,
Your Excellencies,
Ladies and Gentlemen,
Dear Students,

It is a great honour to be invited by the leaders of this university to be here today before such a distinguished audience, to whom I convey my respect and my most sincere appreciation.

Hunan University is known throughout the world not only for its academic excellence but also because it has educated many renowned professionals who have held, and currently hold, leading roles in academic institutions, the government and the private sector, contributing to make China the superpower it is today.

I am also aware that seniority in China is respected and is a mark of wisdom. As such, I could not feel more privileged to have been chosen by this prestigious one-thousand-year-old institution to receive this great honour. Whilst I do not feel I deserve it, I would nevertheless like to share with you some of my life experiences, which have shaped my very personal view of the world and its international relations.

I was born one year after the end of World War II, during which Timor-Leste became a battlefield in the war between Japan and Australia. Indeed, many Timorese assisted the Australians in this war, and around 70,000 Timorese lost their lives. For an important part of my life I endured a difficult 24-year struggle, and watched the years roll by as we entered today's modern world – a world in which technology has become a driving force in a way unthinkable mere decades ago, and which is contributing to a new geopolitical uncertainty.

Today, we are witnessing incredible moments in the history of humankind, where so many events around the world are affecting the daily lives of common citizens, institutions, and states.

Wherever we are in this globalised world of ours, we can sense the relationship between people – and between people, history and nature – being redefined. The past and future are converging into the present, with everything interrelated and in which the physical distance separating local and global events is circumvented by technological advances.

In this context,

we cannot continue to ignore the complexity of today's environment and the manner in which financial, economic, and political crises and their impacts intertwine and reverberate across the world. We cannot continue perpetuating old mistakes because we do not take the time to learn from history and to reflect on its consequences, even though the root causes of many of today's problems can be found there. And because we do not learn from history, we cannot make a proper effort to predict the future.

We are living in times of great tension. This is in part due to the consequences of actions being compressed in both time and distance, and to abrupt changes in the international landscape, both in terms of climate as well as the political and financial environment.

Ladies and Gentlemen,

Those who know me will surely know that my 'schooling' did not involve academic institutions. Instead, it was what I call the school of life. Although I did not have the opportunity to enrol in academic studies, I was nevertheless given the mission to lead, for over 20 years, the complex journey of a resilient people who dared to dream of freedom.

My people taught me that, with sacrifice, consistency, and perseverance towards the common good, it is possible to change the course of difficult, even painful processes.

The mountains, where I lived a good part of my life during the time of the resistance, taught me to see the world from a particular perspective, learning from the successes and failures of other countries, and from victories and losses in other wars, which enabled me to adapt my mindset to the realities of our own war.

And so, my time in the mountains taught me about the dynamics of international relations and power relations, since these considerations were essential to the survival of my people – the Timorese people. As you will all recall, a new geopolitical scenario emerged after World War II. This was called the Cold War, with two superpowers dividing the world. Wars that persisted were not exactly between capitalism and socialism, but, rather, wars to free people from colonial oppression. Consequently, European countries began granting independence to their territories in Asia and in Africa, albeit sometimes reluctantly. So, too, did Timor-Leste free itself from European colonial domination in the 1970s, embracing the hope of living in freedom.

However, nine days after we unilaterally declared our independence on 28 November 1974, we were brutally invaded and annexed by Indonesia. Instead of having the time to heal the wounds caused by centuries of colonisation, we found ourselves in a war of liberation that lasted for 24 years.

Over this period we fought alone against Indonesia, a giant supported by the United States of America, the United Kingdom, France, and Germany. These countries supplied the Indonesian military with weapons, gunships, tanks, aircraft, mortars, cannons, and even counter-guerrilla training, so that they could increase their fighting ability and more quickly crush the resistance of the small Timorese guerrilla force.

The battle tactics of direct engagement with the enemy that we adopted at the start of the Indonesian invasion led to a major strategic defeat at the end of our first three years of fighting. Our military leaders were either killed or imprisoned, and our military capacity was drastically reduced. Meanwhile, the people who had taken refuge in the mountains, under our protection, were now under enemy control.

Since I was a mere soldier in the Portuguese army during the colonial period, I could never have led a war over the next 21 years against Indonesian career generals if not for the teachings on theories of warfare by the great Mao Tsé-Tung. From those theories, I learned to separate the general principles of war from the individual circumstances of particular wars, both in terms of the different historical time as well as the geographical characteristics. I learned the importance of understanding my country, including the characteristics of our land, the way our people thought and behaved, and our own technical and military capacity.

I studied guerrilla wars the best I could, including in the former Portuguese African colonies, in Cuba, and in Vietnam. This enabled me to develop the principles for a guerrilla war that was adapted to the reality of Timor. This in turn forced me to review our successes and failures every year, so that I might better understand our enemy and its strengths and weaknesses, both in the military sector and in other sectors, in Timor, in Indonesia, and in the world.

In practical terms, we were reduced to little over 700 poorly armed guerrilla fighters, without ammunition, ill equipped and barefoot, sometimes having to contend with as many as five battalions, in operations that would last between four and six weeks.

While the large military apparatus of our enemy tried to cover the entire territory, shooting blindly so as to try to scare us, the unpredictability of our small actions worked in our favour. The Indonesians could not anticipate where and when we would show up, in small numbers, in hit-and-run style. Meanwhile, our clandestine organisation enabled us to develop our intelligence assets and other mechanisms to gather information on the enemy. We never received any type of military support from abroad, as our principle was always that of relying on our own strengths - our human, psychological, and ideological resources - and consequently this meant that we fought with a minimum of military hardware.

Even at that time, wars no longer just entailed the concept of military victory through the force of arms. There was already a major psychological component resulting from human nature, where someone shoots to kill, knowing that they, in turn, can be shot and killed.

And still we fought! Needless to say we lost many battles and many valiant soldiers, but we won the war. On the 20th of this month, Timor-Leste will be celebrating its 15th anniversary as an independent state.

Rector,
Ladies and Gentlemen,
Students,

At the time of perestroika and glasnost, we in the mountains of Timor-Leste hailed Gorbachev, because he brought about the end of the Cold War, and we believed that when we finally achieved our independence, the world would be living under a new world order.

Today I am saddened to see that this hope for a new world order has led to the realisation of true world disorder.

One needs only to look at the interventions in Iraq and Afghanistan, where wars started in the name of democracy and human rights expanded, rather than reaching a positive conclusion, taking on increasingly problematic aspects.

When the Arab Spring started, heralded enthusiastically by the 'musketeers of democracy and human rights', I stated publicly at an International Forum in Jakarta that those mass mobilisations spoke of troubling times ahead. A few years later, we see how the social and political fabric of those countries has broken down.

I have repeated at international forums on democracy that democracy is a process, and not a formula that one can apply without considering the specific realities and circumstances of each country. Democratic movements cannot be manipulated or influenced by outside factors, nor fuelled by pressure from other (state or non-state) parties that seek to impose the 'higher interests' of others.

Other wars have broken out, connected to the Arab revolution, and have been applauded by large powers that intervened, directly or indirectly, in the name of 'democracy and human rights'. This only suggests that world leaders cannot change their policy of assisting processes of transitioning to democracy without waging wars; nor can they refrain from interfering in the internal affairs of other countries.

In addition to those endless wars caused by regional and global interferences, today's world is powerless in the face of a new climate of tension: ethnic rivalries, religious rivalries, and extremism, which are taking on worrying proportions.

The most critical threat today is insecurity, which entails risks and dangers far greater than during the Cold War period.

Additionally, these are risks and dangers that no one quite understands yet. Meanwhile, distrust and uncertainty undermine relationships among people, between people, and within states and among states.

In the name of democracy and human rights, we are forcing everyone all over the world to be good disciples of the large powers in which there is also violence, racism, and human rights abuses. As if this rhetoric were not enough, these countries, the self-proclaimed paladins of democracy, have weak and corrupt institutions that fail to adapt to changes that seek to balance the international system, while they also have millions of homeless without social assistance. The disasters caused by this cascade from those countries onto the rest of the world.

We see Europe insecure about acts of terrorism here and there, while conflicts in the Horn of Africa and in the Middle East go unresolved because international powers want to perpetuate their dominance, indifferent to the exodus of millions of people into Europe.

And yet, Europe is not the one that is on the brink of its capacity. It takes courage to admit that the refugee problem is not a European problem, but, rather, a world problem. It takes honesty from the major powers, inside and outside Europe, to admit that their international policies contributed to this problem.

There is a global inability to seek proper solutions for the problems affecting humankind, with social inequalities, poverty, lack of access to basic subsistence services, and wellbeing continuing to affect millions of people.

And if we are talking about democracy and human rights, we should remember the many people who try to reach those 'lands of freedom', only to be held hostage to that dream and detained in camps from the Pacific to Europe.

In 2015 I was invited by a European Parliamentary Commission to take part in a Conference at Expo Milan, in Italy, on the subject of 'Human Rights, Right to Food and Land Rights. What is missing?', I said at the conference that the one thing missing was peace.

At that time, Europe was already witnessing the arrival of hundreds of thousands of people travelling in fragile vessels, many of which sank in the Mediterranean. This was so because the international community prefers to intervene to impose democratic values over handling the root causes of problems.

The universalisation of these democratic principles and values must be considered carefully. Indeed, it often happens that the things being universalised are the interests of the strong, and of their allies. The powerful of the world turn a blind eye to the absence of democracy and breaches of human rights when their allies share their interests. Meanwhile, disasters are created in the name of core principles and core values.

In Milan, like in other forums in which I have taken part,

I have urged world leaders to stop funding wars abroad. The cost of war is steep in every aspect and it would obviously be much safer if they would invest in the fight against poverty. Among other things, that would actually make a positive contribution towards world peace.

Instead, we have seen the wave of refugees continue to swell. Indeed, some countries have built electrified walls to keep away the millions who are, after all, merely fleeing from the wars that ravage their own land. All they need to return home is peace, and I am sure that after so much suffering and deception upon being refused entry into the 'wonderful world' where, after all, their minimum rights to live in security and peace were denied, that in every heart and in every soul, I believe, they are thinking that to go back home would be a journey of hope for their future.

Your Excellencies,
Ladies and Gentlemen,
Young Students,

There is an atmosphere of tension and unease that is causing the lack of trust and mutual respect between states and within states. Elections all over Europe, a continent that seems unable to think clearly about its own future, show that Europeans tend not to trust the system and rhetoric, instead falling under the sway of manipulation, manoeuvres, and diversionary exercises that nurture xenophobic feelings. The traditional ideological currents that governed Europe are suffering from the mistrust of the voters, who no longer know exactly whom to believe and which has led them to question the validity of the European Union itself.

Dialogue is either completely non-existent or does not even bother to hide the fact that it serves only to ensure that each power maintains its influence. It is never the warring sides that win, since the real interested parties are those in the background, defending their interests – which are mainly economic – to be used later on as 'debts to be settled' in return for the military support provided, which always comes at a cost.

I have mentioned the psychological element of war, and our tactic of unpredictability in our attacks. Now I see that the acts of extremism, which cause destruction where one would least expect, serve a more powerful agenda and will persist until world leaders change their perspectives of this complex reality.

With the current policies of prominent global leaders of 'An eye for an eye, a tooth for a tooth' causing even greater distance between people and a desire for revenge and destruction, I truly believe that this nightmare will continue plaguing the world for many years to come.

Your Excellencies,
Ladies and Gentlemen,
Students,

We all know that there are conflicts, whether armed or not, in many parts of the world that reveal the evidence of intolerance, hatred, and ethnic and/or religious divides, or reveals the fragility of states whose institutions do not properly function.

Regardless of our perspective of conflicts, the approach of the international community, if we can't say it was always negative, at least we can say it was always wrong.

The large amounts spent on peacekeeping operations that, instead of making peace, end up prolonging conflicts, so as to justify the continued presence of those very same peacekeeping operations, only reveal how bad the policy approach of the international community is.

People who are tired because of war, misery, and hunger are naturally not ready for an approach that is too doctrinal. When someone is thirsty for peace, it is first necessary to quench that thirst, that is, to create the conditions for establishing peace.

Think with with me for minute: imagine a rural area in any poor country, where access to the local town is very difficult. Are we going to talk of human rights? Sure, they may be a fundamental right, but what about the right to food? The right to health care? The right to live without fear? The right to peace, including peace of mind?

And so, I would dare to say that people living in these circumstances are not ready to be lectured on human rights or free speech. It is first necessary to make them safe and to provide them with access to the most essential goods that are required for their survival and their dignity.

Therefore, I say that the approach of the international community is indeed misguided, with the so-called developed countries, which cannot ensure the full respect of human rights back home, lacking the sensibility to understand that recipient countries do not have the psychological conditions to learn all of those values all at once. Instead, they should be introduced step by step, in accordance with the ability of the people to absorb them.

I know that this offends the drafters of the global indexes of this and that, who put all the countries of the world in the same basket, measuring and weighing them in the same manner, from economics to social policies, from finance to human rights, from democracy to inflation, and from welfare to the environment, with exactly the same rules, even, for example, if a small island hasn't contributed at all to climate change.

Timor-Leste is a small country that fought essentially alone to achieve its independence, dreaming of being part of a better world.

The path we have walked since our independence has had its ups and downs, and I acknowledge the assistance by many great nations who have supported, and continue to support, our development. Here, I must highlight the great support and cooperation from the People's Republic of China. Still, we also had some setbacks.

Our obvious inexperience and immaturity during our transition from decades of conflict into a stable state and nation took us not only towards a cycle of internal crisis but also to a dependence on international aid and institutional assistance, including human resources.

In truth, someone who is dependent on another will never be free.

We learned at our expense that without peace, there can be no development, and that without development, there is no room for peace.

It was also during this process that we realised that international assistance is not always directed to the actual needs of the recipient countries, since donors – those who spout principles and values – also spout in their own interests.

Here, history also matters, as it is not difficult to understand that a new country, with young and inexperienced institutions, will not sit at the table of negotiations with the same weight, the same knowledge, or even the same institutional dignity as other countries, simply because it has not had the time to mature its institutions. Our history shows that the crisis that was shaking the society and the young state, until its climax in 2006, was engendered by external agents, as this served the interests of their countries.

This is one of the reasons why Timor-Leste has been working with other fragile countries, and countries in conflict or post conflict situations, as a founding member of g7+. This is a group consisting of around 20 countries across the world that have come together as one in order to try and change global development policies, which is to say g7+ seeks to make international assistance more effective.

The Secretary-General of the United Nations, Mr António Guterres, is committed to reforming international assistance practices, so as to focus on results that truly benefit the populations of recipient countries.

As we try to place the needs of these countries on the global development agenda, sharing experiences and knowledge, our primary effort is to promote peace in our societies and in the world, following the motto of 'Nothing about us without us'.

Conflict, poverty, and intransigence are evils that affect many people in the world, like a serious transmissible disease that spreads across borders. I advocate that ensuring common security entails strategic alliances in favour of reconciliation and tolerance, with proactive diplomacy for peace.

Your Excellencies,
Ladies and Gentlemen,

In 2013, Indonesia co-hosted a United Nations international conference in Bali on the 'Alliance of Civilisations'. I recall that, at that time, everyone urged mutual respect for the culture, diversity, religion, history, and identity of others, asking for dialogue to bring parties closer together, and for reconciliation to ensure mutual acceptance. Unfortunately, a few years after that conference, we have seen that intolerance, hatred, and vengeance are rampant in several parts of the world, breeding fear and distrust.

Needless to say, hundreds of thousands of Timorese people died during the struggle for independence. Some were killed directly on the battlefields; others were gunned down in systematic cleansing operations. And others still, who managed to survive aerial bombing, ended up dying of starvation, exhaustion, and disease. Meanwhile, history shows that without regard to international law, some legitimated the illegal occupation of Timor-Leste with agreements to take over our resources.

It took us a few years and much destruction before we realised the need to bring the Timorese together around the common ideal of independence. This implied reconciling our differences. As such, and although we always urged the Indonesians to make peace with us, we were faithful to the motto of 'Independence or death'. Indeed, we knew that only by resisting together could we could prevail.

The Timorese youth wanted to have a more active participation in the struggle, through actions they would call the 'Timorese intifada'. I did not agree and I urged them to study in Indonesia, so that they would be prepared for a future independent Timor-Leste. The larger motive, however, was that I did not want violence to escalate and breed hatred and intolerance, since that would be ineffective and counterproductive in a situation where they would have to learn to 'live with the enemy' without ever betraying our ultimate goal of liberation.

While we always urged the Indonesians to choose peace, we were always faithful to our struggle, believing that all Timorese were resisting, and ready to accept either independence or total extermination.

This existential commitment came from the people themselves. Despite the physical, moral, psychological, and political destruction we suffered, upon achieving independence we were ready to forgive and to reconcile. We knew that the sacrifices made liberating our homeland would be for naught if we allowed hatred and vengeance to take root in our hearts. One cannot heal the deep wounds caused by war while harbouring those feelings. Living in peace means more than living in the absence of war; it also means living free from corrosive feelings and distrust of one another.

And so, the Timorese reconciled not only with the Indonesians but also with their Timorese brothers and sisters who had opted to advocate for integration, as well as with themselves. I should add, as a good demonstration of our reconciliation, that I twice visited cemeteries of Indonesian soldiers to pay my respects to the Indonesian victims of the struggle. In turn, two Indonesian presidents of the Republic also honoured our fallen national heroes.

When President Suharto died, I went to his funeral with a group of young Timorese citizens, showing the Indonesian people that the past should not stand in the way of our present.

That does not mean we forgot that over two hundred thousand Timorese died as a result of that illegal and criminal occupation. Nor do we say that reconciliation was an easy process. It is much harder to fill one's heart with peace than to instil a few drops of hatred.

However, the Timorese people showed once again just how big their souls are. And today we have the best of relations with Indonesia.

Rector,
Ladies and Gentlemen,
Students,

In the world, there are over 1.5 billion people living in extreme poverty and misery. We also witness the enormous suffering of children, women, and millions of people directly affected by shelling, wounded or dead, and those surviving without food, without water, and without shelter, not knowing where to go.

Asia needs peace!

Every country in Asia has its own problems and challenges, which are different not just in terms of their nature but also in the impacts on their societies. Timor-Leste, as a small country that suffered from a Japanese invasion during World War II and from international complicity during a 24-year resistance struggle, knows all too well what it means to live in war.

Timor-Leste recognises that China is a powerhouse that has much to teach to countries like Timor-Leste about its economic miracle and its development. I was here, at Changsha, back in 2014, at the invitation of the Chinese government, to take part in a conference on investment cooperation in Timor-Leste that enabled the strengthening of the economic and commercial ties between our two countries. During that trip, I also went to Boao, for the Boao Forum for Asia, where we discussed international social and economic cooperation. On another occasion I visited Macau, participating in a conference on infrastructure.

China is also a member of the United Nations Security Council. Being a new country, Timor-Leste favours honest and sincere dialogue so that we can bring safety, peace, and stability to all people in our region and across the world.

Multilateral actions by world leaders must be tireless in pursuing this goal. The way of dialogue is unquestionably the only weapon that can ease tensions and settle disputes.

Timor-Leste also advocates the principle, often violated by large and rich countries, of having good cooperation. However, relations between countries should be guided by the principles of good faith, justice, and respect for international law.

Large and rich countries should be expected to respect smaller countries as equals, instead of imposing their interests on them, often using the tactic of divide and rule.

This is even more important when we speak of relations between close neighbours. It is our differences that make us unique, but it is by reconciling those differences, and having honest cooperation without hidden agendas, that we can strengthen peace and stability in the region. Indeed, that is what we have achieved with Indonesia.

Your Excellencies
Dear Students,

I would like to leave with a few final words to the young students who have the privilege of attending this unique institution of many talents, in which one of the mottos is 'Dare to be pioneers'.

I would add: Dare to be pioneers of peace, as well. The future, which belongs to you, depends on that, and the region and the world can only benefit.

Thank you very much.

Timor-Leste, History to Present Day: *How Does Timor-Leste Embrace International Law and Institutions to Advance National Objectives?*

Abu Dhabi, United Arab Emirates
13 January 2019

Ladies and Gentlemen,

It is a pleasure for me to be your guest at the Emirati Diplomatic Academy.

This remarkable academy, known for its excellence in training the next generation of diplomats of the United Arab Emirates, stands out for promoting and teaching principles that I consider to be fundamental in today's ever-changing and unpredictable world: innovation, tolerance, diversity, cooperation, and, last, but not least, peace.

Now, more than ever, the world requires competent and professional diplomats who, in addition to pursuing the national interests of their countries, also contribute to making the world a better place.

The world needs more dialogue builders and peace workers and the UAE is stepping up to provide them.

As such, it is an honour to share with this distinguished audience the history of my small, young country, Timor-Leste, and how that history underscores the importance of diplomacy and international law.

Dear Students,

Timor-Leste, a half island nation with a land area a little over 15,000 square kilometres, located at the crossroads of Asia and the Pacific and between two regional giants, Australia and Indonesia, is one of Southeast Asia's poorest countries.

Not unlike your own history before 1966, Timor-Leste's history includes centuries of colonial rule. While this made us yearn for freedom, it also provided us with a meeting of cultures and civilisations, and a unique identity in Asia. Indeed, through being a Portuguese-speaking country, we share our cultural and linguistic identity with eight other nations in the world, nations that, while distant, are joined in solidarity.

The Portuguese Revolution of 1974 made the Timorese believe that independence could finally be achieved. And so, we organised together to decide the political destiny of our nation.

However, the inexperience and lack of preparation by our young revolutionaries led to a brief civil war that, while painful, made every Timorese identify with their homeland and their people.

More than ever, we were determined to see Timor-Leste become a sovereign nation. And so, on 28 November 1975, we unilaterally declared independence from Portugal.

Nine days later, however, we were invaded and subsequently occupied by Indonesia.

And so, in the same year that the Vietnam War ended, a new war started in Southeast Asia. This war lasted 24 years and was perhaps the cruellest in modern history. For a quarter of a century the Timorese were the victims of massacres, torture, induced starvation, intimidation, and violence.

While this was happening to our people, the international community watched with indifference – and in the case of some world powers, with complicit cooperation. This was, of course, during the period of the Cold War, when all too often the end was taken to justify the means....

Still, you all know that in international relations, there are realists and idealists. For the realists, international relations are decided by might. For the idealists, they must be guided by principles of justice.

The fact that Timor-Leste exists today as an independent, democratic nation is evidence that the realists are sometimes wrong and the strong do not always prevail over the weak.

Indeed, while our people stood firm, and our guerrilla fighters resisted the military dictatorship, other brave Timorese fought a diplomatic and political battle in the United Nations and other international institutions. The weapon we wielded was international law.

We had to rely on the diplomacy of the countries that stood with us, as well as of people who had the courage to support Timor-Leste even against the policies of their own governments, which supported, or were silent in the face of, our illegal occupation.

Nearly a quarter of a century after the invasion of our country, and after lengthy negotiations, we finally succeeded in breaking the siege. In addition to the strength of our people and the vital role played by the Timorese resistance, we had another major force on the side of Timor-Leste:

international law and the international system.

United Nations Secretary-General Kofi Annan said, 'Never before has the world united with such resolve to help one small nation establish itself'. But other words from the Secretary-General resonated strongly with us: 'Independence will not mean the end of the world's commitment to you'.

In August 1999, the Timorese people voted overwhelmingly for independence at a referendum organised and supervised by the United Nations.

Dear Students,

After our vote for independence, we had to build our nation from the ashes of destruction, overcoming psychological trauma as well as a lack of financial resources, and having no institutions for building a state.

We had to learn as we went along. And we watched the challenges faced – ones that continue to be faced – by many fragile nations in the world, countries in conflict or post-conflict situations that are unable to see even a ray of hope to allow them to believe that change is possible.

In Timor-Leste, we believe that maintaining peace and stability, while focusing on a long process of reconciliation with Indonesia and internal dialogue amongst the Timorese, are key factors for our development.

Furthermore, establishing ties of cooperation and friendship with both our closest neighbours and other countries in the region and around the world was essential to putting our nation on a safe path.

I cannot overstate how thankful Timor-Leste is to all of the countries that contributed to peace and stability in our nation, as well as to the building of the institutions of the Timorese state.

While rebuilding a country that was born out of the ashes, we realised that we were but one million among hundreds of millions of people all over the world who have to face the challenge of development.

Fortunately, in addition to the nature and resilience of our people, we also hold significant oil and gas reserves, and we grow world-class coffee.

Eight years ago, we prepared a 20-year Strategic Development Plan, to diversify our economy, develop our human capital, and make our country grow sustainably.

Students,

International law was created by the community of nations to regulate relations between states and contribute to the constructive and peaceful resolution of international disputes.

The rules-based international system gives hope to many nations around the world, and particularly to our country, which depended upon it to restore our independence in the first place.

I would like to share with you a more recent case that made Timor-Leste rely once more on international law and international institutions to defend the interests of its people.

Globally, Timor-Leste is remembered, first and foremost, for its difficult fight to free itself from Indonesian occupation, a country whose resources and means were incomparably superior to ours. However, at a time when we were still fragile and dealing with the colossal task of rebuilding our nation, we were forced to start a new fight for sovereignty. This time our adversary was our other large and powerful neighbour, Australia.

The Timor Sea holds important oil and gas reserves, which we believe can transform our nation's economy. Access to these resources will be a powerful driving force for development for our country.

And so, delimiting our maritime boundaries means more to us than the obvious fulfilment of our political and economic independence. It also means ensuring that the sacrifices of our people have not been made in vain.

More than 60% of our population is under the age of 25 and in need of food, education, health care, and jobs. We knew that their generation would never be truly free unless we led a transition from fragility to resilience and stability.

Indonesia, with which we have an excellent relationship of friendship and cooperation, immediately agreed to negotiate maritime boundaries with us in accordance with international law.

However, our ally and neighbour Australia refused to negotiate maritime boundaries with us, and for two decades we used every procedural means available to find a way forward.

Just two months before Timor-Leste regained its independence on 20 May 2002, the Australian Government withdrew from the binding procedures under UNCLOS for resolving maritime boundary disputes.

We were also unable to negotiate bilaterally. The best we could do, thanks to the 'benevolence' of our neighbours, was to sign temporary resource-sharing arrangements, so as to enable us to access and exploit the resources in the Timor Sea. Although these arrangements provided us with important revenues for rebuilding our country through our well managed petroleum fund, they were not fair and did not uphold the sovereign rights of Timor-Leste.

Therefore, after assessing every option, Timor-Leste chose to initiate the first ever compulsory conciliation, under the United Nations Convention on the Law of the Sea (UNCLOS).

The complex issues concerning the oceans and the seas led to a broad multilateral treaty in 1982: UNCLOS. This international treaty is one of the most finely tuned and complex international legal instruments in force today, and forms the basis of the legal order protecting our oceans.

Timor-Leste is a strong advocate of this convention and of the international legal order, created around the principle that all nations are equal before the law, regardless of whether they are large or small, developed or developing, old or young.

The conciliation was no easy process. It was a struggle that tested us every step of the way. Although we initiated the process in April 2016, we only signed the historic Maritime Boundary Treaty with Australia on 6 March 2018. The final outcome provides Timor-Leste with a permanent maritime boundary that is consistent with international law, thereby guaranteeing our sovereign rights as a coastal state under UNCLOS.

The United Nations conciliation model is particularly important today, when geopolitical tensions concerning maritime disputes are on the rise worldwide. Timor-Leste's experience as a small, fragile, and developing country that challenged a large and powerful maritime neighbour shows that the international legal order can be successful.

This process also showed that it may be necessary to support other developing countries in order to promote equal access to international legal mechanisms for solving maritime disputes. This is an initiative that Timor-Leste is determined to promote, alongside other like-minded countries.

We hope to work with our friends around the world to create an international and independent trust fund that would provide financial, legal, and technical support to developing countries on their maritime disputes.

What a fitting time this would be to come together and prove to the world that the international system still works. Timor-Leste achieved its independence with the help of the international system. Today, on maritime boundary disputes, we have a chance to prove that the international system can still deliver.

This is because, apart from these maritime disputes, there are events that question the effectiveness of the implementation of international principles and the moral obligations of global decision makers. For example, the international community is currently failing to analyse the root cause of problems around the world that affect millions of people, including many women and children, while wasting time and resources focusing only on responding to the fatal consequences of the tragic events which we see happening year after year.

Dear Students,

I want to conclude by wishing you all the best in your studies and in your future careers.

You young men and women are the ones who will write a new chapter of diplomacy. You are the next guardians of international law and the next safeguards of our international institutions.

Institutions are not good or bad, fair or unfair. Institutions are but a reflection of the people who work within them. Be the promoters of peace, be the promoters of dialogue, to reduce potential war and conflict. Be the promoters of justice, fairness, and mutual respect among cultures, religions, and peoples, and among nations.

I see before me intelligent, dedicated, and enthusiastic young people – all of you – representing a future that you will shape for a better world of tolerance and a real world of peace.

I wish you the very best in your future.

Thank you.

Acceptance Speech Upon Receiving Honored Doctorate Degree in International Peace: *Promoting Peace in Fragile and Conflict-Affected States*

Phnom Penh, Cambodia
20 November 2019

H.E. Dr Kao Kim Hourn, Founder, Chairman of the Board of Trustees and President of the University of Cambodia,

H.E. Sam Raing Kamsan, Member of the Board of Trustees,

H.E. the Vice-President of the University of Cambodia,

H.E. Prof Dr Chhun Vannak, Director of ASEAN Study Center,

Excellencies, Members of the Academic Council,

Faculties and Students from University of Cambodia,

Distinguished Guests,

Ladies and Gentlemen,

First of all, I would like to thank the University of Cambodia for organising this ceremony and, very humbly, I feel honoured to be here to receive the Honorary Doctorate Degree in International Peace.

And I feel privileged to receive this title in this vibrant nation, the Kingdom of Cambodia, which inspires us all with its breathtaking history of resilience in moving from a turbulent past to rebuild a nation of peace through cultural belief, dialogue and tolerance, as the Honourable Prime Minister Samdech Hun Sen described so well in the inaugural session of Asia Pacific Forum, yesterday, at the Palace of Peace.

I cannot, therefore, miss this opportunity to congratulate the Government of the Kingdom of Cambodia on its efforts to consolidate peace, and its vision for a successful path of development. I was, in my first time to Phnom Penh, in the early 2000, an international observer for the elections that took place in Cambodia. Now, in 2019, I'm simply astonished by the progress made. Really amazing! Actually, Cambodia is on the move.

Well, as someone who has known more war and seen more tragedy than I can ever forget, I am convinced that, as the nations of the world, their leadership and their people, we are not doing enough to achieve international peace.

Peace often depends on a deeply personal commitment. And here, in the university with so many young and talented people, is where we can start to make a difference.

Education for peace should start in our schools, in our universities, and it will have a tremendous impact in every sphere of public and private life. This is the hope that the youth gives us - you can learn skills and knowledge, but you also can learn how to seek tolerance and justice for everyone and, by learning from the mistakes of history, you can build a better future.

And the future needs PEACE.

What a challenge this is - and what a beautiful dream.

It's a dream built on principles that are being challenged and tested, every day, in this disordered and chaotic world - the principles of tolerance, reconciliation, diversity, equality, diplomacy, and cooperation are not yet well assumed by politicians and civil society.

I believe that everyone present here today shares this same sentiment. We all want more peace and more harmony in the lives and hearts of every human being.

However, this is not what is happening.

All of us want to believe in the global architecture, the promises and certain goodwill, or at least certain concern, of world leadership, and all of us try to believe in a global system that effectively promotes peace - beyond what is written in international resolutions and reports - but, regrettably, most of the time what we all see is interference of the great powers and indifference from the decision makers.

I know that we all want to believe in the seriousness of the commitments made in the 2030 Agenda, where the United Nations chose peace as a fundamental pillar, recognizing its importance for global development.

And yet, more than 1.5 billion people are still living in countries where development is compromised by fragility and violence. We can imagine that innocent people who suffer under conflict, both within and between countries, keep asking themselves: Why? Why can't we simply live in peace with each other, with our neighbors, within our communities, in our country and with other countries?

Excellencies.

Ladies and Gentlemen,

This month, we celebrate the 30th anniversary of the fall of the Berlin Wall, leaving behind a critical period in human history in which the world was divided into two blocks during the Cold War.

After the fall of the Berlin Wall, the world changed. We were now in a world that was to be guided by the market, and where political and social issues would be subordinate to the economy. And yet, what happened was growing inequalities between rich and poor.

The great international ideas and theories that have plagued us since that time have brought us no hope and no order. After World War II, there were armed conflicts, made by the liberation movements against their colonisers. But after the end of the Cold War, we witnessed more wars in the name of human rights, more conflicts in the name of democracy, and more violence in the name of security, all of them causing despair among the women and children, and the death of innocent people.

From the shocking international economic inequalities that globalisation and new technologies have increased, to civil wars in Africa, conflicts in the Middle East, and the dramatic consequences of climate change. To the challenges of collective security, where terrorism has become an increasingly complex phenomenon, reminding us that even the most powerful countries in the world are equally vulnerable in this globalised world.

We are constantly reminded that there is no oasis of peace and security in places where there is misery, war, and conflict. The western world still does not want to acknowledge or face the consequences of its own policies, encouraging even more mistrust and uncertainty between people and between states.

Today, we can see the repercussions. We have witnessed the proliferation of demonstrations, riots, and crises all over the world – from Chile to Bolivia, from Hong Kong to Spain and France, from Lebanon to Iraq, where lives are lost and property destroyed. The UN Secretary-General called for non-violence and urged protesters to 'follow the examples of Gandhi, Martin Luther King, and other champions of non-violent change'.

Many of these people are in the streets to challenge the discrimination, corruption, and poverty in which they live. And where is the responsibility of the world's leaders? They simply create more mistrust and discredit in the international order. In the morning, they talk about peace, but in the afternoon, they seal billions of dollars in arms trade.

World decision makers need to do more than articulate their speeches with empty words. They need to change their own minds and put an end to their demagogy by teaching democracy and human rights.

Restoring people's confidence and avoiding conflict depends on the courage to change global policies. Reflection and restraint, ladies and gentlemen, is what the world needs.

As you know, the history of Timor-Leste is a difficult one. For 24 years we struggled for our independence, fighting for a world that would allow us control of our own future. Our resistance came at great cost, but we were determined to be a free people, exercising our sovereignty over our land and our sea.

The path was not an easy one, and we were fighting without the support of the great western powers, which had forsaken us. When we achieved our independence, we recognised that reconciliation was the first thing that we had to do, so that we could heal our country.

First, Timor-Leste had to reconcile with its former occupiers, Indonesia. Today, Indonesia is one of the largest democracies in the world and has a large emerging free-market economy.

We recognise that Timor-Leste not only shares an island with Indonesia, we share a future, and we now walk together in friendship and solidarity. We view the strength of our relationship as an important model of how, with goodwill, with a focus on the future and development, a history of bitterness and conflict can be overcome.

We also had to look inwards. What we found was that sometimes reconciliation between our own people has proved more difficult than with our former occupiers. This led to the realisation that we had to come together and reconcile our internal differences. As a nation, we recognised that we could not build a state without building peace within ourselves. This meant that we needed to come to terms with, and then address, our fragility. And so, we came together and began to honestly deal with our problems. We began reconstructing a country from the ashes.

But we still weren't truly free. We did not have permanent maritime boundaries with either of our neighbours, Australia and Indonesia. We could not claim our seas and those resources which, under international law, belonged to us. We couldn't secure our own future.

After years of trying and failing to negotiate maritime boundaries with Australia, in 2016 we turned to compulsory conciliation. The compulsory conciliation was the last resort we had – designed for countries like ours where a neighbour refuses to negotiate bilaterally but has also withdrawn from the binding dispute resolution mechanisms under UNCLOS.

The compulsory conciliation process had never been used before, and came with no guarantees of success. But after 18 months, we managed to reach an agreement with Australia and, in March of 2018, we signed a treaty at the headquarters of the United Nations.

You may find it odd that I am mentioning this when we are talking about peace, but it is because the United Nations conciliation process is an important model for the peaceful resolution of issues at a time when geopolitical tensions concerning maritime disputes are rising across the world.

The experience of Timor-Leste as a small, fragile, and developing country that faced a large and powerful maritime neighbour helped identify the need for support to be given to developing countries to promote equal access to the international legal mechanisms for solving maritime disputes. It therefore helped to promote peace, instead of instability, and development, instead of dependency.

During our journey, we understood in Timor-Leste, that we were but one million among hundreds of millions of people all over the world who yearn for peace, stability, and dignity, but whose intrinsic fragility does not always allow for it.

Allow me to share with you what we have tried to do to promote peace in the world.

My country, Timor-Leste, was one of the founding members of the g7+. This group is an inter-governmental organisation that brings together 20 conflict-affected countries across Africa, Asia, the Pacific, and the Caribbean, transitioning from conflict into resilience. The g7+ members are Afghanistan, Burundi, Central African Republic, Chad, Union of Comoros, Côte d'Ivoire, Democratic Republic of Congo, Guinea, Guinea-Bissau, Haiti, Liberia, Papua New Guinea, Sao Tomé and Principe, Sierra Leone, Solomon Islands, Somalia, South Sudan, Timor-Leste, Togo, and Yemen.

We established the g7+ in 2010 in Díli, Timor-Leste, with two main missions:

> *To facilitate peer learning and sharing of experience on peace and reconciliation under our flagship program of fragile-to-fragile cooperation (F2F); and*

> *To serve as a platform to speak with one voice to our international partners in relation to changing the delivery of aid.*

Timor-Leste's experience in peace and reconciliation with Indonesia, where we agreed to put the past behind us and focus on development for the future, has become one of the lessons that we shared with other member countries.

We believe that dialogue and reconciliation is the most affordable means to resolve conflict; it should not be resolved with bitterness, hatred, and violence.

Excellencies,
Ladies and Gentlemen,

Sustaining peace has become the main agenda for g7+. However, this can be only be achieved if it is led and owned by us, the people of the country, in order to resolve the conflict and violence that have cost the lives of innocent citizens in our countries.

From the experience of the g7+ countries in achieving peace, we have three main lessons that I would like to share with you today:

Our people are resilient, even if they continue to experience conflict. Our people have survived colonisation, foreign aggression, and interference, civil war and terrorism, natural disasters, famine, and disease. However, people still dare to hope for a better tomorrow. They still believe that they can achieve peace and a better legacy for the coming generations. This means that with the right support for their country and their people, it is possible to succeed.

The state has the ultimate responsibility for service delivery. Statebuilding is instrumental. There is no doubt that we need to build our institutions so that they are capable of serving our people's needs, but for that we need durable peace; otherwise, our efforts of building the state are all in vain.

How do you do it? Peace should be the number one priority upon which all actors have to be united. We need to foster country-led dialogue and reconciliation that brings about peace. The political leadership should put aside all their differences and aim to make and build peace. The mindset of rich and developed countries and their agents, including diplomats and experts, is to maintain dependence. They assert that the people of poor and underdeveloped countries cannot think for themselves, and therefore do not have the right to make decisions, and they proclaim their right to determine the future of these people.

There is a need for support to nurture the evolution of states, instead of imposing imported solutions. Academics know this fact very well, that the transformation of institutions takes time.

Peace cannot be imposed from outside. There is no solution and no nationbuilding without local ownership, from civil society to the media, from academia to the private sector, from culture and traditions to our religions. I believe that involving the local community in the reconciliation process, or in the development process, is not just a way for nationbuilding – it is the only way.

And that is why we, the g7+, strongly advocated for the inclusion of Sustainable Development Goal (SDG) 16 – to promote peaceful and inclusive societies – and SDG 17 – to strengthen global governance and partnership for sustainable development.

To be more effective, the g7+ is in the process of obtaining permanent observer status at the United Nations. I believe that when we achieve this later this year, we will be better able to pursue international peace.

Therefore, I feel humbled to receive this honorary doctorate degree and would like to dedicate it not only to those who have worked to promote peace but also to the children, women, and men who are suffering in wars and conflicts.

And while we are at the heart of ASEAN, I cannot finish without recognising ASEAN as an international success story, having established a region of peace, cooperation, and development.

Since Timor-Leste is part of Southeast Asia, we look forward to becoming a full-fledged member of ASEAN. We believe we have a lot to learn and we have experiences to share, strengthening the cooperation and peace in the region.

Let us all share in the hope that, in 30 years' time, the world achieves the true new international order, where peace is a reality for generations to come.

Thank you very much.

Kyoto University of the Arts, Honorary Award Ceremony Commemorative Speech.
Peace and Culture: The Arts in the Service of Peace

Tokyo, Japan
23 November 2021

Faculties, Departments, and Students from Kyoto University of the Arts,
Distinguished Guests,
Ladies and Gentlemen,

It is a great pleasure for me to be here at this University of the Arts to share a little of my vision on Culture and Peace with you, young artists.

I would like to start by thanking the Kyoto University of the Arts for the academic award it has bestowed upon me today. It is a great honour - and perhaps a source of inspiration for me to dedicate more time to painting, which is something I always loved, but which circumstances did not allow me to pursue.

Arts provide human beings with knowledge, harmony, and happiness. Arts build citizenship and consolidate development. This is true for any period of history, but never truer than in the most critical times, both for individuals and for the world as a whole.

However, not everyone has the gift possessed by you, my dearest students of the Kyoto University of the Arts. Sadly, creativity is a talent that is increasingly rare and that is not nurtured enough in our societies.

Faced with many competing priorities, politicians tend to pay little attention to culture. While they may consider it a less critical sector, I believe it is just the opposite. Culture is an important structural element in any society. I say that culture and the arts should be present in the lives of everyone, from toddlers to senior citizens, and particularly those in the higher echelons of leadership.

You, the creatives, may assist humankind in achieving what it needs the most: a world of peace, tolerance, mutual respect, and solidarity. You, my dear students, have the ability to work in a context of ambivalence, contradiction, complexity, and change, so common in today's world.

You have a superpower! You are able to transform the unpleasant world around us into something beautiful and stunning, which imbues us with hope. Culture, and particularly the arts, brings people and ideas closer and can have a liberating effect.

I think that is why I went back to painting and poetry during my seven long years as a political prisoner. I went from an idealistic guerrilla fighter to an idealistic prisoner, and it was culture that helped me to endure imprisonment.

While the Timorese resistance continued to fight against a dictatorial regime and an illegal occupation, I felt powerless, and the only place where I could find relief from my frustration and anguish was in the arts.

It was during this search for lost dignity and the determination to continue fighting the powers that be of an international system that was indifferent to the Timorese suffering that some people were kind enough to label me as a 'painter and poet'.

Back then I used to proclaim:

(...) Cultivate love
and love Peace!
We were brothers, we are brothers
In the pain of THE STRUGGLE
We are brothers, we will be brothers
In the freedom of PEACE.[4]

My dream of finding a world of peace did not grow dim, neither when I was inside a prison cell nor now that I am free once more. But there are others who remain prisoners – imprisoned in lives of poverty and conflict.

Millions of men, women, and children yearn for freedom. The world cannot take any more violence and misery. The world does not need more hubris, ambition, or opportunism. The world needs dialogue, and passions that mobilise people towards the common good.

The world needs the arts. And the world needs peace – what an enormous challenge and what a beautiful dream!

Your creativity may therefore be instrumental in establishing a world of peace, since nothing is more attractive than messages that appeal to our senses. Use that creativity to make a world of peace go viral.

---

4. *Mar Meu, poemas e pinturas* (1998), Xanana Gusmão.

Today's world is challenged and tested every day, in a state of disorder and chaos. World leaders, as well as their agencies and multinationals, are lost amongst rambling and selfish priorities.

In all global conferences, such as the latest climate conference in Glasgow, world leaders come together to smile and make statements asking the poor to become even poorer, while the countries polluting the planet the most, and which have achieved a comfortable level of development, sleep peacefully because they have banned plastic straws and drive electric cars to work.

And still, one cannot say that the summit was a failure. Despite everything, a few steps were taken to actually protect the planet, and a few commitments were strengthened. There was environmental awareness, and there was dialogue and communication seeking to respond to the most serious threat looming over the future of humankind.

Even though there is still some time left before the upcoming catastrophe, there is an increasing awareness as to the urgency of climate matters.

But what about the urgency to resolve migratory crises? Thousands of men, women, and children die in the Mediterranean trying to reach Europe, or in the Indian and the Pacific oceans trying to reach safe havens. At the US–Mexico border, people despair in overcrowded shelters, living in miserable conditions. But the height of cynicism is the Poland/Belarus border today, where thousands of people freeze at the doors of Europe.

What cultural legacy is this that creates monsters unable to respect human life? These are human beings – like you and me – running from war, hunger, and political persecution. How can they be used as political weapons?

And even understanding the pressure placed upon destination countries, how can we let people living in inhumane conditions slip from our minds for hours, days, months, even years?

World leaders insist on remaining steadfast in their perceptions. Mistrust and uncertainty undermine relations between people, between people and states, and even between states. Meanwhile, new areas of conflict arise throughout the world.

There is fear that refugees will bring their background of suffering and violence to recipient countries; that they will alienate rights and that they will take jobs, education, health care, and even principles and values from the citizens of those countries. Still, our powerlessness and passiveness on such vital matters make us all more inhumane.

While the supremacy of the strongest and the richest prevails, we will see the growth of the most fragile and the poorest. As long as the world continues to harbour feelings of ethnocentrism, racism, and xenophobia, as well as other types of prejudice and fundamentalism, stability will be under threat everywhere.

Still, the International Community insists on ignoring the root causes of problems. Instead, it continues to hold that the endless wave of refugees is only a by-product of wars, which is to say the absence of peace in the countries of origin.

We are constantly reminded that there is no oasis of peace and security in places where there is misery, war, and conflict. And yet the West continues not to acknowledge and face the consequences of its own policies, preferring instead to continue stoking the fires of mistrust and uncertainty in the future — your future.

You will recall that over these nearly two years of COVID-19 pandemic, there were many who wanted to believe that this was a unique opportunity for building a better world. There was much talk about cooperation and scientific breakthroughs. There was talk about solidarity inside and across borders – that once a vaccine was created, no one should be left behind.

Unfortunately, vaccination rates in Africa are extremely low. This is a flagrant example of the failure of international solidarity. It is a failure because we continue to lack the capacity to assist those who need it the most. It is also a failure because our selfishness makes us blind to the risks of a new public health crisis.

It turns out that the pandemic did not bring the cure for all the ills of humankind. Neither did the climate emergency, nor watching the suffering of thousands of people through the media to which we all have access. It seems there is no ill in the world that is able to build sound and disinterested international cooperation that puts people at the centre of every agenda.

On the contrary, international solidarity in action quickly turns into forgetfulness in action.

Tragedies keep occurring, one after the other, while the number of victims keeps piling up.

A couple of months ago, there was much talk about the Afghan tragedy. Much was said about the Afghan women and girls who, after having lost so much, were now about to be deprived of their most precious asset: hope.

After nearly two decades of an intervention that failed to produce lasting results, the US called 'mission accomplished' in Kabul and departed, leaving behind a country in chaos. Almost two decades preaching democracy and human rights, only to end up with more deaths and a terrifying void.

This is why it is time to revise engagement paradigms encapsulated into civilising missions that seek to implement exotic concepts that never had roots in the target countries.

And yet, this is not merely a matter of human rights and freedom. The Taliban government inherited a miserable country without drinkable water, sufficient food, or the most basic conditions for people to survive. This happens in many places of the world, not just in the Middle East.

Let us please take notice to see whether geo-strategic influence and realpolitik will once again prevail. And let us see whether those who publicly talked about the duty of solidarity will not be the first ones to close borders on a problem that is just starting.

I believe it is essential to have greater international cooperation well beyond the global public health crisis. Inequalities across and inside our borders are appalling. We must eliminate the disparities in the access to knowledge, education, modern technologies, and tools for human development, which became even clearer during the pandemic.

If we truly want to build a world of peace, then we must focus on capacity building.

Without reducing instability and economic inequalities within countries and between countries, any global sustainable development plan, like the one featured over the 17 Sustainable Development Goals, will be merely a pipe dream.

We want to believe in the commitments made in the 2030 Agenda, in which the UN elected peace as a cornerstone, acknowledging its importance to global development. And yet, in the countdown to this common agenda goal, over 1.5 billion people live in countries where development is compromised by fragility and violence.

I know from experience in my country that 'Without peace, there is no development', and that 'Without development, there is no peace'.

It is urgent that we improve multilateral diplomacy and that we adopt preventive diplomacy, so that events do not escalate into conflicts, particularly since the reaction time of the international community is slower than the speed at which events unfold. A more fruitful relationship between the international community and its agencies on one side, and fragile and conflict or post-conflict countries on the other, might correct this time lapse.

Your Excellencies,
Ladies and Gentlemen,

The experience of Timor-Leste as a small and fragile country without resources that decided to fight for its independence based on international law, and which, after achieving that goal, chose reconciliation over past grievances, opting to leave the past behind in order to focus on the future, led us to take another key step years later: that of fighting for our full maritime sovereignty.

In this final delimitation of maritime boundaries, we faced once again a powerful neighbour, this time at the negotiation table. Whether dealing with Indonesia or Australia, our perception remains the same. The purpose of international law is to lead to peaceful solutions, and as such we believe in the basic principle that all states are equal.

Previously, we knew that we were but one million amongst the hundreds of millions of people all over the world who yearn for peace, stability, and dignity, but whose intrinsic fragility does not always allow it. Now, we also know that fragile countries must be supported in terms of achieving equal access to international legal mechanisms, including the ones for resolving maritime disputes.

Our experiences in the struggle for liberation and in breaking away from a situation of instability and fragility led us to want to share experiences on reconciliation, statebuilding, and peacebuilding. Thus, in 2010, we joined a group, the g7+, which shares the same challenges and ambitions. This is an intergovernmental group that brings together 20 conflict-affected countries from Africa, Asia, the Pacific, and the Caribbean, which are transitioning from conflict to resilience.

Our member states have very different backgrounds and geographic, historical, cultural, and political characteristics. Still, they all have people suffering and dreaming of a world of peace.

Amongst our various goals, we want to:

- Share experiences on reconciliation and peace, through the Fragile-to-Fragile (F2F) Cooperation program;
- Take part in the global discussion on sustainable development in fragile states and contribute to a new world order where states like ours are represented, and where our voice is heard, particularly when discussions are about us.

- Strengthen internal resilience and the relationship with international partners. In addition to civil war, terrorism, natural disasters, hunger, disease, and despair, our people also have to deal with foreign condescension and interference. And yet, we hold on to the hope of a better tomorrow – a brighter future for the next generations.
- Build our states according to the best practices, while respecting our realities and idiosyncrasies. We are aware that we need to invest in consolidating our agencies, so as to respond to the needs of our people.
- Promote country-led dialogue, both internally and with foreign partners. This requires political leaders to set aside all their antagonisms and to fight the status quo of internal dependency. We are the ones most responsible for our fate, and it is up to us to contribute the most to any solution. As such, it is concluded that peace can never be imposed by mechanisms that are alien to us. Instead, it must be an internal process that engages every agent in our society towards the collective interest.

Dear Students,

The g7+ is but a meeting of cultures from countries that are already multicultural, in view of their common history of mostly European colonisation.

And while our meetings are almost always difficult, because we are speaking about our own past or present hardships, they still have their beauty. Indeed, when we open our hearts to talk about stories of hatred towards others or towards ourselves, stories of intolerance and despair, stories of tiredness in words and actions... we become closer to those others.

We understand the beauty of other people. The beauty of other practices, cultures, and arts. We understand their weaknesses and expectations. It becomes a process of reconciliation, something that is so direly needed in many parts of the world.

That which is a condition of fragility may be transformed into trust and create space for dialogue and mutual respect. And where there is dialogue and respect, there are conditions for negotiating and resolving divergences, and for moving forward with the ambition of achieving peace and sustainable development.

Your Excellencies,
Ladies and Gentlemen,

It is time to cultivate a culture of interdependence, which is something that we already have. It is time to return to multilateralism, which does not threaten the sovereignty of different countries. In fact, it does just the opposite.

The key problem today is the complete lack of trust between people, and particularly between people and the agencies that lead them, both at the national and international level. This mistrust and disbelief in agencies and their policies is detrimental to the creation of conditions for building peace, or even combating the global pandemic.

People do not look after one another. Societies do not look after one another. This leads to global despair, instead of consolidating a culture of general benevolence.

It is when our problems are not met with a response that our actions become increasingly individualised, in accordance with our cultural roots. Hence, the importance of knowing and respecting the culture of each individual and each society.

These cultural roots must also be taken into account when it comes to climate matters.

If we are indeed serious about mitigating climate change, then over a period of little more than three decades we will have to change our culture all over the world. This goes from the manner in which we see our subsistence or market economies, to the manner in which we eat, dress, travel, and even warm ourselves.

This is an enormous challenge. It is a collective challenge. However, those who contributed the most to this situation of environmental fragility must also be the ones to take the first step forward, respecting the needs and situation of others in the world.

We do not want to leave anyone behind. Still, due to inequalities built over hundreds of years, there are countries that should take the lead in this fight and carry most of the weight. This is the only way we will be able to save humankind.

The reason why I am telling you about all of this is that art, in its various shapes, is also a mode of intervention and demonstration.

Works of art may lead us to expose, question, and even change various issues in our daily lives, which may address both individual or global concerns.

You know this better than anyone. You know that while art may be contemplative, it is also often expositive or provocative. Art wakes and shakes consciousness to different realities, and can thus cause positive ruptures in attitudes, behaviours, and systems that need to be changed.

Dear Students,

In addition to breath-taking beauty, my half-island of Timor-Leste has magnificent cultural wealth. With a strong connection to nature and our ancestors, but also with the fusion of several ethnicities, cultures, and civilisations, we can say that we have the perfect raw materials for a world of art.

Another key aspect of our wealth is our youth, which represents over half of our population. Many of our young people are hugely creative and talented. Sadly, most lack access to opportunities to develop their abilities.

I say that all young people living in free and democratic societies today cannot forget those who have yet to attain those rights. I urge you not to forget those young people all over the world who possibly have talents like yours, but who lack the opportunity to explore and develop those talents.

In view of this, we are trying to develop partnerships with education establishments in order to enable Timorese young people to achieve their potential. As such, I would like to congratulate the Kyoto University of the Arts for its initiative of establishing a partnership with one of our art institutions in Timor-Leste.

We must work together to create a new civilisation moved by artistic culture and a philosophy based on constant love for nature and humankind.

Most importantly, let us not continue responding to hatred with more hatred. Let us instead respond with knowledge and art.

As the great Mahatma Gandhi once said, 'The art of living is about making life a work of art'.

It is here at this university that your work begins. May that work – all of your works – have a foundation of peace.

Thank you very much.

Sophia University, Honourary Award Ceremony, Commemorative Speech: *Shaping a New Era of Peace and Development in a Post-COVID World*

Tokyo, Japan
26 November 2021

H.E. Prof. Dr. Yoshiaki Terumichi, President of Sophia University,
H.E. Prof. Dr. Tsutomu Sakuma S.J., Chancellor of Sophia School,
H.E. Prof. Dr. Shintaro Fukutake, Professor of Faculty of Global Studies,
Excellencies, Members of the Academic Council,
Faculties, Departments, and Students from Sophia University,
Distinguished Guests,
Ladies and Gentlemen,

I would like to start by thanking the Sophia University for hosting this ceremony.

It is a great honour and an enormous privilege for me to receive this academic award. I am humbled to accept the Honorary Doctorate from this Catholic institution of higher education, in the amazing city of Tokyo.

In addition to internationally acknowledged academic excellence, your century-old institution has a long history of promoting humanist values and principles that are vital for the young people of today. Living up to the legacy of Saint Ignatius of Loyola, who worked with dedication to make the world a better place, Sophia University is making its contribution to a more peaceful world.

This university cannot be separated from the resiliency of the Jesuits; nor from Japan and the Japanese people. Japan, with its impressive post-war reconstruction, is an inspiration to the world in general, and to Timor-Leste in particular.

Ever since it was established, this most beautiful sanctuary of global education has been promoting globalisation and the internationalisation of human development, cooperation, and peace, so that no one is left behind in this unequal and ever-changing world.

Those who know a little about me know that I was never able to attend higher education. Instead, I had to enrol in the 'school of life'.

1. Post-war

My childhood was a happy one, even though I was poor. I ran freely on soft green grass in one of the many beautiful areas of my country. At the time, two sisters of mine attended the boarding school of the Canossian Mothers, who made me believe in angels …

My father was a primary school teacher. He would read me Catholic magazines and teach me many things, including stories from World War II. My father was involved in politics, although not a politician. He was one of those people who, in exchange for a pittance, helped the colonial power – the Portuguese – rekindle the notion of 'cross and sword', while never reneging on his own origins and traditions.

I think that is why I am starting my speech this way. My father was a man of principles. A mild-mannered man, yet sure of himself. He wanted to break away from the vision of a small world where children grow without ambition.

My father wanted his children to be able to dream of something more than a life of poverty.

That is how I came to study at the Dare seminary, which was headed by Jesuit priests. Although a rebellious youngster, much of what I am today developed during that time. I got the taste for reading from my father, but my taste for languages, numbers, and cultures came from the time I spent at the seminary. I learned values and principles. I also learned about the importance of trust and the will to serve – particularly those most vulnerable and most in need of solidarity.

As you know, I grew up during the post-war period.

While the world was dividing into two sides to fight for global dominance, we Timorese were uniting around a collective sense of identity.

A unique identity that, despite being indigenous, allowed itself to adopt moral and Christian tenets; an ancestral, historical, and cultural identity that allowed itself to merge with new cultures, habits, and traditions; and an identity that, even while supressed by the colonial power, became increasingly pro-independence.

Even during Portuguese rule, which lasted for centuries, we managed to create a territorial notion associated with our people with a specific personality, creating the spark for a people–nation that wanted to be sovereign. All this in a small half-island, plus an enclave in the other half, out of the more than 17,000 islands, both large and small, in the enormous archipelago that is Indonesia.

The story of our brutal occupation, which continued for almost a quarter of a century, is well known. I believe that so is our resilience and the sacrifices we made for independence. And yet we now know that, for some time, we too were victims of the Cold War. In addition to boasting great resources, Indonesia relied on a geopolitical alliance and the international hypocrisy of the time.

I believe that people everywhere were hoping for a new world order that would bring stability, economic and social stability, and development.

As such, we Timorese learned to look at the world with critical thinking, understanding that the disintegration of the ideals of European superiority and the fragmentation of the bipolar world might enable us to continue to fight for self-determination.

This concept was not invented by the Timorese. Indeed, while nationalist ambitions have led to many bloody wars in the past, this could still not subjugate the will of the people to be free.

Even back in World War II, when the Timorese woke up to find a war being fought by others in our own land, we were ready to make sacrifices for something that was not yet truly ours – our homeland.

Even though the United Nations, the UN, supported the decolonisation movements back in the '60s, it was only in the '70s, with the fall of the Portuguese dictatorship, that we knew for sure that the right to freedom and independence was not just a pipe dream. It had a legal and political basis that was founded in international law.

Still, at the time we did not know the universal principles of the right to independence. We resisted, because the alternative was extermination or total domination by a foreign power. As such, we proclaimed that 'To resist is to win'.

It was only in 1986, once the necessary political conditions had been met, that Portugal began to do everything in its power – in the spheres of diplomacy and international law – to enable self-determination in Timor-Leste.

And it was in 1989 that our world – everyone's world – began to change. The fall of the Berlin Wall heralded a new international system marked by multilateralism.

2. New World Order

For a certain period in history there was honest and serious dialogue between states and nations, in the search for peace. However, in Timor-Leste, we had to wait another long decade.

In 1992, I went from an idealistic guerrilla fighter to an idealistic prisoner at Cipinang prison, in Jakarta. This was precisely one year after the infamous Santa Cruz massacre, where Indonesian soldiers killed almost 300 young people who were attending the funeral of another young man. That massacre was 30 years ago this month.

While I continued to declare myself a Portuguese citizen, in accordance with international law, in my mind I was a citizen of Timor-Leste who was a victim of illegal imprisonment in the same way that my country was a victim of illegal occupation.

In my defence, in the Indonesian courts, I said to the international community that it was 'time to prove we are facing the new world order. We need actions that indicate a break with the situations inherited from the past'.[5]

Sadly, nearly three decades later, I continue to make the same plea.

Still, during that new dawn, states which had never shared the Western traditions of the Rule of Law, democracy, human rights, economic rights, social rights, and a market economy started to become infused with new concepts. It was during this period that the European Union was formally established, that the number of democracies grew, and that societies and nations were pacified through negotiation and processes of technical assistance.

From Latin America to Africa and Asia, we can find positive examples on virtually every continent. This includes the normalisation of the situation between Iraq and Kuwait, the autonomy plan for the West Bank and Gaza Strip, the independence of Namibia, the end of apartheid in South Africa and, as we saw, the start of the democratic transition in Indonesia, which walked hand in hand with the right of the Timorese to vote for their independence.

Still, what we need to highlight about this period are the movements in favour of peace and a collective effort towards greater diplomacy when resolving crises and conflicts, as opposed to a paradigm of mistrust, imposition, and menace.

It is not a coincidence that Timor-Leste earned its right to independence through a referendum held in 1999 and formally acknowledged in 2002. This was a decade when a number of problems across the world were resolved and when the relationship between peoples and nations became healthier.

I can say that my country is a result of the success of multilateralism.

'The independence of Timor-Leste owes much to the UN. Still, Timor-Leste also gave much to the UN and to the world, at a time when the UN needed this help. Timor-Leste proved that international law can be put into practice. It proved that the UN and multilateralism work; that they are relevant; and

---

5. *Xanana Gusmão* (1994), Timor-Leste, Um Povo, Uma Pátria, Edições Colibri.

that they have a positive impact in the lives of thousands of people. It also proved that conflicts can be resolved at the negotiation table.' I did not say this; it was the UN Secretary-General, António Guterres.[6]

After the destruction left by our occupiers, who were enraged at the victory we achieved through democracy, Timor-Leste rose from the ashes. This was thanks to the heroic resiliency of the resistance and all of the Timorese people, who worked from scratch to build a country where they could finally dream of something more than a life of poverty for their children.

As you know, I was the first elected President of the Republic of Timor-Leste. I can honestly say that the first few years of independence were not easier than the years of occupation. We had to learn how to be a state and how to be a nation. This was no small feat, since our people were hurt and scarred from years of occupation. This resulted in a period where we had cyclical crises of violence.

Fortunately, we were able to rely on the United Nations, development partnerships, and international solidarity. With great effort, we succeeded in keeping the promise we made to the West during the years of occupation. We never wanted to jeopardise stability in the region.

Not only did we keep our word, but we advocated dialogue and peaceful political actions in the region and in the world, namely through the g7+, a group of around 20 fragile and conflict-affected states that share their experiences and promote peacebuilding and statebuilding, reconciliation, and sustainable prosperity in an unequal world.

We were also able to acknowledge that we do not just share an island with Indonesia – we also share a future. Today we walk side by side, in friendship and cooperation. Our reconciliation is a model of good will, focusing on the future and on development, rather than being a tale of bitterness and conflict.

We also had to look inwards. We recognised that it is sometimes harder to reconcile amongst ourselves than with our 'enemies'. This led us to realise that we had to come together and work on our internal differences. As a nation, we acknowledged that we could not build a state without building peace within ourselves.

And so, we started a process of dialogue, seeking to engage all of our people. We adopted a new political stance when dealing with our people and our institutions, searching for solutions. We dealt honestly with the root causes of our problems, through a bottom-up approach, putting the interests of the whole above any individual interests.

6. *Bárbara Reis & Fernando Neves* (2019), 'O Negociador – Revelações Diplomáticas sobre Timor Leste (1997-1999)', D. Quixote, Lisboa.

Across the world, however, and despite some improvements, too many people remained trapped by hunger, poverty, conflict, war, and dire inequality. This only became worse, following the attack on the World Trade Center in September 2001.

3. From 9/11 to the COVID-19 pandemic

The new world order turned into a new world *disorder*.

The world became governed by political and economic supremacy. Despite the military power of the United States of America, which reacted ferociously to the 2001 attacks, we were left with a multipolar world, where a new orchestra set the world's trends – or divisions.

The truth is that the new world order resulted in an appalling contrast between the rich North and the poor South, but for a few exceptions. And worse than this disparity is the 'colonialist' condescension of the rich, telling others what they should do in their own countries.

As someone who has known more wars and witnessed more tragedies than I can forget, I am convinced that the nations of the world — their leaders and their peoples — are not doing enough to achieve international peace.

Every action by government agents, the private sector, development partners, and each private citizen should seek to advance peacebuilding and statebuilding. Dialogue and preventive diplomacy are much more likely to succeed than any type of military action, and will prevent the sacrifice of countless lives.

In 2011, UN Secretary-General Ban Ki-Moon defined preventive diplomacy as 'diplomatic action taken, at the earliest possible stage, to prevent disputes from arising between parties, to prevent existing disputes from escalating into conflicts, and to limit the spread of the latter when they occur'.[7] And yet, there are world leaders who discuss peace agreements at lunch and sign arms deals at dinner.

Most conflicts in fragile countries are the result of hegemonic policies by powerful nations and/or their multinationals. Fragile countries are often used as battlefields in which other parties wage their wars.

On the other hand, peace often depends on a deeply personal commitment. And it is in universities such as this one, with so many talented young people, that we may start to make a difference. Education for peace must begin in our schools and our universities. It will have an enormous

---

7. Report of the Secretary-General, UN (2011), 'Preventive Diplomacy: Delivering Results'.

impact on every aspect of public and private life. That is the hope that young people give us – that your skills and knowledge may contribute to a more just and tolerant world.

You can learn from past and current mistakes to build a better future.

I know it must be tiring for you, the 'men and women of tomorrow', to listen to the same things over and over again. That you will be the ones to put into practice what the 'men and women of today' only said in words. Still, that is what hope is all about.

Looking at history, one cannot forget the interventions in Iraq and Afghanistan, where wars were started in the name of democracy and human rights – wars that are yet to end.

We cannot forget the movements of the Arab Spring, which challenged dictatorial regimes, only to become, instead, a 'long winter'.

We cannot forget South Sudan, Somalia, the Central African Republic, Mozambique, Ethiopia, Yemen and so many other countries. Africa is wounded from the inside and despised from the outside.

The conflict between Palestine and Israel, one of the longest in history... are we really to believe that divides are so deep as to leave no room for understanding?

How much longer will democracy continue to be a mirage in Myanmar? Tensions in this country have been high for decades, and are made worse by the Rohingya issue, which is strongly condemned by Western countries.

I had the opportunity of visiting Myanmar, like I have visited Afghanistan, the Central African Republic, South Sudan, and others. There I met with the leaders of state and civil society. The conclusion was always the same: There are always different perspectives on the same problem, and regardless of the perspective, one cannot look at a problem through only one lens.

The Rohingya minority is not the only problem in Myanmar. The Burmese are also subject to the pressure of alienation of their cultural and identity. And in Afghanistan, the problem goes beyond the relationship with the Taliban. There are many other causes and factors that sometimes escape the Western lens.

It is known that wherever there is conflict, misery, and violence, there are people who need to flee. I refuse to accept the international community's selfishness on this matter. Timor-Leste has had thousands of refugees. In this century alone, we have had many internally displaced persons. Would anyone in their right mind abandon their home and all that they know, unless they are in a desperate situation?

From the people in detention centres in Australia, to the Mexico–US border and those trying to enter Europe, they are all human beings – like me and you – desperately in search of peace.

I understand that the latitude and longitude of these crises is such that they do not cause us to lose sleep over them.

Still, let us not fool ourselves. We are all responsible for our passiveness in preventing crises.

Indeed, we are complicit, whether due to impotence or indifference, electing leaders who promote war and conflict. More recently, at the Polish border of the EU with Belarus, refugees have become pawns in the hands of political interests. This is complete disregard for human life!

We also have climate change, an issue that led to over 100 world leaders holding a two-week meeting in Glasgow. Based on scientific evidence, climate change is being felt in various countries and threatens the survival of the small island developing states (SIDS), and, ultimately, all humankind.

These are threats to peace and development like no other. If people commit atrocities over oil and minerals, imagine what they would do for a few drops of water or a handful of cereal.

And you, young students, know this. Japan is one of the countries most affected by climate change: storms, heat waves, and typhoons, causing death, destruction, and huge financial losses. Meanwhile, there are people in Madagascar reduced to eating grasshoppers, and even mud.

Your Excellencies,
Ladies and Gentlemen,

We see world leaders and organisations trying to respond to humanitarian crises, increasing hunger and misery, and the impacts of climate change, and still we continue not to address the root causes of problems. We continue not to apply the concept of 'diplomatic action taken, at the earliest possible stage', which is to say that we continue not to act pre-emptively.

Even those who did not have the opportunity of attending school know that there can be no lasting peace and no development solutions without first casting seeds and tending the roots, so that the plants may grow. Furthermore, each seed requires different care, and each fruit may turn out to be promising or disastrous.

To make an already tragic scenario even worse, it seems to me that the previous US administration - a key country in the international system - decided that multilateralism was a limitation to its sovereignty. As if any country, no matter how powerful, could prevail alone against the challenges that afflict all of humankind in today's interconnected world!

It pains me to see that some human beings have difficulty accepting that an international system of open dialogue and genuine negotiation may be more advantageous than a system of confrontation and of 'Me first'.

Everyone wants to be sovereign, and Timor-Leste is no exception. We all have national interests to protect and voters who hold us accountable. Still, without dialogue across borders, there is no peace and no sustainable development within borders.

I am currently the Chief Negotiator for the Final Delimitation of Maritime Boundaries with Australia and Indonesia. We continue to rely on the international system to achieve full sovereignty over our maritime jurisdiction. Indeed, while we are a small country in size and population, we believe in the basic principle that all states are equal.

After years of failed negotiations with Australia on where the boundary should lie, we managed to achieve a satisfactory result through the compulsive conciliation process under the United Nations Convention on the Law of the Sea (UNCLOS). This negotiation mechanism was difficult, and sometimes downright exasperating, but with good will and mutual respect for the interests of both parties, we succeeded in defending our respective sovereignty.

We are currently holding consultations on delimitating boundaries with Indonesia, agreeing that these negotiations will also be held in accordance with international law and UNCLOS. Although it is expected that such a negotiation process will necessarily entail some tension, we know that nothing must jeopardise the peace and stability we sacrificed so much to achieve.

In the international arena, everyone 'must give some and take some from the other', so that no one loses everything, particularly their life, their dignity, and their hope.

4. A new era of peace and development in a post-COVID world

History gives us no great reasons to be optimistic. There is not a favourable planetary climate, in every sense of the word 'climate'.

Still, today, I want to be an optimist.

I want to believe in the extraordinary intelligence of human beings and in their ability to do good things. At a time when we hear about a new industrial revolution based on artificial intelligence, how could we not be optimistic that we will be able to find solutions for the common good, instead of increasing disparities?

As some countries move on from the disaster brought by the COVID-19 pandemic and the geopolitical map is redrawn, it is imperative that we move towards global peace and development.

The pandemic interrupted the normal flow of history and exposed many of the weaknesses of the international order. And yet, despite the closing of borders and the economic, social, and institutional crises all over the world, despite the fact that the poorest countries became even poorer, and despite the overall weakening of democracy, there was a special moment in this tragedy that must be seized upon.

So many people rightly believed that the pandemic was a unique opportunity to build a better world.

So many people responded collectively to the need for isolation and social distancing, and understood the value of collective action. Many people suddenly found their children deprived of access to education and/or the necessary technologies to pursue that education, and therefore feared for their future. Many people suffered with the interruption of access to raw materials, goods, services, markets, and consumers. For many people, it was the first time they were unable to cross borders at will.

Did we learn anything from this? Do we now feel more empathy towards others for whom these difficulties are part of their daily lives? I doubt it.

Perhaps we will understand better if we know that some countries in Africa have vaccination rates below 1%. Not only is this tragic for these countries, but it also creates a risk of new variants emerging, which may lead to a new public health crisis and render useless the higher vaccination rates achieved in the richest countries. Perhaps it is time to understand that no one is safe until everyone is safe.

This is the time to revise engagement paradigms so that they contribute to peace. This is the time to act pre-emptively, together, in order to resolve crises that affect us all.

No one can do everything alone and no one knows everything about everything. Some know what it is to live in inequality, while others know what is like to theorise about it. We need to build a bridge between these two groups. We must have greater representation and more perspectives from all corners of the globe when discussing issues and challenges, so that solutions are indeed global. This can only be achieved by bringing fragile states closer to the international community and its agencies.

While only the vision of the strongest prevails, development will never be for everyone.

Thus, we must return to multilateralism.

Last September, the UN Secretary-General, António Guterres, launched a document titled 'Our Common Agenda', focusing on crisis prevention instead of 'business as usual', where we pay the price for the inability to foresee crises and to plan responses in good time. I should add that this price is always steeper for those who are actually living through the crises. I believe that a common agenda that is centred on the dignity of the human person is a good starting point, provided that it is taken seriously.

It is undeniable that the UN and the Security Council need to be reformed in order to be more efficient and effective. The permanent members of the Security Council should favour international diplomacy over confrontation. The UN is still the key arena for multilateralism, and it can be improved with everyone's contribution.

People speak about a changing world, but they do not say much about what has to be changed individually, or as a society. There are no right or wrong perspectives – instead, there are tensions that do not result in the reconciliation of perspectives, actions, and intents.

We need individual change in human beings. One Greta Thunberg is not enough; we need several Gretas, and for every issue that troubles us. If we do not want extremist acts on our borders, then we cannot allow extremist positions within our own borders. We must work to ensure a new international order that serves everyone's interests.

We need new heroes such as Mahatma Gandhi, Nelson Mandela, Kim Dae-jung, Martin Luther King, Kofi Annan, Malala Yousafzai, and a recently deceased Portuguese man called Jorge Sampaio, who among other things created the Global Platform for Higher Education, which was initially meant to assist Syrian students and was recently expanded to include, as well as Afghan students, all students who have refugee status or who have been affected by humanitarian emergencies or crises.

We need the courage of those who dare to defend causes that are not just theirs but everyone's. This is the way we can move towards a world of peace.

This world needs more courage. We need to dream of the impossible, until the impossible becomes real.

Everyone has this power – or maybe even this mission – particularly the young people in attendance today. You must never forget that even in the most complex game of chess, a simple pawn can change the course of the game and secure a win.

Your Excellencies,
Ladies and Gentlemen,

I know that I have already taken much of your time, but before I conclude I would like to raise two more aspects that I believe to be essential.

First, the importance of education to a world of peace and development. In my view, educating children and young people is part of preventive diplomacy. Enabling access to the tools that allow young people to fulfil their destiny of participating in a more developed and peaceful future is the best investment any country can make, particularly in the case of young people coming from situations of fragility.

In Timor-Leste, the St. Ignatius of Loyola College has been making a difference. Established in 2014, it has already produced its first graduates. More than just a school, the St. Ignatius of Loyola College may be a significant part of the future of a country where a third of our population is illiterate and over 50% of our population are under 20 years old.

We appreciate the support of the Jesuit Education Project, particularly the support from Japan, which allows our young people to continue their higher education in order to make a difference. This means more young people who can now play their part in achieving the impossible.

Secondly, the Climate Summit, which concluded around two weeks ago.

We cannot consider that this summit was a success in terms of commitments for mitigating the major threats looming over our future. This should come as no surprise. Indeed, if we cannot solve the pressing issues of today, we could hardly be expected to solve those of the near future.

If we are not troubled by children who die of malnutrition today, then the idea of children dying a few decades from now should trouble us even less. Still, at least world leaders are becoming aware and are negotiating. We even had some progress in some areas.

Civil society was well represented, like the thousands of individuals who took to the streets to put pressure on political decision makers all over the world.

As much as this summit failed, it is still a success. To bring together almost 200 countries to discuss agreements to address a crisis that many have not yet felt is no easy task, particularly since national interests will always prevail. I say this because I have some experience of negotiations, albeit just between two countries.

When catastrophes arrive at our borders it is likely that the leaders who sat in Glasgow will no longer be among us. However, *you* will be. You and your children, and your children's children. Collective action must start today. Unfair as it may be, this is once again in your hands.

We all know that an alliance on climate requires a good relationship between the states entering that alliance. In view of the 'important absentees', it seemed to me that there were more smiles than pacts and commitments. It is the reflection of how things are today.

Those smiling tend to be the ones who have contributed the most to climate degradation, rather than those who are suffering as a result of those actions, since the latter could not even convey their voices properly, let alone their smiles. Thus, developing countries can very well see this summit as a failure.

Nevertheless, and because I want to be an optimist, we cannot lose heart as long as we do not go another six years until the next agreement, like we did between the Paris Agreement and COP26, and provided that negotiations made in good faith continue, correcting mistakes and amending commitments to make them more ambitious, but still feasible.

And speaking of commitments, as the Special Representative of the Government of Timor-Leste for the Blue Economy, I must ask what commitments have been made concerning the health of the ocean – just one ocean, because it connects us all.

This asset of humankind represents over 70% of the planet's surface and absorbs one third of the world's carbon dioxide. Its grass, seaweed, and mangrove forests have the potential to contribute, with over 20% of the necessary carbon emission reductions. However, I do not think the ocean is being taken into account when discussing ways to protect the planet from global warming. We are also failing to address the issue of increasing ocean pollution, particularly from plastics.

Protecting the ocean is protecting the planet, and protecting humankind is not leaving anyone behind. This is achieved through responsible economic development.

Hopefully, the opportunity to protect our planet will not be neglected in the next summit. Incidentally, the word 'opportunity' derives from the Latin seafaring expression *ob portum veniens*, meaning 'coming towards a port'. It was created by sailors who had to wait for the right combination of wind, currents, and tide to be able to navigate successfully into port. That is to say, they had to make the most of the right opportunity.

When will we have the opportunity to offer individual effort towards a collective benefit? Humankind needs cooperation towards the common good, the sooner the better.

If I may quote something I wrote back when I was a political prisoner:

Today, in the shackles of anger, I recall guerrilla fighters who died in battle. And I want to die in a life free from prison. So that I may give life to those who knew how to die.[8]

There is a lot going on in the world that merits our anger – issues much more serious than refusing to be administered a vaccine that is the outcome of cooperation by the world of science towards the common good. In the post-COVID world, my only wish is that our efforts may honour all the victims of poverty, violence, war, and climate change, as well as the more than five million people who died as a direct result of the pandemic.

Thank you very much.

---

8. Xanana Gusmão (1994), 'Timor-Leste, Um Povo, Uma Pátria', Edições Colibri

Upon Being Awarded an Honorary Doctorate Degree in Humane Letters by The American University of Phnom Penh

Phnom Penh, Cambodia
6 May 2023

Your Excellency Dr Chea Vandeth, Minister of Post and Telecom of the Kingdom of Cambodia, Founder of AUPP,

Honourable Dr Guido Gianasso, Member of the AUPP Board of Trustees,

Dr Raymond Leos, AUPP Vice President for Academic and Student Affairs,

Dr Vereonia Lane Dasom, Director of Students Affairs, AUPP,

Dr Jose E Mora, Professor and Global Affairs Chair, AUPP,

Faculty Staffs, Dear Graduate Students,

Ladies and Gentlemen,

I would like to start by thanking the American University of Phnom Penh for hosting this ceremony in which I will be awarded an honorary doctorate degree that I am humbled and honoured to accept.

It is a great privilege for me to visit this modern academic institution located in the vibrant capital city of Cambodia. The Kingdom of Cambodia has provided inspiration to the world and, in particular, its youngest Southeast Asian neighbour, Timor-Leste.

We are inspired not only by the beauty and spirituality of Cambodia but also its history of overcoming suffering. The strong cultural values of Cambodia, along with dialogue and tolerance, enabled your country to rebuild itself as a peaceful and modern nation.

As we are at a university, surrounded by talented and promising young people, I think it is fitting to tell you how precious peace is. Indeed, it is the most important universal principle.

We are living in troubled times where global challenges are overwhelming. Recently, we have endured a global pandemic, climate emergencies, humanitarian and security crises, and social and economic disparities. And yet, humanity has no plight more decadent than war.

I believe that every problem created by humans can be solved by humans. We have both an individual and collective responsibility to promote peace, to educate towards peace, to learn from history's mistakes, and to build a peaceful future for each and every one of us.

I am speaking to you from experience, having endured a quarter century of war. The tragedies, sacrifices, and suffering caused by war scar not only us, who have lived through them, but also future generations, who have their social and economic development compromised.

In a way, this explains why so many post-conflict countries continue to be what we call fragile states. And that is provided they do not have the misfortune of becoming failed states.

While throughout the world there is poverty, as well as war and conflict, not much is done to prevent this. Even though we are more than six decades on from the moment when the concept of preventive diplomacy was born. (In the 1950s, the Secretary-General of the United Nations was already advocating crisis prevention.)

One of the battlefields in which Timor-Leste fought to gain its independence was the halls of the UN, an organisation dreamed by idealists seeking to achieve consensus between states towards peace, security, and collective development. It was precisely under the banner of the UN that our people had the opportunity to vote for independence at a popular consultation held in 1999.

When Timor-Leste became the 191st member state of the UN, back in 20 May 2002, we were a country that was small, poor, and deeply traumatised by war. Our first steps as an independent nation were supported by the international community and international agencies. We shall never forget their solidarity at such a difficult time.

As such, when the 2030 Agenda for Sustainable Development was approved back in 2015, we rejoiced because the United Nations had made peace a cornerstone, and in doing so, acknowledged its importance to sustainable development.

We believed in the global architecture and in the promises and commitments of world leaders. We wanted to believe in a global system that promotes peace beyond the rhetoric of international resolutions and reports. Unfortunately, whether by inertia or hubris, whether by economic, financial, political, or ideological ambition, around two billion people are currently living in areas affected by conflict. That is to say that a quarter of the world's population have their development compromised by fragility and violence.

I believe that you, young people, have the courage to ask why this is. Why is it that people, communities, and countries cannot simply live in peace with one another?

Excellencies, Young Students,

I do not claim to have a response for you today. Instead, I would like to share the experience of Timor-Leste, whose history shares common traits with many other fragile and/or conflict-affected countries, particularly those that, like us, have lived through colonialism and imperialism, which is to say, have endured the greed and power of others.

History tells us that policies of domination and exploitation usually breed revolt and resistance, as well as political awareness that feeds national identity and the desire for freedom and independence.

In the 1960s, Timor-Leste and other colonies entered the radar of the UN and other pro-decolonisation movements, becoming considered as 'Non-Autonomous Territories'. This took place in a rather adverse geopolitical context governed by the vested interests of the Cold War.

We recall the role of key global players, such as the US, France, Germany, and the UK. Alongside their regional allies, these countries decided on the supposed 'best solutions for world peace'.

In the case of Timor-Leste, the fall of the Portuguese dictatorship in 1974 had the Timorese hoping for freedom and independence. This feeling was short-lived, since we were invaded by Indonesia in 1975, while the West turned a blind eye.

Although lacking any significant military capability, the Timorese fought a guerrilla war against this brutal occupation. This new war in Southeast Asia began months after the US had lost the war in Vietnam. Back then, the West lived in fear of the expansion of socialist regimes.

This explains why Indonesian military were trained in the United States of America, in addition to the US providing Indonesia with fighter jets and napalm bombs, surplus from the war in Vietnam, to be used against the defenceless Timorese population which was resisting in the mountains. The Indonesian military were also provided with weapons, tanks, and navy boats by European countries. Meanwhile, we were waging a guerrilla war without proper military means or any form of outside assistance.

While the world ignored, or pretended to ignore, the plight of the Timorese people, Australia – the only country in the world to recognise our illegal annexation – started maritime boundary negotiations with Indonesia, leading to an agreement in 1989 to divide the revenues from the exploitation of the valuable natural resources located in the Timor Sea.

These were resources that belonged to Timor-Leste and were vital to our feasibility as an independent state.

Our 24-year struggle for freedom continued to adapt to the specific circumstances of the time, as we witnessed the dawn of a new world order. Within that context we sought a peaceful solution to end the suffering of the Timorese people.

It was in March 1983 that we began to advocate that a referendum be held under the banner of the UN, in which the people of Timor-Leste would have the opportunity to freely decide their own future.

This referendum finally came to pass in 1999 as a result of a concentration of wills by states and international solidarity organisations throughout the world, which played a vital role in helping Timor-Leste become independent. At the same time, the Asian Financial Crisis led to a democratic transition in Indonesia, forcing President Suharto to resign in 1998.

Excellencies,

People never fight for their independence alone. They do not fight for a flag, an anthem, a president, their own government, or periodic elections. There are other dreams that come together around the ideal of independence, such as enabling the development and progress of both country and people.

As the first elected President of the Republic of Timor-Leste, I can tell you that the hardships of the first years of peace were not easier than those we had to endure during the struggle.

We started with nothing: we had no experience, no human or financial resources, no infrastructure, no legal framework, and no public or private agencies. Meanwhile, our people were in pain and wanting for everything, including inner peace.

Living in peace means more than merely not living in war. It also implies that wounds must be healed by way of pragmatic decisions and policies that put an end to hatred, vengeance, and mistrust.

And so, there is great importance in investing in reconciliation processes. This reconciliation is two-fold. Firstly, there must be reconciliation between citizens who have run afoul of each other due to the divisionary policies of the occupying country. Secondly, there must be reconciliation with Indonesia so that, with openness and solidarity, both Indonesians and Timorese may prosper.

Indonesia is now more than a close neighbour with which we are linked by ties of friendship and cooperation. It is also a role model of stability, democracy, and economic growth which inspires Timor-Leste.

Excellencies,
Ladies and Gentlemen,

In order for a country to develop, it must first overcome its weaknesses. A country taking its first steps on the path to development while carrying a heavy burden resulting from a past of conflict will necessarily make mistakes and experience setbacks. That is why, after independence, we suffered a vicious cycle of conflicts and quarrels, which prevented us from moving forward and even from living in peace.

It became necessary to force state agencies to cooperate among themselves in the search for solutions.

We had to find and address the root causes of problems and we had to build the capacity of our communities by way of ongoing and genuine dialogue.

We also had to ask our people to make another ultimate sacrifice: to once again put collective interests above their individual needs, and to continue to fight hard – this time for national development.

Step by step, we gave back dignity to those who fought for independence, including their demobilisation and reintegration, while taking care of orphans and widows with welfare and social justice measures, so as to protect the most vulnerable groups in our society. Additionally, we prioritised stability and security in our country, by way of thorough reforms in our law enforcement agency and our military, reconciling the differences between the two and correcting errors in terms of their capacity building and training.

In 2009, on the 10th anniversary of the referendum, we launched the motto for our nation: 'Goodbye conflict, welcome development'. Since then, I am happy to say that we have started living in a new environment of safety, stability, and confidence in the future.

We have a long-term *Strategic Development Plan* and we have achieved economic and social development outcomes that, while modest, show us that we are on the path to stability.

We are also increasingly prepared to achieve our goal to attain full membership in the Association of Southeast Asian Nations (ASEAN). In fact, I would like to use this opportunity to publicly convey my appreciation to Cambodia for being such a strong supporter our application.

Excellencies,
Dear Students,

Before I conclude, I want to share with you two experiences from my country's recent history which, even though we are small and fragile, make us a country that defends international order and that contributes to peace.

The first concerns our relationship with Australia, which had gone sour after a dispute over maritime boundaries, before we managed to overcome these divergences with dialogue and diplomacy.

Timor-Leste, which had relied on international law and in international organisations to achieve its independence, once again put its trust in international law and international organisations to gain full sovereignty over our maritime jurisdiction.

A short explanation is required. For years the Australian government and multinational companies turned a blind eye to the tragedy unfolding in Timor-Leste, since having control over natural resources was a priority for Australian economic policy.

A mere two months before Timor-Leste regained its independence, Australia withdrew from every binding resolution mechanism concerning maritime boundary disputes, and in doing so, it prevented Timor-Leste from asking an international tribunal to decide on a permanent maritime boundary with Australia.

On the first day of our independence, we were led to sign a treaty to re-establish the agreements that Australia had made with our former occupier, so that Australia might maintain its rights and benefits over the Timor Sea.

Furthermore, two years after our independence, the Australian government planted illegal listening devices in the Timorese cabinet office during negotiations on the sharing of resources. By the time we learned of these actions, we had already signed a treaty imposing a 50-year moratorium on any maritime boundary negotiations.

As I explained earlier, at that time, Timor-Leste was a young and inexperienced country that was starved for revenues that were needed to rescue our people from extreme poverty.

Upon learning of these illegal wiretaps, we felt we had been deceived into signing a treaty that, for us, meant the difference between a future of hope or misery, but for our rich and powerful neighbour, merely meant more wealth and more power.

Delimitating maritime boundaries means full sovereignty for the Timorese. As such, we refused to give up. Instead, we made use of international law, particularly UNCLOS, to start a compulsory conciliation process with Australia, the first time in history that such a process was attempted.

After several rounds of negotiation guided by the UN Conciliation Commission, an agreement was finally reached with Australia on a permanent maritime boundary between both countries.

This achievement made our young country proud. We had the courage to use a mechanism that had never been used before, and in doing so, we became a role model for other countries in a similar situation, particularly small and less powerful countries.

Additionally, after overcoming the dispute that cast a shadow over our relationship, Timor-Leste and Australia showed that it is possible to, at the same time, resolve divergences peacefully and decolonise the legal order and international relations.

We want to believe that the process with Indonesia, with which we will soon be starting maritime boundary negotiations, will likewise prove to be a tale of success for the world to see. We want to show that while we share a bitter past, our present is one of reconciliation and cooperation, and our future holds prosperity and sovereignty for both our countries.

The second experience concerns a group of fragile and/or conflict-affected states of which Timor-Leste has been a founding member since 2010. This group, the g7+, consists of around 20 countries that have come together to promote peace, reconciliation, and sustainable prosperity, as well as to contribute to preventive diplomacy.

This is a story of union, sharing and cooperation between fragile countries that, by coming together around common goals, have created a strong group. This group managed to become part of the global discussion on sustainable development and to advocate a new world order. Recently it has been granted Permanent Observer Status by the United Nations.

If world leaders come together to decide the future of fragile states, then we have the right to come together to demand a global development partnership where nothing is discussed about us without us.

We are moved by the common suffering of our peoples and by the dream of a world of peace.

Thank you very much.

Lecture at Zhejiang Gongshang University.
The Changing Shape of Asia:
From China to Timor-Leste

Hangzhou, China
22 September 2023

Your Excellencies,
Ladies and Gentlemen,

First and foremost, I would like to thank Zhejiang Gongshang University for granting me the opportunity to address these talented youngsters who are looking to shape their future and, who knows, create a better future for all humanity.

It is an honour to be here today at this century-old university. This academic institution boasts a prestigious reputation and has the good fortune to be located in this stunning city.

And so, here I am, surrounded by a glorious culture, an enthusiastic and innovative spirit, and a dynamic landscape, to speak to you about change.

Dear young students,

We live in uncertain times where global challenges are disruptive. From pandemics to climate emergencies, from humanitarian and security crises to abject poverty and social and economic inequalities. And from conflict to war, this great worldwide scourge that brings suffering to millions of people.

If we are intent on changing the global landscape, then each of us must take responsibility for promoting peace and building a developed and peaceful future for all human beings. The effort is collective, but the first step is individual.

Without peace and stability, there is no room for change. There is no room for a strong, united, developed, and prosperous Asia.

I speak from personal experience, having lived through a quarter-century of war during which I witnessed the suffering of my people and the destruction of my country.

As you know, Asia, and particularly Southeast Asia, has not always been a region of unity and cooperation. Not so long ago, our region was a victim of colonisation and the Cold War. The greed, conflict, and wars of other nations found their way to our side of the world, far from their origins, but close to their interests.

The dynamics of the Cold War and the demands of Western powers led to my country, Timor-Leste, being subjected to a brutal occupation, which left us no choice but to courageously fight for our self-determination.

Perhaps it is because of this, and of the deep scars this period left on our society, that not only we refuse to take sides in the geopolitical disputes of the world's major powers but are also committed to promoting world peace.

We believe that only by working to build trust among countries, reconciling diverse cultures, ideologies, and histories, can we achieve a shared commitment to tolerance, friendship, and cooperation.

The Global Security and Development Initiatives proposed by His Excellency President Xi Jinping are in perfect alignment with what Timor-Leste stands for:

'The world needs peace, not war; it needs development, not poverty; it needs openness, not closure; it needs cooperation, not confrontation; it needs unity, not division; and it needs justice, not intimidation.'

Fortunately, thanks to China's international status and its global influence, there is an active voice capable of driving the desired change. However, this ambition to evolve is far from being achieved in many parts of the world.

Many countries struggle to integrate significantly into the global economy. There are too many people without hope for a more comforting future. Poverty, instability, and despair are still the defining features of the lives of over a billion people.

To exacerbate this situation, we face increasingly extreme weather conditions – floods, droughts, cyclones, and rising sea levels – also due to the failure of global powers to respond to climate change.

It is always the poorest and most fragile states that suffer the worst effects of climate change, just as they were the ones who suffered with the impacts of any disruption in the world order.

The failure of the global economic system to develop the poorest parts of the world is resulting in fragility and dangerous declines in the capacity of states. It is fuelling mass migration and the tragedies we witness on the shores of Europe's entry points. It is fuelling extremism, transnational crime, and the growth of overall instability.

Your Excellencies,
Ladies and Gentlemen,

Dear Students,

It is, of course, easier to blame fragile and poor countries, as well as their peoples. Still, to do so is to turn a deaf ear to the echoes of history.

This would be like ignoring the impact of conflict, economic exclusion, and foreign intervention that keeps these countries trapped in a state of fragility.

After achieving full independence in Timor-Leste in 2002, and having had the opportunity to better understand the world, we were left with the distressing feeling that the much-touted new world order was but a slogan, as wars and conflicts continued to emerge, perhaps even more than before.

As such, when we talk about the new world order today, we are talking about an order that does not exist, because what actually exists is total disorder, perpetuated by the conflicting interests of the powerful in the world.

Independent countries reveal the weaknesses of democratic society; European countries also reveal weaknesses in democratic values; and countries that believe themselves to have hegemony in democratic lessons reveal so much weakness within their societies, especially among their politicians, that it becomes urgent to seek new options, so that every population in every country can exercise their freedoms with greater awareness.

The obsession with hegemonies, be they political, military, or economic, is, in my humble opinion, the cause of this global disorder.

The truth is that the world's main leaders, in order to secure a top position in the global hierarchy, are unable to look at the suffering of their own populations. They suffer from inflation, from an energy crisis, from declining purchasing power, and from the real impoverishment of families and communities.

There is uncertainty, there is fear, there is discontent in societies – we are not heading towards a safe place, we are not heading towards freedom, because being free means living in safety.

So, I say, instead of reinforcing war, we must create conditions for peace.

And whatever may be the new world order that is looming, it will not be 'new' if it does not prioritise world peace.

Perhaps what we need is to establish an order based on a vision of human solidarity and shared prosperity. This is the change that is required, for Asia and for the world.

We need an international order that helps fragile states build resilience and stability.

It was with this realisation – and after a period of turmoil in our own country – that Timor-Leste joined other least-developed countries that also faced conflicts and fragilities.

We believed that it was important for our collective voice to be heard – especially when decisions were being made about our countries without our perspectives being taken into account.

In view of this, we established a group of countries that we call the g7+. This is an intergovernmental organisation consisting of about 20 countries from Africa, Asia, the Middle East, and the Pacific.

The g7+ works to make its voice heard on the international stage. We have observer status at the United Nations, which allows us to provide a collective perspective on the agenda and work of the United Nations.

Above all, we want to reduce conflicts in each country. We see that the West is increasingly obsessed with modernising its military apparatus, which now culminates in the war in Ukraine, where millions of US dollars go towards providing new weapons to Ukraine, and the desire of all Western countries is to continue the war in order to defeat Russia.

The g7+ naturally condemns Russia's invasion. However, the g7+ also regrets the lack of willingness on the part of world leaders to do their utmost to pursue a path to a peaceful solution, instead of increasing the need to maintain the war.

Your Excellencies,
Ladies and Gentlemen,

China has been playing an increasingly crucial role in supporting multilateralism and in promoting international cooperation and sustainable development. China offers a vision and presents solutions to effectively address current challenges and create a world of peace.

Fragile states, like those in the g7+, fragile and devastated countries like those in Africa, and even countries like Timor-Leste, committed to lifting their people out of poverty and moving towards resilience and economic growth, need global development initiatives that lead to the realisation of the 2030 Sustainable Development Agenda.

China has been an important partner in achieving this agenda. The Belt and Road Initiative builds avenues that contribute to global development and peace, especially in the most neglected areas of the world, 'or by the world'.

This new proposal for the international system, this spirit of cooperation and dialogue, brings prosperity to all, interlinking the world in an infrastructure of hope.

Timor-Leste needs this hope.

As soon as we became independent in 2002, we focused on building the state. This meant constructing and consolidating public institutions, which were non-existent in the country.

We faced challenges of every type and nature: scarce human and financial resources, non-existent infrastructure, and limited access to technology, know-how, and basic qualifications for nation building. Still, we are conquering these challenges, and the Timorese people now have security, stability, and determination to overcome adversities.

We have a young population, frustrated by the lack of qualifications and access to employment, but resilient and capable of overcoming the obstacles encountered in this process of building our young nation.

And it is precisely for this reason that we cannot rest. Our young people need opportunities for developing this country which was conquered with so much sacrifice.

I am impressed by the dynamism of the young people in this university, and of the Chinese young people in general. And I can say that the youth of my country are also talented and resilient in the face of adversity, but they need more opportunities to develop their skills and abilities.

Investing in their education, training, and qualifications is not just a way to invest in the country's development; it is the only way.

Our young people are our hope, not only because of their vigour and adaptability to change but also because they can look at history and the future through different lenses, with a new perspective that is essential for development.

Fortunately, our young people, both Chinese and Timorese, live in the most promising region in the world. We are aware that Asia will become the dominant economic space in the world.

And China, as the largest country in Asia, has an important place in our region, which should be recognised and respected.

We look at this country with admiration. As the largest developing country in the world, it is also a partner that seeks not hegemony but, rather, the common development of all countries.

Between China and Timor-Leste, there are also the countries of Southeast Asia. This association of countries has made extraordinary achievements, not only through their economic miracles but also through strong state capacity, effective governance, the rule of law, public order, and the healthy and qualified workforces they have been establishing.

More importantly, ASEAN has adopted a people-centred approach that emphasises tolerance, mutual respect, and peace in this region.

ASEAN can provide models of sovereign development for building strong communities, social infrastructure, and economic resilience. ASEAN has shown the world the power of dialogue and what can be achieved when nations come together around a common purpose.

And it has shown us the benefits of more inclusive economic growth, in which prosperity is widely shared.

For all these reasons, Timor-Leste has been working towards full membership in this organisation, capacitating its technical staff and support infrastructure in order to enter this Asian community which promotes trust and preventive diplomacy in the region, with the enhancement of the people-centred community.

Timor-Leste wants to be part of ASEAN, not only because it wants to benefit from economic cooperation, trade, services, and investment advantages but also because it wants to be part of the solution to the challenges that we face.

Due to our history of overcoming adversity and friendship with our two neighbouring countries, Timor-Leste is a model of reconciliation in the region. We are still living proof that resorting to the rules-based international system can lead to the peaceful resolution of international disputes.

We want to be part of the joint work for peace, prosperity, and inclusion in the region and in the world.

I conclude by recognising and thanking China not only for its support to Timor-Leste's accession to ASEAN but also for all the support provided by the People's Republic of China to Timor-Leste so far.

As the Chinese proverb says, 'Carry a handful of earth every day and you'll make a mountain'.

This is the challenge I leave with you: A handful of commitment from each of us, and we can change history – we can change the world for the better.

Thank you very much.

www.ingramcontent.com/pod-product-compliance
Lightning Source LLC
Chambersburg PA
CBHW051256020426
42333CB00026B/3227